Springer Series in Statistics

Advisors:
P. Bickel, P. Diggle, S. Fienberg, K. Krickeberg,
I. Olkin, N. Wermuth, S. Zeger

Springer

New York
Berlin
Heidelberg
Barcelona
Budapest
Hong Kong
London
Milan
Paris
Santa Clara
Singapore
Tokyo

Springer Series in Statistics

Andersen/Borgan/Gill/Keiding: Statistical Models Based on Counting Processes.
Andrews/Herzberg: Data: A Collection of Problems from Many Fields for the Student and Research Worker.
Anscombe: Computing in Statistical Science through APL.
Berger: Statistical Decision Theory and Bayesian Analysis, 2nd edition.
Bolfarine/Zacks: Prediction Theory for Finite Populations.
Borg/Groenen: Modern Multidimensional Scaling: Theory and Applications
Brémaud: Point Processes and Queues: Martingale Dynamics.
Brockwell/Davis: Time Series: Theory and Methods, 2nd edition.
Daley/Vere-Jones: An Introduction to the Theory of Point Processes.
Dzhaparidze: Parameter Estimation and Hypothesis Testing in Spectral Analysis of Stationary Time Series.
Fahrmeir/Tutz: Multivariate Statistical Modelling Based on Generalized Linear Models.
Farrell: Multivariate Calculation.
Federer: Statistical Design and Analysis for Intercropping Experiments.
Fienberg/Hoaglin/Kruskal/Tanur (Eds.): A Statistical Model: Frederick Mosteller's Contributions to Statistics, Science and Public Policy.
Fisher/Sen: The Collected Works of Wassily Hoeffding.
Good: Permutation Tests: A Practical Guide to Resampling Methods for Testing Hypotheses.
Goodman/Kruskal: Measures of Association for Cross Classifications.
Gouriéroux: ARCH Models and Financial Applications.
Grandell: Aspects of Risk Theory.
Haberman: Advanced Statistics, Volume I: Description of Populations.
Hall: The Bootstrap and Edgeworth Expansion.
Härdle: Smoothing Techniques: With Implementation in S.
Hartigan: Bayes Theory.
Heyer: Theory of Statistical Experiments.
Huet/Bouvier/Gruet/Jolivet: Statistical Tools for Nonlinear Regression: A Practical Guide with S-PLUS Examples.
Jolliffe: Principal Component Analysis.
Kolen/Brennan: Test Equating: Methods and Practices.
Kotz/Johnson (Eds.): Breakthroughs in Statistics Volume I.
Kotz/Johnson (Eds.): Breakthroughs in Statistics Volume II.
Kres: Statistical Tables for Multivariate Analysis.
Le Cam: Asymptotic Methods in Statistical Decision Theory.
Le Cam/Yang: Asymptotics in Statistics: Some Basic Concepts.
Longford: Models for Uncertainty in Educational Testing.
Manoukian: Modern Concepts and Theorems of Mathematical Statistics.
Miller, Jr.: Simultaneous Statistical Inference, 2nd edition.
Mosteller/Wallace: Applied Bayesian and Classical Inference: The Case of *The Federalist Papers.*

(continued after index)

Christian Gouriéroux

ARCH Models and Financial Applications

With 26 Figures

 Springer

Christian Gouriéroux
Centre de Recherche en Economie et Statistique
Laboratoire de Finance-Assurance
Bâtiment Malakoff 2-Timbre J320
15 Boulevard Gabriel Péri
92245 Malakoff Cedex, France

Library of Congress Cataloging-in-Publication Data
Gouriéroux, Christian, 1949–
    ARCH models and financial applications/Christian Gouriéroux.
        p.   cm. − (Springer series in statistics)
    Includes bibliographical references and index.
    ISBN 0-387-94876-7 (alk. paper)
    1. Finance − Mathematical models.   2. Autoregression (Statistics)
    I. Title.   II. Series.
    HG176.5.G68   1997
    332 − dc20   96-33588

Printed on acid-free paper.

Production managed by Hal Henglein; manufacturing supervised by Jacqui Ashri.
Camera-ready copy prepared from the author's LaTeX files.
Printed and bound by Maple-Vail Book Manufacturing Group, York, PA.
Printed in the United States of America.

9 8 7 6 5 4 3 2 1

ISBN 0-387-94876-7 Springer-Verlag New York Berlin Heidelberg   SPIN 10551079

Contents

1
Introduction

1.1 The Development of ARCH Models

Time series models have been initially introduced either for descriptive purposes like prediction and seasonal correction or for dynamic control. In the 1970s, the research focused on a specific class of time series models, the so-called autoregressive moving average processes (ARMA), which were very easy to implement. In these models, the current value of the series of interest is written as a linear function of its own lagged values and current and past values of some noise process, which can be interpreted as innovations to the system. However, this approach has two major drawbacks: 1) it is essentially a linear setup, which automatically restricts the type of dynamics to be approximated; 2) it is generally applied without imposing a priori constraints on the autoregressive and moving average parameters, which is inadequate for structural interpretations.

Among the field of applications where standard ARMA fit is poor are financial and monetary problems. The financial time series features various forms of non-linear dynamics, the crucial one being the strong dependence of the instantaneous variability of the series on its own past. Moreover, financial theories based on concepts like equilibrium or rational behavior of the investors would naturally suggest including and testing some structural constraints on the parameters. In this context, ARCH (Autoregressive Conditionally Heteroscedastic) models, introduced by Engle (1982), arise as an appropriate framework for studying these problems. Currently, there exist more than one hundred papers and some dozen Ph.D. theses on this topic, which reflects the importance of this approach for statistical theory, finance and empirical work.

From the viewpoint of statistical theory, the ARCH models may be considered as some specific nonlinear time series models, which allow for a quite exhaustive study of the underlying dynamics. It is therefore possible to reexamine a number of classical questions like the random walk hypothesis, prediction intervals building, presence of latent variables [factors] etc., and to test the validity of the previously established results.

The introduction of models with path dependent volatility also requires a refinement of the standard financial theory. In parallel with the development of ARCH modelling, we observe an evolution of the structural models used for dynamic portfolio management as well as an increased interest in issues like derivative assets pricing with stochastic volatility, estimation of path dependent 'betas' in the regression of the basic assets return on the market portfolio return or studies of the impact of asymmetric information on volatility.

The success of ARCH modelling is also due to the failure of some standard practices based on a static analysis of financial phenomena. For example, a serious difficulty was encountered in the implementation on the French market of standard software for determining hedging portfolios proposed by Roll and Ross. This is certainly due to the fact that it is based on the static APT (Arbitrage Pricing Theory) model.

We may distinguish two main categories of potential applications. The first one involves testing several economic or financial theories concerning the stock, bond and currency markets, or studying the links between the short and long run (e.g., the term structure of interest rates). The second one is basically operational and related to the interventions of the banks on the markets [choice of optimal portfolios, hedging portfolios, values at risk (VaR), the size and times of block trading]. This second category is often subject to some confidentiality restrictions, contrary to the first, which is of a more global use. A careless reader of the existing literature could however be misled and mistakenly believe that the main application of ARCH models is for theoretical purposes. Although at the beginning of the 1990s, it was still possible to consider the ARCH models as decision tools in an experimental phase, several institutions have now developed the necessary skills to use them, for instance, for updating hedging portfolios.

As is the case with many mathematical models, ARCH-based computer softwares for portfolio management, for example, are readily available on the market. However, a potential user should remain cautious in drawing inferences from some output provided by these pre-programmed procedures. They should rather be thought of as a useful source of supplementary advice for decision making. In particular, adjustments are necessary before any test of practical interest is performed. There is a potential danger in relying extensively on the computed results and ignoring the simplifying assumption imposed on the estimated ARCH model. Indeed, different specificities of the data, of the market, or even of traders' behavior have to be accounted for by an efficient analyst.

For example, the possibly omitted relevant features may involve the following issues:

- In some markets, automated electronic quote systems were initiated that allow for price announcements even if no trading takes place at these prices.

- There may exist different prices on the same market, for the same asset, at the same date. This may be due to stripping of large orders on stock markets or to the intermediation activity of the so-called market-makers.

- The announced price may be only an indicator that is used as a basis for bargaining that leads to the true price.

- The prices take only discrete values and, for instance, their increments are multiples of some basic unit like 0.05.

- There may exist transaction costs that depend on the quantities to be traded or on the characteristics of the investors.

- The trades occur only if some supply responds to some demand. It is the problem of the liquidity of financial assets, which will not be discussed in this book.

- At a given date, and for a given asset, the number of active investors may be rather small. The traditional approach based on the competitive equilibrium is not appropriate for describing such situations, and some insights from game theory might be useful.

On the other hand, one also should be aware of the limitations to the assumptions on the underlying ARCH models. They can be summarized as follows.

- ARCH models are fitted to return series. As we know, the financial decisions depend not only on expected returns and volatilities but also on market shares, on the search for balanced allocations among several categories of assets (legal constraints may exist for mutual funds), and on volumes.

- The ARCH model assumes a rather stable environment and fails to capture irregular phenomena such as crashes, mergers, news effects or threshold effects, opening and closing of the markets, price evolution for an option close to maturity, etc.

- The price evolution is modelled using the common knowledge contained in lagged prices. It does not take into account the possibility of information withheld by individuals or explain how to deal with it.

This list of practical limitations provides some insights on the limits of ARCH models and explains why they generally should be supplemented by more traditional inference methods.

1.2   Book Content

In chapter 2, we first present precise definitions of nonlinearity in dynamic systems. We distinguish between different kinds of nonlinearities, with conditional heteroscedasticity as an example of primary interest. We show different modelling strategies to accommodate these nonlinearities and describe various test procedures to detect them.

Univariate ARCH models are introduced and studied in chapter 3. We derive the main probabilistic properties of the associated time series (stationarity conditions, analytical forms of the first and second order moments) and study the tail behaviors of the distribution.

Chapter 4 is devoted to statistical inference: estimation of ARCH models by the quasi (pseudo) maximum likelihood method or by two step estimation methods, with a distinction being made between the parameters of the conditional mean and the parameters of the conditional variance. We also present a comparison of the asymptotic properties of these estimators. Two other questions are also studied, namely, the determination of path dependent prediction intervals and test procedures of the null hypothesis of conditional homoscedasticity.

Several extensions are collected in chapter 5: the leptokurticity of financial series, the link between stochastic volatility models in discrete time (ARCH model) and in continuous time (stochastic differential equation), test corrections for the random walk hypothesis to accommodate conditional heteroscedasticity, the nonparametric estimation of the volatility function, the threshold effects (TARCH models), and finally ARCH models with unit roots and volatility persistence.

The multivariate framework is considered in chapter 6. The direct multivariate extensions of ARCH models yield a very large number of parameters, which cannot be estimated precisely without additional restrictions imposed accross and within the equations. We first present some constraints proposed in the literature, and finally we discuss statistical inference on the example of factor ARCH models.

In chapter 7, we describe the standard financial theory explaining how to determine efficient or hedging portfolios. This theory is conceived for myopic agents, but we stress the path dependence to establish links with the previous chapter. It reveals some interesting applications of ARCH models for solving a number of problems (chapter 8).

Finally, in chapter 9 we discuss the equilibrium models. We first present the capital asset pricing model (CAPM) and describe the implied constraints on the conditional moments of the returns. We then discuss the test of the CAPM against some maintained ARCH hypothesis. We end this chapter with a discussion of the effect of heterogenous information in equilibrium models.

2
Linear and Nonlinear Processes

2.1 Stochastic Processes

The analysis of dynamics in economics is based on observations of relevant processes. Generally, the resulting time series shows that are some regularities that are present in explosive or cyclical components (see the evolution of unemployment in figure 2.1) or comovements of different series (see figure 2.2, which displays the behavior of short and long term interest rates, where the two series have approximately the same trend and differ from one another in terms of their variabilities).

In order to study these regularities, an observed time series is viewed as a realization of a stochastic process. A stochastic process is a sequence of random

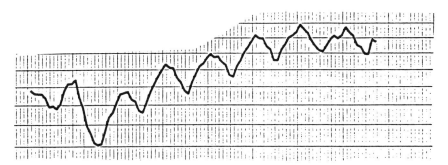

FIGURE 2.1. Number of unemployed workers.

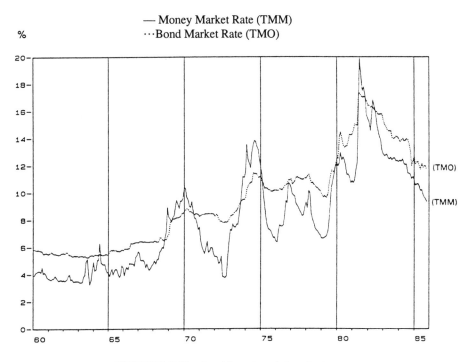

FIGURE 2.2. Short and long term interest rates.

variables that are defined on a set Ω, called the state space. These random variables may be unidimensional or multidimensional (see figures 2.1 and 2.2, respectively) and are indexed by time in our applications. To simplify our discussion, we suppose that the times at which the observations are recorded are regularly spaced, which allows us to consider an index by taking only integer values. The stochastic process is denoted by

$$Y = (Y_t, t \in \mathcal{T}), \tag{2.1}$$

where the index set $\mathcal{T}$ is $\mathbb{N}$ or $\mathbb{Z}$. When the process is multivariate, its components are denoted by

$$Y_t = (Y_{jt}, j = 1, \ldots, n).$$

Each series $Y_j = (Y_{jt}, t \in \mathcal{T})$ defines a univariate process.

The chronology observed corresponds to $Y_t(\omega), t = 1, \ldots, T$, where ω is a particular state and $[1, \ldots, T]$ the period of observation; such a realization $(Y_t(\omega), t \in \mathcal{T})$ is often called the *path of the process*. The regularities that can be observed in the path are often due to some particularities of the underlying distribution of the whole process. According to *Kolmogorov's theorem*, this distribution is entirely characterized by the finite dimensional distributions that correspond to $(Y_{t_1}, \ldots, Y_{t_n})$ for any $n, t_1, \ldots, t_n$. This distribution can also be described using the marginal distributions of Y_t and the successive conditional distributions of Y_t given $Y_{t-1} = y_{t-1}, \ldots, Y_{t-k} = y_{t-k}$, k varying. In the case of continuous distributions, the corresponding marginal and conditional probability density functions can be considered and will be denoted by, respectively,

$$f(y_t, y_{t-1}, \ldots, y_{t-k}),$$

and

$$f_{t/t-1,\ldots,t-k}(y_t/y_{t-1}, \ldots, y_{t-k}). \tag{2.2}$$

The probability density function (pdf) of $(Y_t, Y_{t-1}, \ldots, Y_{t-k})$ can be obtained as a product of the successive conditional distributions:

$$f_{t-k}(y_{t-k}) \quad f_{t-k+1/t-k}(y_{t-k+1}/y_{t-k}) \cdots f_{t/t-1,\ldots,t-k}(y_t, y_{t-1}, \ldots, y_{t-k}).$$

When the components are square integrable, the process is said to be of second order, and its distribution may partly be summarized by the two first order moments. The first moment generally depends on time and provides an idea of the average evolution of the series. This moment is denoted $m_t = E(Y_t)$, and in a multivariate framework it may be described component by component: $m_{jt} = E(Y_{jt})$. The second moment summarizes the variability of the series and the lagged and instantaneous dependence between the variables. The matrix of second moments can be defined as

$$\Gamma(t, h) = E[(Y_t - E(Y_t))(Y_{t+h} - E(Y_{t+h}))'], \quad t, h \in \tau, \tag{2.3}$$

where Y' denotes the transposed vector of Y, and $\Gamma(t, h)$ is a square matrix of dimension (n, n). The off diagonal elements of $\Gamma(t, 0)$ are the variances of the different components and the out of diagonal elements are their instantaneous covariances. When h is different from zero, the $\Gamma(t, h)$'s elements indicate linear dependence with delay h. Let us now restrict the class of stochastic processes that will be considered. Two types of conditions are often introduced: the stationarity condition and the assumption that the process is a Markov process (a third condition, which assumes that the process is linear, is often considered and will be discussed in the next subsection).

Definition 2.4. *i) A process is said to be strictly (or strongly) stationary if and only if the joint distribution of $(Y_{t+t_1}, \ldots, Y_{t+t_n})$ is the same as the joint distribution of $(Y_{t_1}, \ldots, Y_{t_n})$ for every n, t, t_1, t_n.*

ii) A process is said to be weakly stationary (or second order stationary) if and only if

(*) the mean does not depend on time: $m_t = m, \quad \forall t$;

(**) the covariances depend only on the difference between the time indices of the two variables: $\Gamma(t, h) = \Gamma(h), \quad \forall t$.

$\Gamma(.)$ *is called the autocovariance function.*

A strictly stationary second order process is obviously weakly stationary. On the contrary, a weakly stationary process may not be strictly stationary, for instance, if the third and fourth moments are not time invariant. These two notions coincide if the process is Gaussian, that is to say, if all finite dimensional distributions are normal.

In practice, the rough series are often transformed in order to eliminate some possible nonstationarities. Such transformations include, for instance, the differencing

$$Y_t \longrightarrow \Delta Y_t = Y_t - Y_{t-1},$$

or taking the logarithms

$$Y_t \longrightarrow \log Y_t.$$

The Markov assumption means that the informational content of the entire past of the process can be summarized by a finite number of variables, the so-called state variables. In the simplest case, where the state variables are lagged values of the process, the Markov condition is defined as follows.

Definition 2.5. *The process is Markovian of order k if and only if:*

$$f_{t/t-1,\dots,t-k}(y_t, y_{t-1}, \dots, y_{t-k}) = f_{t/t-1,\dots,t-K}(y_t, y_{t-1}, \dots, y_{t-K}), \quad \forall t, \forall k \geq K.$$

All past information is then included in the most recent K values.

In analogy with the weak and strict stationarity, it would be interesting to introduce the notion of a weak Markov condition. Such a concept may be defined using the conditional expectation of Y_t given the past values $\underline{Y_{t-1}} = \{Y_{t-1}, Y_{t-2}, \dots\}$ or the linear regression of Y_t on these values. The conditional expectation $E(Y_t/\underline{Y_{t-1}})$ is the best approximation of Y_t in the mean-square error sense by a function of the past values $Y_{t-1}, Y_{t-2}, \dots$; this approximation is generally a nonlinear function of these values. The linear regression $LE(Y_t/\underline{Y_{t-1}})$—LE for linear expectation—is the best prediction of Y_t by means of an affine function of $Y_{t-1}, Y_{t-2}, \dots$

Definition 2.6. *A second order stochastic process is*
i) an autoregressive process of order K if and only if

$$E(Y_t/\underline{Y_{t-1}}) = E(Y_t/Y_{t-1}, \dots, Y_{t-K}), \forall t;$$

ii) a linear autoregressive process of order K if and only if

$$LE(Y_t/\underline{Y_{t-1}}) = LE(Y_t/Y_{t-1}, \dots, Y_{t-K}), \forall t.$$

Such processes are denoted *AR(K)*, usually without distinguishing between the two autoregressive notions.

2.2   Weak and Strict Stationarity

A large number of contributors to the literature on time series consider linear models and in particular autoregressive moving average processes (ARMA). The current value Y_t of this process is expressed as a linear function of the past values of Y and of current and past values of a white noise process ε, i.e., of a sequence of uncorrelated and homoscedastic variables with zero mean .

An ARMA representation is

$$Y_t = C + \Phi_1 Y_{t-1} + \ldots + \Phi_p Y_{t-p} + \varepsilon_t - \Theta_1 \varepsilon_1 - \ldots - \Theta_q \varepsilon_{t-q}, \tag{2.7}$$

where $\Phi_1, \ldots, \Phi_p, \Theta_1, \ldots, \Theta_q$ are square matrices and C is a vector. One can introduce the autoregressive and moving average lag-polynomials:

$$\Phi(L) = Id - \Phi_1 L + \ldots + \Phi_p L^p \tag{2.8}$$
$$\Theta(L) = Id - \Theta_1 L - \ldots - \Theta_q L^q,$$

where L describes the lag operator $LY_t = Y_{t-1}$. Now the ARMA representation can be written as:

$$\Phi(L)Y_t = C + \Theta(L)\varepsilon_t. \tag{2.9}$$

The coefficients $\Phi_j, j = 1, \ldots, p, \Theta_j, j = 1, \ldots, q$ usually are subject to stability constraints. These restrictions concern the roots of the equations:

$$\det(\Phi(z)) = 0 \quad \text{and} \quad \det(\Theta(z)) = 0, \tag{2.10}$$

which are supposed to lie outside of the unit circle, that is, $|z| > 1$. Under these stability restrictions, the polynomials $\det(\Phi(z))$ and $\det(\Theta(z))$ can be inverted, yielding two alternative representations of the process:

an infinite moving average representation:

$$Y_t = \Phi(L)^{-1}C + \Phi(L)^{-1}\Theta(L)\varepsilon_t \tag{2.11}$$
$$= \Phi(1)^{-1}C + \Phi(L)^{-1}\Theta(L)\varepsilon_t,$$

and an infinite autoregressive representation:

$$\Theta(L)^{-1}\Phi(L)Y_t = \Theta(1)^{-1}C + \varepsilon_t. \tag{2.12}$$

The success of ARMA models is due to the tractability of the model, which is linear in the variables and some of the parameters at the same time. This first linearity feature yields the forecast formulas that are easy to implement, and the second one allows for estimation of the parameters using linear least squares methods. Moreover, the ARMA model is a parsimonious approximation of an infinite moving average model, whose main theoretical background is Wold's decomposition theorem.

Wold's Theorem (2.13). *A weakly stationary process* $(Y_t, t \in T)$, *such that* $\lim_{h \to \infty} E(Y_{t+h}/\underline{Y_t}) = E(Y_t)$, *always admits an infinite moving average representation*

$$Y_t = C_0 + \varepsilon_t - A_1\varepsilon_{t-1} \ldots - A_j\varepsilon_{t-j} \ldots$$
$$= C_0 + A(L)\varepsilon_t,$$

where $(\varepsilon_t, t \in T)$ *is a sequence of homoscedastic noise variables,* $V\varepsilon_t = \Omega$, *which are uncorrelated,* $Cov(\varepsilon_t, \varepsilon_{t'}) = 0$, $\forall t \neq t'$, *with zero mean*, $E\varepsilon_t = 0$, *and where the coefficients* $A_1, \ldots, A_j \ldots$ *satisfy the stability condition*

$$\sum_{j=0}^{\infty} A_j\Omega A'_j < \infty.$$

The condition $\lim_{h \to \infty} E(Y_{t+h}/\underline{Y_t}) = E(Y_t)$ means that the observations prior to t do not provide any information to forecast at an infinite horizon. When this condition is satisfied, the process is said to be *regular*. The sequence ε appearing in the preceding moving average decomposition has an interesting interpretation. Indeed, ε coincides with the linear forecast error:

$$\varepsilon_t = Y_t - LE(Y_t/\underline{\varepsilon_{t-1}}). \tag{2.14}$$

Hence ε is called the *innovation process*.

The moving average representation may thus be considered as a linear model in which the current value is a function of the current and past values of ε. If the polynomial $A(L)$ is invertible, the previous formula implies an autoregressive representation:

$$A(L)^{-1}Y_t = A(1)^{-1}C_0 + \varepsilon_t, \tag{2.15}$$

which is also a linear model, with Y_t a linear function of the current innovation and of the lagged values of Y.

Different notions of linearity are thus associated with Wold's decomposition theorem, and these notions are the ones that we intend to clarify. As usual, different definitions may be introduced depending on the assumptions imposed on the error term ε. Some more stringent assumptions are described below.

Assumption A1:

Let $\varepsilon = (\varepsilon_t, t \in T)$ be a *weak white noise*, that is, a sequence of uncorrelated, homoscedastic variables with zero mean. It may be interpreted in terms of linear forecast:

$$\begin{cases} LE(\varepsilon_t/\underline{\varepsilon_{t-1}}) = 0, \\ V(\varepsilon_t) = \Omega, \text{ independent of } t. \end{cases}$$

Assumption A2:

Let $\varepsilon = (\varepsilon_t, t \in T)$ be a *homoscedastic martingale difference sequence* :

$$\begin{cases} LE(\varepsilon_t/\underline{\varepsilon_{t-1}}) = 0, \\ V(\varepsilon_t) = \Omega, \text{ independent of } t. \end{cases}$$

Assumption A3:

Let $\varepsilon = (\varepsilon_t, t \in T)$ be a *conditional white noise* :

$$\begin{cases} E(\varepsilon_t / \underline{\varepsilon_{t-1}}) = 0, \\ V(\varepsilon_t / \underline{\varepsilon_{t-1}}) = \Omega, \text{ independent of } t. \end{cases}$$

Assumption A4:

Let $\varepsilon = (\varepsilon_t, t \in T)$ be a *strict* (or independent) white noise, that is, a sequence of independent and identically distributed (i.i.d.) random variables where finite second order moments exist.

Assumption A5:

Let $\varepsilon = (\varepsilon_t, t \in T)$ be a *Gaussian white noise*, where we suppose in addition that the ε's are normally distributed.

Each of the aforementioned white noise sequences is associated with a notion of moving average or autoregressive representation. For instance, we know that every regular weakly stationary process admits a moving average representation with a weak white noise. However, in general, it does not admit a moving average representation with a strict white noise. In such a case, the best forecast $E(Y_t / \underline{Y_{t-1}})$ is a nonlinear function of the past values of the process. In order to clarify the difference between assumptions A1 and A5, it may be useful to recall a classical result concerning strictly stationary processes. One could establish that every strictly stationary process may be approximated as closely as desired by a polynomial in Gaussian white noise [see Nisio (1960, 1961)]. This implies that every strictly stationary time series admits an expansion of the form:

$$Y_t = \mu + \sum_{i=-\infty}^{\infty} \theta_i \varepsilon_{t-i} + \sum_i \sum_j \theta_{ij} \varepsilon_{t-i} \varepsilon_{t-j}$$
$$+ \sum_i \sum_j \sum_k \theta_{ijk} \varepsilon_{t-i} \varepsilon_{t-j} \varepsilon_{t-k} + \dots,$$

where $\varepsilon = (\varepsilon_t, t \in T)$ is a Gaussian white noise. This expansion is called *Volterra's expansion*. The process Y is also clearly second order stationary and, according to Wold's theorem, admits a weak linear representation:

$$Y_t = \mu + \sum_j \theta_j^* u_{t-j},$$

where $u = (u_t)$ is a weak white noise.

These two representations coincide, that is, u equals ε, if and only if the terms of order greater than two disappear in Volterra's expansion:

$$\theta_{ij} = 0, \quad \forall i, j, \qquad \theta_{ijk} = 0, \quad \forall i, j, k \dots.$$

In the following subsection, we give different examples of weakly stationary processes (that is, "weak linear" processes according to Wold's decomposition theorem) with linear innovation $Y_t - LE(Y_t/Y_{t-1})$ not being strong white noise. Therefore, these processes show some nonlinear aspects that may be taken into account to improve the results.

2.3   A Few Examples

There exist different ways to model nonlinearities in time series. The most important ones are pointed out in this section.

i) Linear Transformation of a Strict Linear Process

Let us consider a (strict) moving average process of order one:

$$X_t = \varepsilon_t - \frac{1}{2}\varepsilon_{t-1}, \tag{2.16}$$

where (ε_t) is a Gaussian white noise with unitary variance. The process X is also Gaussian with a mean zero, and its autocovariance function is

$$\gamma_x(0) = 1 + \frac{1}{4} = \frac{5}{4}, \qquad \gamma_x(1) = -\frac{1}{2}, \qquad \gamma_x(h) = 0, \quad \text{if} \quad h \ge 2.$$

The sign of X defines another stochastic process:

$$Y_t = \begin{cases} +1, & \text{if} \quad X_t \ge 0, \\ -1, & \text{if} \quad X_t < 0. \end{cases} \tag{2.17}$$

As the transformation yielding the new process is time independent, Y is also strictly stationary (see exercise 2.1). Besides, Y_t with a bounded modulus is a second order process. One can then deduce that Y is also weakly stationary and admits an infinite moving average representation. Since X_t is independent of $X_{t-2}, X_{t-3}, \ldots$, Y_t is a function of X_t and is independent of $Y_{t-2}, Y_{t-3}, \ldots$. In particular, the autocovariance function of Y is zero when the delays are greater than or equal to two: $\gamma_Y(h) = 0$ if $h \ge 2$. It implies that Y's moving average representation is reduced to a pure moving average representation of order one, which in turn can be written

$$Y_t = \eta_t + \theta\eta_{t-1}, \tag{2.18}$$

where (η_t) is a weak white noise.

Nevertheless, (η_t) is not a strict white noise. It is easy to show that, if η_{t-1} and η_t were independent, the conditional distribution of η_t given η_{t-1} would be independent of the values taken by η_{t-1}. However, as $\eta_t = Y_t - \theta\eta_{t-1}$, the only possible values of η_t are $1 - \theta\eta_{t-1}$ and $-1 - \theta\eta_{t-1}$. This means that the support of the conditional distribution clearly depends on η_{t-1}. In figure 2.3, the paths of the initial and transformed series X and Y are plotted. They have been computed using a reduced Gaussian noise and setting the parameter θ equal to 0.5.

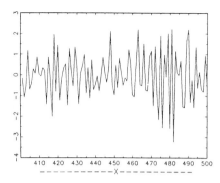 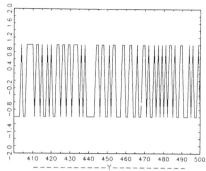

FIGURE 2.3. Sign function.

ii) Threshold Autoregressive Models (TAR)

Some nonlinearities may be accommodated by expressing the current value of the process as a nonlinear function of the past values (Tong and Lin 1980). For instance, let us consider the model:

$$Y_t = \mathbb{I}_{Y_{t-1}>0} + \varepsilon_t, \tag{2.19}$$

where ε is a reduced Gaussian white noise and $\mathbb{I}_{Y_{t-1}>0}$ is the indicator function:

$$\mathbb{I}_{Y_{t-1}>0} = \begin{cases} 1, & \text{if } Y_{t-1} > 0, \\ 0, & \text{otherwise.} \end{cases}$$

The preceding process is built from observations on the state variable $Z_{t-1} = \mathbb{I}_{Y_{t-1}>0}$, and we will study this qualitative process in the first stage. We have

$$P[Z_t = 1/\underline{Y_{t-1}}] = P[Y_t > 0/\underline{Y_{t-1}}]$$
$$= P[Z_{t-1} + \varepsilon_t > 0/\underline{Y_{t-1}}] = \Phi(Z_{t-1}),$$

where Φ denotes the cumulative distribution function (cdf) of the standard normal distribution. We can see from the expression of this conditional probability that Z is a homogeneous Markov chain with a transition matrix given by

$$\begin{pmatrix} P[Z_t = 1/Z_{t-1} = 1] & P[Z_t = 1/Z_{t-1} = 0] \\ P[Z_t = 0/Z_{t-1} = 1] & P[Z_t = 0/Z_{t-1} = 0] \end{pmatrix} = \begin{pmatrix} \Phi(1) & \Phi(0) \\ 1 - \Phi(1) & 1 - \Phi(0) \end{pmatrix}.$$

It is known that a transition matrix always admits one as the first eigenvalue, the second one being obtained from the trace of the matrix, i.e., $\Phi(1) - \Phi(0)$. Besides Φ being the cumulative distribution function of a symmetric distribution, this eigenvalue lies between 0 and 1/2; its modulus is in particular lower than 1. It implies that the Markov chain Z is ergodic and, according to equation (2.19), the process Y is also (asymptotically) strictly stationary. According to Wold's theorem

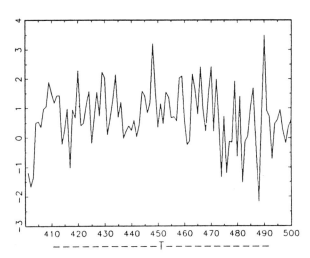

FIGURE 2.4. Threshold autoregressive process.

(see exercise 2.3), Y_t may be written as

$$Y_t = \mu + \sum_{i=1}^{\infty} \varphi_i Y_{t-i} + u_t, \qquad (2.20)$$

where u_t is a weak white noise.

This example shows that the weak linear formula (2.21) is compatible with a nonlinear optimal forecast, since

$$E(Y_t/\underline{Y_{t-1}}) = \mathbb{I}_{Y_{t-1}>0} \neq LE(Y_t/\underline{Y_{t-1}}).$$

A simulated path of such a process is plotted in figure 2.4. The process is not of zero mean because of the translation $\mathbb{I}_{Y_{t-1}>0}$. In particular, the mean is equal to

$$EY_t = P[Y_{t-1} > 0] = P[Z_t = 1],$$

i.e., to the marginal probability of the invariant measure of the Markov chain Z.

iii) Deterministic Autoregression

Second order stationarity may also be obtained using deterministic recursive equations. We present below two well known examples: the first one is similar to the threshold model and is known as the tent map; the second one is used to derive classical random number generators.

a) **The tent map**

Let us consider the deterministic dynamic model

$$Y_t = g(Y_{t-1}), \qquad (2.21)$$

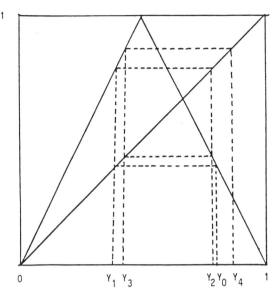

FIGURE 2.5. The tent map.

where the map g, defined on the interval $[0, 1]$, has a tent shape (see figure 2.5).

Using the 45 degree line and the g curve, we draw a dotted line displaying a path of (Y_t). The tent map is piecewise linear and defined by

$$g(y) = \begin{cases} 2y, & \text{if } 0 \le y \le \dfrac{1}{2}, \\ -2y + 2, & \text{if } \dfrac{1}{2} \le y \le 1. \end{cases}$$

If Y_0 is a random variable and equation (2.21) holds, we obtain a stochastic process with very particular properties: the best forecast of Y_t given Y_{t-1} is nonlinear and equals $g(Y_{t-1})$, with zero forecast error. It may be interesting to investigate if the equation (2.21) is compatible with the second order stationarity of the process Y. Mathematically, the question is the following: does a Y_0's distribution exist such that the Y_1's distribution coincides with the Y_0's? We must therefore search for the distributions defined on $[0,1]$ invariant with respect to the transformation g. For simplicity, let us focus on the continuous invariant measures and denote by f the corresponding density function (pdf). The invariance condition for the tent map is

$$f(y) = \frac{f(y) + f(1-y)}{2}, \quad \forall y \in [0, 1]$$
$$\Leftrightarrow f(y) = f(1-y), \quad \forall y \in [0, 1].$$

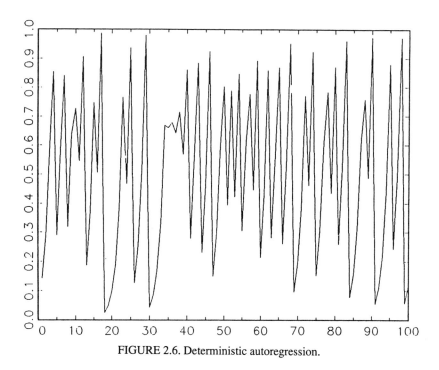

FIGURE 2.6. Deterministic autoregression.

For instance, it holds for the uniform distribution on [0,1]. If Y_0 is randomly drawn from [0,1], the associated stochastic process is stationary. The (unique) path associated to the initial condition $y_0 = 0.14$ is described in figure 2.6.

b) **The Fractionary part**

Another example is described in Whittle (1963). Let us consider a uniformly distributed random variable X on [0,1], and the following process defined on X:

$$\begin{cases} X_0 = X, \\ X_t = (2X_{t-1})\text{'s fractionary part, if } t = 1, 2, \dots \end{cases} \tag{2.22}$$

It is a deterministic recursive equation. Its stochastic properties are easily described, noting that the variables of this process have a binary representation. More precisely, let us introduce the binary expansion of X_0:

$$X_0 = \frac{a_0}{2} + \frac{a_1}{2^2} + \frac{a_3}{2^3} + \dots.$$

The variables a_j, $j = 0, 1, \dots$ are independent and have the same distribution:

$$P[a_j = 1] = P[a_j = 0] = \frac{1}{2}.$$

Furthermore, any X_t can be written in terms of a_j, $j = 0, 1 \ldots$:

$$X_t = \frac{a_t}{2} + \frac{a_{t+1}}{2^2} + \frac{a_{t+2}}{2^3} + \ldots.$$

Taking expectations on both sides of the equations yields

$$EX_t = \frac{1}{2}\left[\frac{1}{2} + \frac{1}{2^2} + \ldots + \frac{1}{2^j} + \ldots\right]$$

$$= \frac{1}{2}\frac{1}{2}\frac{1}{1 - (1/2)} = \frac{1}{2};$$

therefore, the mean is time independent. The second order moments are shown by the formula below, namely, for $h \geq 0$,

$$\mathrm{Cov}(X_t, X_{t+h})$$
$$= \mathrm{Cov}\left(\left[\frac{a_t}{2} + \frac{a_{t+1}}{2^2} + \ldots + \frac{a_{t+h}}{2^{h-1}} + \frac{a_{t+h+1}}{2^h} + \ldots\right], \left[\frac{a_{t+h}}{2} + \frac{a_{t+h+1}}{2^2} + \ldots\right]\right)$$
$$= \frac{1}{2^h}V(a_{t+h}) + \frac{1}{2^{h+2}}V(a_{t+h+1})\ldots$$
$$= \frac{1}{2^h}.$$

This means that the process is second order stationary, and, since the correlogram shows an exponential decay, it admits an AR(1) linear representation

$$X_t = \frac{1}{4} + \frac{1}{2}X_{t-1} + \eta_t,$$

where η is a weak white noise.

iv) ARCH Model

The Autoregressive Conditionally Heteroskedastic models have been introduced by Engle (1982) to take into account time dependent conditional variances. An example of an ARCH model is

$$Y_t = \varepsilon_{t-1}^2\varepsilon_t, \tag{2.23}$$

where ε is a Gaussian white noise with variance σ^2. The second order properties of the process Y are easy to derive. We have

$$E(Y_t) = E(\varepsilon_{t-1}^2\varepsilon_t) = E(\varepsilon_{t-1}^2)E(\varepsilon_t) \text{ (because } \varepsilon_{t-1} \text{ and } \varepsilon_t \text{ are independent)}$$
$$= 0 \text{ (because } \varepsilon \text{ has zero mean);}$$

$$E(Y_t^2) = E(\varepsilon_{t-1}^4\varepsilon_t^2) = E(\varepsilon_{t-1}^4)E(\varepsilon_t^2)$$
$$= 3\sigma^6, \text{ where } \sigma^2 = V\varepsilon_t;$$

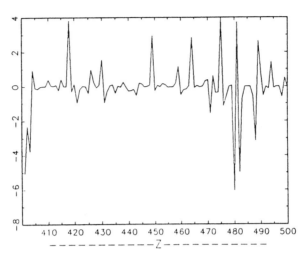

FIGURE 2.7. ARCH model.

$$E(Y_t Y_{t-h}) = E(\varepsilon_{t-1}^2 \varepsilon_t \varepsilon_{t-h-1}^2 \varepsilon_{t-h})$$
$$= E(\varepsilon_t) E(\varepsilon_{t-1}^2 \varepsilon_{t-h-1}^2 \varepsilon_{t-h}) \quad \text{(if} \quad h > 0)$$
$$= 0.$$

We see that the process Y is weakly stationary and is indeed a weak white noise:

$$Y_t = u_t, \quad E u_t = 0, \quad V u_t = 3\sigma^6, \tag{2.24}$$
$$\text{Cov}(u_t, u_{t-h}) = 0, \quad \text{if} \quad h \neq 0.$$

Its unconditional variance, which is equal to $3\sigma^6$, is time independent, whereas its conditional variance given the past,

$$V(Y_t / \underline{Y_{t-1}}) = V(\varepsilon_{t-1}^2 \varepsilon_t / \underline{Y_{t-1}}) = \sigma^2 \varepsilon_{t-1}^4,$$

depends on the lagged residuals.

A simulated path of this noise process is plotted in figure 2.7. As expected, it shows different variabilities depending on the subperiod.

v) Bilinear Models (Granger and Andersen 1978; Subba Rao 1981)

A bilinear model is linear in Y_t and ε_t but not in the two variables taken together. Its representation is

$$Y_t = \mu + \sum_{i=1}^{\infty} \varphi_i Y_{t-i} + \sum_{j=0}^{\infty} \theta_j \varepsilon_{t-j} + \sum_{i=1}^{\infty} \sum_{j=1}^{\infty} c_{ij} Y_{t-i} \varepsilon_{t-j},$$

with $\theta_0 = 1$.

Some bilinear processes have properties that are similar to those of an ARCH model. For instance, let us consider the process defined by

$$Y_t = \varepsilon_t + 0.5Y_{t-2}\varepsilon_{t-1}, \tag{2.25}$$

where ε_t is a Gaussian white noise. It has zero mean:

$$\begin{aligned} EY_t &= E(\varepsilon_t) + 0.5E(Y_{t-2}\varepsilon_{t-1}) \\ &= E(\varepsilon_t) + 0.5E(Y_{t-2})E(\varepsilon_{t-1}) = 0. \end{aligned}$$

Moreover, we have

$$\begin{aligned} E(Y_t Y_{t-h}) &= E(\varepsilon_t \varepsilon_{t-h}) + (0.5)^2 E(Y_{t-2}\varepsilon_{t-1}Y_{t-h-2}\varepsilon_{t-h-1}) \\ &\quad + (0.5)E(\varepsilon_t Y_{t-h-2}\varepsilon_{t-h-1}) + (0.5)E(\varepsilon_{t-h}Y_{t-2}\varepsilon_{t-1}). \end{aligned}$$

If $h \geq 2$, we see that

$$\begin{aligned} E(Y_t Y_{t-h}) &= E(\varepsilon_t)E(\varepsilon_{t-h}) + (0.5)^2 E(Y_{t-2})E(\varepsilon_{t-1}Y_{t-h-2}\varepsilon_{t-h-1}) \\ &\quad + (0.5)E(\varepsilon_t)E(Y_{t-h-2}\varepsilon_{t-h-1}) + (0.5)E(\varepsilon_{t-h}Y_{t-2})E(\varepsilon_{t-1}) = 0. \end{aligned}$$

If $h = 1$, we have

$$\begin{aligned} E(Y_t Y_{t-1}) &= E(\varepsilon_t)E(\varepsilon_{t-1}) + (0.5)^2 E(Y_{t-2})E(\varepsilon_{t-1}Y_{t-3}\varepsilon_{t-2}) \\ &\quad + (0.5)E(\varepsilon_t)E(Y_{t-3}\varepsilon_{t-2}) + (0.5)E(\varepsilon_{t-1}^2)E(Y_{t-2}) = 0. \end{aligned}$$

Finally, the equation written for $h = 0$ describes the variance

$$\begin{aligned} E(Y_t^2) &= E(\varepsilon_t^2) + (0.5)^2 E(Y_{t-2}^2\varepsilon_{t-1}^2) + E(\varepsilon_t \varepsilon_{t-1}Y_{t-2}), \\ E(Y_t^2) &= \sigma^2 + (0.5)^2 E(Y_{t-2}^2)\sigma^2. \end{aligned}$$

Therefore, $\sigma_t^2 = VY_t$ satisfies the recursive equation

$$\sigma_t^2 = \sigma^2 + (0.5)^2\sigma_{t-2}^2\sigma^2.$$

The solutions of this equation converge if $(0.5)^2\sigma^2 < 1$. This inequality is an ergodicity condition to ensure that the equation (2.25) has a second order stationary solution This bilinear process features heteroscedasticity at horizon 2. We have indeed

$$V(Y_t/\underline{Y_{t-2}}) = \sigma^2[1 + (0.5)^2 Y_{t-2}^2],$$

so that the conditional variance depends on the lagged values of the process.

A simulated path is displayed in figure 2.8.

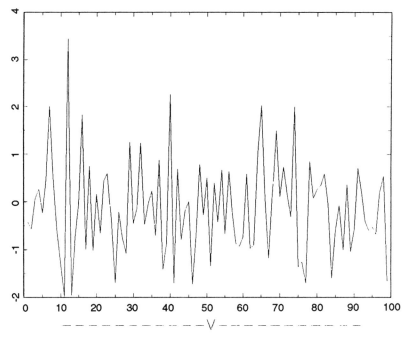

FIGURE 2.8. Bilinear process.

vi) Stochastic Autoregression

This example describes duration data, where the marginal distribution of the process is an exponential distribution with mean one. This autoregressive model has been proposed by Lawrance and Lewis (1985):

$$Y_t = \varepsilon_t + \begin{cases} \beta_1 Y_{t-1}, & \text{with probability } \alpha_1, \\ \beta_2 Y_{t-2}, & \text{with probability } \alpha_2, \\ 0, & \text{with probability } 1 - \alpha_1 - \alpha_2. \end{cases} \qquad (2.26)$$

If $\alpha_1 > 0, \alpha_2 > 0, \alpha_1 + \alpha_2 < 1, 0 < \beta_1, \beta_2 < 1$, the distribution of the i.i.d. sequence (ε_t) may be chosen such that the marginal distribution of Y_t is exponential and has a mean equal to 1. This particular distribution of the white noise is

$$\varepsilon_t = \begin{cases} u_t, & \text{with probability } 1 - p_2 - p_3, \\ b_2 u_t, & \text{with probability } p_2, \\ b_3 u_t, & \text{with probability } p_3, \end{cases}$$

where u_t has an exponential distribution with a mean equal to 1, and the auxiliary parameters b_2, b_3, p_2, p_3 are fixed relatively to $\beta_1, \beta_2, \alpha_1, \alpha_2$.

vii) Time Deformed Process

The existence of data bases, where prices and traded volumes are observed tick by tick, provides a rationale for distinguishing between the so-called transaction time determined by the counting process of the ticks and the usual calendar time. Some models have recently been introduced in the literature to take into account this feature (Clark 1973; Stock 1988; Dacarogna et al. 1994; Ghysels et al. 1995).

Let us consider the price process defined in transaction time: Y_n^*, $n \in \mathbb{N}$, where n denotes the tick and N_t, $t \in \mathbb{N}$ is the number of ticks observed at or before t. The price process in calendar time is

$$Y_t = Y_{N_t}^*.$$

For illustration, let us assume that the two processes Y^* and N are independent, such that Y^* is a Gaussian AR(1) process:

$$Y_n^* = \rho Y_{n-1}^* + \sigma \varepsilon_n^*, \quad \varepsilon_n^* \ IIN(0, 1),$$

while N has i.i.d. increments: $N_t - N_{t-1} = \mu_t$ (say). We can write

$$Y_{N_t}^* = \rho^{N_t - N_{t-1}} Y_{N_{t-1}}^* + \sigma \varepsilon_{N_t}^* + \rho \sigma \varepsilon_{N_t-1}^* + \dots + \rho^{N_t - N_{t-1} - 1} \sigma \varepsilon_{N_{t-1}+1}^*,$$

or

$$Y_t = \rho^{N_t - N_{t-1}} Y_{t-1}^* + \sigma \left[\frac{1 - \rho^{2(N_t - N_{t-1})}}{1 - \rho^2} \right]^{1/2} \varepsilon_t, \quad \varepsilon_t \ IIN(0, 1)$$

$$Y_t = \rho^{\mu_t} y_{t-1} + \sigma \left[\frac{1 - \rho^{2\mu_t}}{1 - \rho^2} \right]^{1/2} \varepsilon_t, \quad \varepsilon_t \ IIN(0, 1).$$

We see that

$$E(Y_t / Y_{t-1}, \mu_t) = \rho^{\mu_t} Y_{t-1},$$

$$V(Y_t / Y_{t-1}, \mu_t) = \rho^2 \frac{1 - \rho^{2\mu_t}}{1 - \rho^2}.$$

By integrating out the time deformation variable μ_t and taking into account the independence between the two processes Y^* and N, we get

$$E\left[Y_t Y_{t-1}\right] = E(\rho^{\mu_t}) Y_{t-1} = r Y_{t-1} \text{ (say)},$$

$$V\left[Y_t Y_{t-1}\right] = E\left[V(Y_t / Y_{t-1}, \mu_t) / Y_{t-1}\right] + V\left[E(Y_t / Y_{t-1}, \mu_t) / Y_{t-1}\right]$$

$$= \sigma^2 E\left(\frac{1 - \rho^{2\mu_t}}{1 - \rho^2}\right) + r^2 Y_{t-1}^2.$$

Therefore, we see that this time deformed process features conditional heteroscedasticity, while the underlying transaction time process does not.

2.4   Nonlinearities

We have seen in subsection 2.2 the complexity of linear time series, and we have introduced different definitions of linearity depending on assumptions on the white noise. Tests are generally carried out in order to check whether the error term ε is a weak white noise. Yet, it is also necessary to employ other procedures to check whether the noise satisfies more stringent conditions. For this purpose, two approaches may be considered. First, some implications of the strongest assumption of a Gaussian white noise may be considered and directly tested. This approach is based on specification tests, where the alternative and the null hypotheses are implicitly defined by means of the test statistic. Another approach considers specific nonlinear models nesting the linear model with a strict white noise. In that case, it is straightforward to test the null hypothesis by one of the classical test procedures, for instance, the Lagrange multiplier test. In this subsection, we essentially discuss the main specification tests.

2.4.1   Portmanteau Statistic

If the observed process (Y_t) admits an ARMA representation with a weak white noise

$$\Phi(L)Y_t = C + \Theta(L)\varepsilon_t,$$

the innovation process must be uncorrelated with the past values of the process or, equivalently, with the past values of the noise. Thus, a natural test of the hypothesis of weak linear representation is to check whether the covariance between ε_t and ε_{t-h} equals zero for every strictly positive value of h.

This idea is the basis of the Portmanteau procedure suggested by Box and Pierce (1970) and Ljung and Box (1978). If $(\hat{\varepsilon}_t)$ denotes the estimated residuals in the ARMA model, the empirical autocorrelations are

$$\hat{\rho}(h) = \sum_{t=1}^{T-h} \hat{\varepsilon}_t \hat{\varepsilon}_{t-h} \bigg/ \sum_{t=1}^{T} \hat{\varepsilon}_t^2.$$

These correlations are used to compute the test statistic:¿

$$Q_H = T(T+2) \sum_{h=1}^{H} \frac{\hat{\rho}(h)^2}{T-h}. \qquad (2.27)$$

Under the null hypothesis of an ARMA(p, q) model with a strict white noise, the Q_H statistic is asymptotically chi-square distributed with $H - p - q$ degrees of freedom. The null hypothesis is then accepted if $Q_h < \chi^2_{95\%}(H - p - q)$ and rejected otherwise, where $\chi^2_{95\%}(H - p - q)$ denotes the 95% quantile of the chi-square distribution with $H - p - q$ degrees of freedom.

2.4.2   Some Implications of the White Noise Hypothesis

i) Additional Regressors

If ε is a Gaussian white noise, the martingale difference assumption is satisfied and ε_t is uncorrelated with any function of the past values. Assumption A2 may then be tested by adding one or more regressor(s) to the ARMA representation, that is, by considering the extended model

$$\Phi(L)Y_t = C + \Theta(L)\varepsilon_t + \alpha h(\underline{Y_{t-1}}) \tag{2.28}$$

and testing for the significance of the coefficient α. Two types of additional regressors may be distinguished:

a) Some are known functions of the lagged values of the observed process. For instance, we could test the null hypothesis of a weak linear AR(1) process

$$Y_t = \rho Y_{t-1} + \varepsilon_t,$$

or of the presence of a threshold effect:

$$Y_t = \rho Y_{t-1} + \alpha \mathbb{I}_{Y_{t-1}>0} + \varepsilon_t.$$

This test can be performed using the classical Student t-statistic for the parameter α.

b) In other cases, the auxiliary regressors are known functions of $Y_{t-1}, Y_{t-2}, \ldots$ and of the latent errors $\varepsilon_{t-1}, .\varepsilon_{t-2}, \ldots$ For instance, if Y is strictly stationary, we know that the series may be suitably approximated by its Volterra's expansion. It is then natural to test for the significance of cross terms. Thus, if the ARMA model is reduced to an AR(1) representation

$$Y_t = \rho Y_{t-1} + \varepsilon_t,$$

the following extended model may be proposed:

$$Y_t = \rho Y_{t-1} + C_{11}\varepsilon_{t-1}^2 + C_{12}\varepsilon_{t-1}\varepsilon_{t-2} + \varepsilon_t,$$

which includes cross terms in ε.

This test relies on the usual Fisher F-statistic for the null hypothesis $H_0 = (C_{11} = C_{12} = 0)$, where the additional regressors ε_{t-1}^2, $\varepsilon_{t-1}\varepsilon_{t-2}$ are replaced by the corresponding residuals $\hat{\varepsilon}_{t-1}^2$, $\hat{\varepsilon}_{t-1}\hat{\varepsilon}_{t-2}$, and where $\hat{\varepsilon}_t = Y_t - \hat{\rho}Y_{t-1}$ is computed under the null hypothesis. Such an approach based on Volterra's expansion was developed by Keenan (1985).

ii) Independence of the White Noise

Another way to proceed is based on a generalized Portmanteau statistic. Indeed, if $\varepsilon = (\varepsilon_t)$ is a sequence of independent and identically distributed variables, the no correlation property holds for any nonlinear function of ε:

$$\forall g, \forall h \neq 0, \quad \mathrm{Cov}[g(\varepsilon_t), g(\varepsilon_{t-h})] = 0.$$

A Portmanteau statistic may then be defined for each of these transformations. McLeod and Li (1983) have suggested a Portmanteau test based on the autocorrelations of the squared residuals. The statistic is

$$\tilde{Q}_H = T(T+2) \sum_{h=1}^{H} \frac{\hat{\rho}_2^2(h)}{T-h}, \tag{2.29}$$

where

$$\hat{\rho}_{(2)}(h) = \left[\sum_{t=1}^{T-h} (\hat{\varepsilon}_t^2 - \hat{\sigma}^2)(\hat{\varepsilon}_{t-h}^2 - \hat{\sigma}^2) \right] \bigg/ \left[\sum_{t=1}^{T} (\hat{\varepsilon}_t^2 - \hat{\sigma}^2) \right],$$

$$\hat{\sigma}^2 = \frac{1}{T} \sum_{t=1}^{T} \hat{\varepsilon}_t^2.$$

iii) Subperiod Analysis

A common way to test for independence and equidistribution is to divide the initial sample $(Y_t, t = 1, 2, \ldots, T)$ [or $(\hat{\varepsilon}_t, t = 1, \ldots, T)$] into two subsamples $(Y_t, t \in T_1), (Y_t, t \in T_2)$ [or $(\hat{\varepsilon}_t, t \in T_1), (\hat{\varepsilon}_t, t \in T_2)$] and study whether the distribution properties are the same on the two subsamples. This approach is adopted in the classical Chow's test. In practice, the subsamples may be exogenously or endogenously determined. As an example, let us consider the idea of variance stability for the noise.

a) The whole sample may be divided into $(\hat{\varepsilon}_t, t = 1, \ldots [t/2])$ and $(\hat{\varepsilon}_t, t = [t/2] + 1, \ldots, T)$, and we can compare the empirical variances:

$$\hat{\sigma}_1^2 = \frac{2}{T} \sum_{t=1}^{[T/2]} \hat{\varepsilon}_t^2, \quad \hat{\sigma}_2^2 = \frac{2}{T} \sum_{t=[T/2]+1}^{T} \hat{\varepsilon}_t^2.$$

b) A partition based on lagged values like ε_{t-1} might be more appropriate. We can consider the two subsamples

$$(\hat{\varepsilon}_t, t \in T_1 = \{t : |\hat{\varepsilon}_{t-1}| > \hat{\sigma}\}),$$

$$(\hat{\varepsilon}_t, t \in T_2 = \{t : |\hat{\varepsilon}_{t-1}| < \hat{\sigma}\}),$$

where $\hat{\sigma}^2$ is an estimator of $\sigma^2 = V\varepsilon_t$.

A comparison of the empirical variances estimated from these subsamples would allow us to detect any kind of conditional heteroscedasticity.

iv) Testing for Normality

Finally, other procedures rely on specific properties of the normal distribution. The following result due to Granger and Newbold (1976) is a basic idea of a large number of tests.

Property 2.30. *Let (Y_t) be a stationary Gaussian linear process. Then*

$$\rho_h(Y_t^2) = [\rho_h(Y_t)]^2, \quad h = 0, \pm 1, \ldots,$$

where ρ_h denotes the autocorrelation of order h.

Proof. The moment generating function of the pair (Y_t, Y_{t-h}) is

$$m(u, v) = \exp[\frac{1}{2}\sigma_y^2(u^2 + v^2 + 2\rho_h uv)],$$

with $\sigma_y^2 = VY_t$ and $\rho_h = \rho_h(Y_t)$. Since

$$E[Y_t^2 Y_{t-h}^2] = \left[\frac{\partial^4 m(u, v)}{\partial u^2 \partial v^2}\right]_{u=v=0} = \sigma_y^4(1 + 2\rho_h^2)$$

and $V(Y_t^2) = 2\sigma_y^4$, we obtain

$$\rho_h(Y_t^2) = \frac{E[Y_t^2 Y_{t-h}^2] - \sigma_y^4}{2\sigma_y^4} = \rho_h^2.$$

Q.E.D.

This relation holds for either the initial series (Y_t) or the residual series $(\hat{\varepsilon}_t)$. An empirical test of this property involves drawing a graph of the correlations of squared residuals:

$$\hat{\rho}_h(\hat{\varepsilon}_t^2) = \left[\frac{1}{T - H}\sum_{t=1}^{T-h}(\hat{\varepsilon}_t^2 - \hat{\sigma}^2)(\hat{\varepsilon}_{t-h}^2 - \hat{\sigma}^2)\right] / \left[\frac{1}{T}\sum_{t=1}^{T}(\hat{\varepsilon}_t^2 - \hat{\sigma}^2)\right],$$

as a function of $\hat{\rho}_h(\hat{\varepsilon}_t)^2$. Under the normality, the points lay approximately on the 45 degree line.

v) The Bispectral Approach

Other tests can be applied directly to the initial series (Y_t). Subba Rao and Gabr (1980) and Hinich (1982) developed test procedures of the strict linearity assumption using the notion of bispectrum. Let us consider a stationary series (Y_t) with a strict linear representation

$$Y_t = \sum_{j=0}^{\infty} \theta_j \varepsilon_{t-j},$$

where (ε_t) is a strict white noise and $\sum_{j=0}^{\infty} |\theta_j| < \infty$.

Let us suppose that the three first order moments of (Y_t) are finite. Hence the cumulant of order three can be defined:

$$C(m, n) = E(Y_t Y_{t+m} Y_{t+n}). \tag{2.31}$$

The bispectrum computed at the frequencies (ω_1, ω_2) is the double Fourier transform of the sequence $C(m, n)$:

$$B(\omega_1, \omega_2) = \sum_{m=-\infty}^{\infty} \sum_{n=-\infty}^{\infty} C(m, n) \exp[-i2\pi(\omega_1 m + \omega_2 n)]. \tag{2.32}$$

Consequently, it is a direct generalization of the spectral density function:

$$f(\omega) = \sum_{m=-\infty}^{+\infty} \gamma(m) \exp(-i2\pi\omega m), \quad \gamma(m) = E(Y_t Y_{t+m}).$$

A direct computation shows that

$$B(\omega_1, \omega_2) = \mu_3 \Theta(\exp[-i2\pi\omega_1]) \Theta(\exp[-i2\pi\omega_2]) \Theta(\exp[2i(\omega_1 + \omega_2)]),$$

$$f(\omega) = \sigma^2 \Theta(\exp[-i2\pi\omega]) \Theta(\exp[i2\pi\omega]),$$

with $\mu_3 = EY_t^3$. It follows that

$$\frac{|B(\omega_1, \omega_2)|^2}{f(\omega_1)f(\omega_2)f(\omega_1 + \omega_2)} = \frac{\mu_3^2}{\sigma^6}$$

is constant. A test procedure may then be based on a comparison between the estimated bispectrum $\hat{B}(\omega_1, \omega_2)$ and the product of the estimated spectra $\hat{f}(\omega_1)\hat{f}(\omega_2)\hat{f}(\omega_1 + \omega_2)$.

2.5 Exercises

Exercise 2.1. Let $(X_t, t \in \mathbb{Z})$ be a strongly stationary process.

1. Let f be a mapping defined on the set of possible values $\mathcal{X}$ of X_t. Show that the process

$$Y_t = f(X_t), t \in \mathfrak{Z}$$

is strongly stationary.

2. Is the stationarity property preserved by a transformation $Y_t = g(X_t, X_{t-1})$ that takes into account the dynamics of X?

Exercise 2.2. Show an example where a process $Y_t = f_t(X_t)$, in which $(X_t, t \in \mathfrak{Z})$ is strongly stationary and f_t depends on time, has the property of weak stationarity.

Exercise 2.3. One considers a threshold autoregressive model defined by

$$Y_t = a\mathbb{I}_{Y_{t-1}>0} + \varepsilon_t,$$

where ε_t is a reduced Gaussian white noise.

1. Verify that the underlying process $Z_t = \mathbb{I}_{Y_{t-1}>0}$ is a homogeneous Markov chain.

2 Find the corresponding transition matrix and conclude that the ergodicity condition holds, that is, the condition on a ensuring that the matrix has an eigenvalue with modulus strictly lower than 1 is satisfied. Determine the invariant measure corresponding to this chain.

3. The ergodicity condition is supposed to be satisfied, and the stationary solution of the threshold autoregressive equation is retained. Specify the form of the mean and covariances of the process Z. Show that the sequence of covariances satisfies a linear recursive equation of a given order and, therefore, Z admits a weak ARMA representation. Find this representation.

4. Follow the same approach to find a weak ARMA representation for the Y process.

3
Univariate ARCH Models

The aim of this chapter is to describe the major specifications with conditional heteroscedasticity found in the literature. We first present an autoregressive model of order one with heteroscedastic errors. This simple example allows us to study in detail the existence conditions of the process and to discuss its main properties. We then discuss the different possible extensions of the basic model and show how the results derived for a simple case may be generalized.

3.1 A Heteroscedastic Model of Order One

3.1.1 *Description of the Model*

i) The Autoregressive Equations

As an illustration, we consider an autoregressive model of order one with a regression coefficient φ and with a modulus assumed to be smaller than one to ensure the stability of the system. The current value of the process is

$$Y_t = \mu + \varphi Y_{t-1} + \varepsilon_t, \quad \forall t, |\varphi| < 1, \tag{3.1}$$

where $\varepsilon = (\varepsilon_t)$ is a weak white noise satisfying the martingale difference sequence condition:

$$E(\varepsilon_t / \underline{\varepsilon_{t-1}}) = 0, \quad \forall t. \tag{3.2}$$

Contrary to the usual practice, we do not assume that the conditional variance of the noise, i.e., $V(\varepsilon_t / \underline{\varepsilon_{t-1}})$, is time independent. Instead, we allow for a time

dependence through an autoregressive equation of order one for the squared innovations:

$$\varepsilon_t^2 = c + a\varepsilon_{t-1}^2 + u_t, \tag{3.3}$$

where $u = (u_t)$ is a strong white noise.

A process that satisfies the three aforementioned conditions is called autoregressive of order one with ARCH(1) errors. Its properties can be obtained directly
from the two recursive equations defining (Y_t) and (ε_t^2).

ii) A Few Conditions Ensuring the Existence of the Process

The restrictions (3.2), (3.3) have been simultaneously imposed on the innovation
process ε, and it is not a priori obvious that they are compatible with each other.

(*) We first notice that the recursive equation (3.3) is not sufficient to define without ambiguity the process (ε_t^2). It has to be complemented by an initial condition.
In this case, the mean of the squared innovations is

$$m_t = E(\varepsilon_t^2) = c + am_{t-1},$$

where m_0 is given.

In order to ensure that this unconditional mean is time invariant, we assume that
the parameter a has a modulus strictly smaller than 1 and that the initial condition
corresponds to the equilibrium value $m_0 = c/(1-a)$.

(**) In addition, the positivity of the process (ε_t^2) must be ensured. Some sufficient conditions for positivity are $a > 0$ and $c + u_t \geq 0$ for any admissible value
of u_t.

(***) Finally, let us consider two independent processes $(Z_t), (\delta_t)$, where (Z_t)
takes positive values:

$$Z_t = c + aZ_{t-1} + u_t,$$

and where the random variables δ_t are independent and identically distributed, so
that:

$$P[\delta_t = +1] = P[\delta_t = -1] = \frac{1}{2}.$$

We note that the process $\varepsilon_t = \delta_t\sqrt{Z_t}$ satisfies both conditions (3.2) and (3.3),
and the compatibility of these conditions follows.

In the following, we assume that these conditions ensuring the existence of a
process satisfying (3.1), (3.2), (3.3) are verified, and we study the probabilistic
properties of the two processes ε and Y.

3.1.2 Properties of the Innovation Process ε

The process (ε_t) must satisfy the orthogonality condition with respect to the past:
$E(\varepsilon_t/\underline{\varepsilon_{t-1}}) = 0$. This constraint has several consequences.

i) We first notice that the error process is also orthogonal to the past values at
any lag:

$$E(\varepsilon_t/\underline{\varepsilon_{t-h}}) = 0, \forall h > 0$$

by the law of iterated expectations. Indeed, the informational content of ε_{t-h} is smaller than that of ε_{t-1}. Hence

$$E(\varepsilon_t/\varepsilon_{t-h}) = E(E(\varepsilon_t/\varepsilon_{t-1})/\varepsilon_{t-h}) = E(0/\varepsilon_{t-h}) = 0.$$

ii) This orthogonality property implies that some conditional correlations are equal to zero. Let us consider two positive integers h and k to show that

$$\begin{aligned}
&\text{Cov}[(\varepsilon_t, \varepsilon_{t+k})/\varepsilon_{t-h}] \\
&= E[\varepsilon_t \varepsilon_{t+k}/\varepsilon_{t-h}] - E[\varepsilon_t/\varepsilon_{t-h}]E[\varepsilon_{t+k}/\varepsilon_{t-h}] \\
&= E[\varepsilon_t \varepsilon_{t+k}/\varepsilon_{t-h}] \\
&= E[E(\varepsilon_t \varepsilon_{t+k}/\varepsilon_{t+k-1})/\varepsilon_{t-h}]
\end{aligned}$$

(according to the law of iterated expectations)

$$= E[\varepsilon_t E(\varepsilon_{t+k}/\varepsilon_{t+k-1})/\varepsilon_{t-h}]$$

(since ε_t belongs to the information ε_{t+k-1})

$$= 0.$$

Therefore, there is no correlation between the present and future values of the innovation process at any lag h.

iii) Other properties of the error process are to be derived from the autoregressive equation (3.3): $\varepsilon_t^2 = c + a\varepsilon_{t-1}^2 + u_t$; they concern the conditional variance. Substituting recursively yields

$$\varepsilon_t^2 = c[1 + a + \ldots + a^{h-1}] + a^h \varepsilon_{t-h}^2 + u_t + au_{t-1} + \ldots + a^{h-1}u_{t-h+1}.$$

By taking expectation on both sides of this equation conditionally on the information ε_{t-h}, we obtain

$$\begin{aligned}
E(\varepsilon_t^2/\varepsilon_{t-h}) &= c[1 + a + \ldots + a^{h-1}] + a^h \varepsilon_{t-h}^2 \\
&= c\frac{1 - a^h}{1 - a} + a^h \varepsilon_{t-h}^2.
\end{aligned}$$

Therefore, the conditional variances are

$$V(\varepsilon_t/\varepsilon_{t-h}) = c\frac{1 - a^h}{1 - a} + a^h \varepsilon_{t-h}^2. \tag{3.4}$$

They depend on the past information only through the most recent value ε_{t-h}^2. When the lag h tends to infinity, those variances converge towards the unconditional variance:

$$V(\varepsilon_t) = EV(\varepsilon_t/\varepsilon_{t-h}) = \frac{c}{1 - a}. \tag{3.5}$$

Since this variance is time independent, we find that the process ε is a weak white noise. The difference between the conditional variance and the unconditional variance is a simple function of the deviations of squared innovations from the mean. We have indeed

$$V(\varepsilon_t/\varepsilon_{t-h}) - V(\varepsilon_t) = a^h[\varepsilon_{t-h}^2 - E(\varepsilon_{t-h}^2)].$$

Let us suppose that the condition $a > 0$ is satisfied. If the modulus of the innovation is large, the conditional variance takes smaller values than the unconditional variance.

3.1.3 Properties of the Y Process

The properties of this process may be derived directly from those of the white noise ε.

i) The nonlinear forecasts of Y coincide with the linear ones. These forecasts are given by the expression

$$E(Y_t/Y_{t-h}) = \mu\frac{1 - \varphi^h}{1 - \varphi} + \varphi^h Y_{t-h} \tag{3.6}$$

and depend in a linear way on the most recent value.

ii) The conditional variances and covariances may thus be computed, by writing Y_t in terms of the most recent innovations,

$$Y_t = \mu\frac{1 - \varphi^h}{1 - \varphi} + \varphi^h Y_{t-h} + \varepsilon_t + \varphi\varepsilon_{t-1} + \ldots + \varphi^{h-1}\varepsilon_{t-h+1}.$$

If h and k are two integers, the first one being strictly positive and the second one nonnegative, we can write

$$\text{Cov}[(Y_t, Y_{t+k})/Y_{t-h}]$$

$$= \text{Cov}\left[\left(\mu\frac{1 - \varphi^h}{1 - \varphi} + \varphi^h Y_{t-h} + \varepsilon_t + \ldots + \varphi^{h-1}\varepsilon_{t-h+1},\right.\right.$$

$$\left.\left.\mu\frac{1 - \varphi^{h+k}}{1 - \varphi} + \varphi^{h+k} Y_{t-h} + \varepsilon_{t+k} + \ldots + \varphi^{h+k-1}\varepsilon_{t-h+1}\right)/Y_{t-h}\right]$$

$$= \text{Cov}[(\varepsilon_t + \ldots + \varphi^{h-1}\varepsilon_{t-h+1}, \varepsilon_{t+k} + \ldots + \varphi^{h+k-1}\varepsilon_{t-h+1})/Y_{t-h}]$$

$$= \varphi^k V(\varepsilon_t/\varepsilon_{t-h}) + \varphi^{k+2} V(\varepsilon_{t-1}/\varepsilon_{t-h}) + \ldots + \varphi^{k+2(h-1)} V(\varepsilon_{t-h+1}/\varepsilon_{t-h})$$

$$= \varphi^k \sum_{j=0}^{h-1} \varphi^{2j} V(\varepsilon_{t-j}/\varepsilon_{t-h})$$

$$= \varphi^k \sum_{j=0}^{h-1} \varphi^{2j}\left\{c\frac{1 - a^{h-j}}{1 - a} + a^{h-j}\varepsilon_{t-h}^2\right\}$$

$$= \frac{c\varphi^k}{1 - a} \sum_{j=0}^{h-1} \varphi^{2j} - \frac{ca^h\varphi^k}{1 - a} \sum_{j=0}^{h-1} \varphi^{2j}a^{-j} + a^h\varphi^k\varepsilon_{t-h}^2 \sum_{j=0}^{h-1} \varphi^{2j}a^{-j}$$

$$= \frac{c\varphi^k}{1-a}\frac{1-\varphi^{2h}}{1-\varphi^2} - \frac{ca\varphi^k}{1-a}\frac{a^h-\varphi^{2h}}{a-\varphi^2} + a\varphi^k \varepsilon^2_{t-h}\frac{a^h-\varphi^{2h}}{a-\varphi^2}.$$

In particular, the unconditional covariances are obtained in a limiting case when h tends to infinity. The usual formulas can then be derived:

$$\mathrm{Cov}(Y_t, Y_{t+k}) = \frac{c\varphi^k}{1-a}\frac{1}{1-\varphi^2} = \varphi^k V Y_t, \quad k \geq 0. \tag{3.7}$$

iii) The precision of the forecast at horizon one is summarized by the variance: $V(Y_t/\underline{Y_{t-1}})$. The expression for this conditional variance is obtained from the formula of $\mathrm{Cov}((Y_t, Y_{t+k})/\underline{Y_{t-h}})$ by setting $k = 0$ and $h = 1$:

$$V(Y_t/\underline{Y_{t-1}}) = V(\varepsilon_t/\underline{Y_{t-1}}) = c + a\varepsilon^2_{t-1}. \tag{3.8}$$

3.1.4   Distribution of the Error Process

Other results may be derived if the distribution of the error terms (ε_t) is specified. Engle (1982), for instance, studied a process ε with a conditionally normal distribution:

$$\varepsilon_t/\underline{\varepsilon_{t-1}} \sim N[0, c + a\varepsilon^2_{t-1}]. \tag{3.9}$$

Note that this process is conditionally Gaussian but not marginally Gaussian. Indeed, if that were the case, the conditional variance would be independent of the past values, which is not true. A few more precise results may be derived concerning the non-Gaussian aspect of the marginal distribution of ε. For instance, we find (see exercise 3.1) that the process (3.9) has stationary moments of order 2 and 4, if $3a^2 < 1$. These moments are, respectively,

$$E(\varepsilon^2_t) = \frac{c}{1-a}, \quad E(\varepsilon^4_t) = \frac{3c^2}{(1-a)^2}\frac{1-a^2}{1-3a^2}. \tag{3.10}$$

This implies that the kurtosis associated with the marginal distribution,

$$k = \frac{E(\varepsilon^4_t)}{[E(\varepsilon^2_t)]^2} = 3\frac{1-a^2}{1-3a^2},$$

is always larger than 3 (kurtosis value of the normal distribution). This reflects fatness tails of the marginal distributions compared to those of the normal. This distribution is said to be *leptokurtic*. The kurtosis as a function of a is represented in figure 3.1.

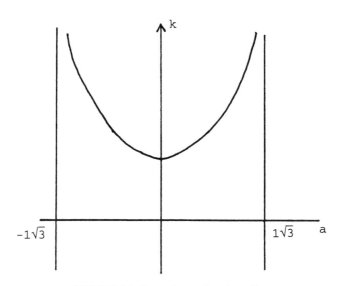

FIGURE 3.1. Kurtosis as a function of a.

3.2   General Properties of ARCH Processes

3.2.1   Various Extensions

As was shown in the previous section, the ARCH model describes simultaneously the evolution of the conditional mean and the conditional variance. Different models have been proposed in the literature in order to obtain past dependent conditional variances. We will briefly discuss these models and the corresponding terminology.

i) ARCH(q) Models (Engle 1982)

These models generalize the ARCH(1) model for the error term presented in the previous section. The basic idea is to increase the order of the autoregressive polynomial. Hence, the ARCH(q) model is defined as

$$\varepsilon_t^2 = c + \sum_{i=1}^{q} a_i \varepsilon_{t-i}^2 + u_t, \quad E(\varepsilon_t / \underline{\varepsilon_{t-1}}) = 0, \tag{3.11}$$

where $u = (u_t)$ is a martingale difference sequence. The conditional variance of ε_t is

$$V(\varepsilon_t / \underline{\varepsilon_{t-1}}) = c + \sum_{i=1}^{q} a_i \varepsilon_{t-i}^2$$

and depends on the past through the q most recent values of ε_t^2.

ii) GARCH (p, q) Models (Bollerslev 1986)

The ARCH model is based on an autoregressive representation of the conditional variance. One may also in a usual way add a moving average part. The GARCH processes (generalized autoregressive conditionally heteroscedastic) are thus obtained. The model is defined by

$$
\left\{
\begin{array}{l}
E(\varepsilon_t/\underline{\varepsilon_{t-1}}) = 0, \\[2mm]
V(\varepsilon_t/\underline{\varepsilon_{t-1}}) = h_t = c + \displaystyle\sum_{i=1}^{q} \alpha_i \varepsilon_{t-i}^2 + \sum_{j=1}^{p} \beta_j h_{t-j}.
\end{array}
\right.
$$

$$(3.12)$$

The GARCH(p, q) model may be rewritten in an alternative form that is easy to compare with the autoregressive representation (3.11). For this purpose, let us introduce the innovation corresponding to the square of the process: $u_t = \varepsilon_t^2 - h_t$. Replacing h_t by $\varepsilon_t^2 - u_t$ in the GARCH representation yields

$$
\varepsilon_t^2 - u_t = c + \sum_{i=1}^{q} \alpha_i \varepsilon_{t-i}^2 + \sum_{j=1}^{p} \beta_j (\varepsilon_{t-j}^2 - u_{t-j})
$$

$$
\Leftrightarrow \varepsilon_t^2 = c + \sum_{i=1}^{\mathrm{Max}(p,q)} (\alpha_i + \beta_i)\varepsilon_{t-i}^2 + u_t - \sum_{j=1}^{p} \beta_j u_{t-j},
$$

with $\alpha_i = 0$ for $i > q$ and $\beta_i = 0$ for $i > p$.

It is an ARMA[Max(p, q), p] representation for the process ε^2 but with an error term u that does not necessarily have a constant variance. We emphasize the fact that the GARCH terminology is similar to that of the ARMA, except that p denotes the order of the moving average part and not necessarily of the autoregressive polynomial.

iii) ARMA–GARCH Models (Weiss 1986)

Finally, the GARCH modelling may be applied to the innovation process instead of the initial process. We may simultaneously introduce several additional effects either in the conditional mean or in the conditional variance. We may consider a linear regression model with GARCH errors:

$$Y_t = X_t b + \varepsilon_t, \text{ where } (\varepsilon_t) \text{ satisfies a GARCH}(p, q) \text{ model;} \qquad (3.13)$$

or an ARMA model with GARCH errors:

$$\Phi(L)Y_t = \Theta(L)\varepsilon_t, \text{ where } (\varepsilon_t) \text{ satisfies a GARCH}(p, q) \text{ model,} \qquad (3.14)$$

or even an ARMA model, where the unconditional variance of Y has an impact on the conditional variance:

$$
\begin{cases}
\Phi(L)Y_t = \Theta(L)\varepsilon_t, \\
E(\varepsilon_t/\underline{\varepsilon_{t-1}}) = 0, \\
V(\varepsilon_t/\underline{\varepsilon_{t-1}}) = c + \sum_{i=1}^{q} \alpha_i \varepsilon_{t-i}^2 + \gamma_0 [E(Y_t/\underline{Y_{t-1}})]^2 + \sum_{i=1}^{s} \gamma_i Y_{t-i}^2.
\end{cases}
\tag{3.15}
$$

For example, Duang and Hung (1991) considered the returns on financial assets with residual maturity not being time invariant and also proposed an ARCH model with maturity as an explanatory variable.

iv) ARCH-M Models (Engle, Lilien, and Robbins 1987)

The ARCH-M models are likely better tools to describe the impact of the volatility on the conditional mean (see chapters 7 and 8). In these models, the conditional variance appears as an explanatory variable in the conditional mean. An example of an ARCH-M model is

$$
Y_t = X_t b + \delta h_t + \varepsilon_t, \text{ where } (\varepsilon_t) \text{ satisfies a GARCH model.} \tag{3.16}
$$

As in the example discussed in section 3.1, the ARCH type models originate from the recursive equations satisfied by the conditional variances. Hence, it may be worth checking to see whether there exist processes that satisfy these equations. As a matter of fact, it is easy to see that this is the case. Let us consider a GARCH model. It may be derived from a (ε_t) process defined as

$$
\begin{cases}
\varepsilon_t = (c + \sum_{i=1}^{q} \alpha_i \varepsilon_{t-i}^2 + \sum_{j=1}^{p} \beta_j h_{t-j})^{1/2} u_t, \\
h_t = c + \sum_{i=1}^{q} \alpha_i \varepsilon_{t-i}^2 + \sum_{j=1}^{p} \beta_j h_{t-j},
\end{cases}
\tag{3.17}
$$

where $(u_t, t \geq 0)$ is a strong white noise and where the initial conditions $\varepsilon_{-1}, \ldots, \varepsilon_{-q}, h_{-1}, \ldots, h_{-p}$ are given.

v) Stochastic Variance Models

In the model proposed by Harvey, Ruiz, and Shepard (1991), the second recursive equation describes the behavior of the log-volatility instead of the volatility itself. A clear advantage of this approach is to ensure the positivity of the volatility process.

This model is defined as

$$
\begin{cases}
\Phi(L)Y_t = \Theta(L) \left\{ \exp\left(\frac{v_t}{2}\right) e_t \right\}, \\
A(L)v_t = B(L)\eta_t,
\end{cases}
\tag{3.18}
$$

where (e_t), (η_t) are two independent Gaussian white noises with variance 1 and σ_η^2, respectively.

3.2.2 Stationarity of a GARCH(p, q) Process

Let us consider a process $\varepsilon = (\varepsilon_t)$ satisfying a GARCH(p, q) model:

$$\begin{cases} E(\varepsilon_t / \varepsilon_{t-1}) = 0, \\ V(\varepsilon_t / \varepsilon_{t-1}) = h_t = c + \sum_{i=1}^{q} \alpha_i \varepsilon_{t-i} + \sum_{j=1}^{p} \beta_j h_{t-j}. \end{cases}$$

The process ε is a martingale difference sequence and admits in particular uncorrelated components with zero mean. In order to study the second order stationarity, it is then sufficient to consider the variance,

$$V \varepsilon_t = V \left[E(\varepsilon_t / \varepsilon_{t-1}) \right] + E \left[V(\varepsilon_t / \varepsilon_{t-1}) \right] = E h_t,$$

and to show that it is asymptotically time independent.

Property 3.19. *A process ε satisfying a GARCH(p,q) model with positive coefficients $c \geq 0$, $\alpha_i \geq 0$, $i = 1, \ldots, q$, $\beta_j \geq 0$, $j = 1, \ldots, p$, is asymptotically second order stationary if*

$$\alpha(1) + \beta(1) = \sum_{i=1}^{q} \alpha_i + \sum_{j=1}^{p} \beta_j < 1.$$

Proof. (*) We have already noted that the GARCH model can be rewritten as an ARMA representation of the process ε^2. We have

$$\varepsilon_t^2 = c + \sum_{i=1}^{\text{Max}(p,q)} (\alpha_i + \beta_i) \varepsilon_{t-i}^2 + u_t - \sum_{j=1}^{p} \beta_j u_{t-j}.$$

Taking the expectation of both sides yields

$$E \varepsilon_t^2 = c + \sum_{i=1}^{\text{Max}(p,q)} (\alpha_i + \beta_i) E(\varepsilon_{t-i}^2).$$

Therefore, if the roots of the characteristic polynomial,

$$1 - \sum_{i=1}^{\text{Max}(p,q)} (\alpha_i + \beta_i) L^i,$$

are strictly outside the unit circle, the sequence $E \varepsilon_t^2$ converges and the process is asymptotically second order stationary.

(**) This condition implies that $\alpha(1) + \beta(1) < 1$. Indeed, if $\alpha(1) + \beta(1)$ were greater than or equal to 1, we would have $1 - \alpha(0) - \beta(0) > 0$ and $1 - \alpha(1) - \beta(1) \leq 0$; there would then be a root of the characteristic polynomial that would be real and lie between 0 and 1.

(***) Conversely, let us assume that $\alpha(1) + \beta(1) < 1$. If the root z of the characteristic polynomial had a modulus strictly smaller than 1, we would have

$$
1 = \sum_{i=1}^{\text{Max}(p,q)} (\alpha_i + \beta_i)z^i
$$

$$
= |\sum_{i=1}^{\text{Max}(p,q)} (\alpha_i + \beta_i)z^i|
$$

$$
\leq \sum_{i=1}^{\text{Max}(p,q)} (\alpha_i + \beta_i)|z|^i \leq \alpha(1) + \beta(1) < 1,
$$

and clearly a contradiction arises.   Q.E.D.

3.2.3 Kurtosis

The difference between the conditional and unconditional distributions arises especially in terms of increased kurtosis. Let us consider a conditionally Gaussian GARCH process. The second and fourth moments of the process are related by

$$
E(\varepsilon_t^4/\varepsilon_{t-1}) = 3[E(\varepsilon_t^2/\varepsilon_{t-1})]^2.
$$

Taking the expectation of both sides, we obtain

$$
\begin{aligned}
E(\varepsilon_t^4) &= E \quad E(\varepsilon_t^4/\varepsilon_{t-1}) \\
&= 3E[E(\varepsilon_t^2/\varepsilon_{t-1})]^2 \\
&\geq 3[E E(\varepsilon_t^2/\varepsilon_{t-1})]^2 \\
&= 3(E\varepsilon_t^2)^2.
\end{aligned}
$$

We deduce that the marginal distribution of (ε_t) has fatter tails than the normal distribution. Moreover, we have

$$
k = \frac{E(\varepsilon_t^4)}{(E\varepsilon_t^2)^2} = 3 + 3\frac{E[E(\varepsilon_t^2/\varepsilon_{t-1})^2] - E[E(\varepsilon_t^2/\varepsilon_{t-1})]^2}{(E\varepsilon_t^2)^2},
$$

$$
k = 3 + 3\frac{V \quad E(\varepsilon_t^2/\varepsilon_{t-1})}{(E\varepsilon_t^2)^2}.
$$

The kurtosis thus is directly linked to a natural measure of conditional heteroscedasticity.

3.2.4 Yule–Walker Equations for the Square of a GARCH Process

Under some regularity assumptions (see exercise 3.6) the square of the process (ε_t^2) may also be second order stationary. The representation

$$
\varepsilon_t^2 = c + \sum_{i=1}^{\text{Max}(p,q)} (\alpha_i + \beta_i)\varepsilon_{t-i}^2 + u_t - \sum_{j=1}^{p} \beta_j u_{t-j}
$$

is a standard ARMA with an innovation process (u_t) that is itself a second order white noise. This noise is generally conditionally heteroscedastic. Hence, classical results on ARMA processes apply.

For example, we may consider the autocovariance function associated with (ε_t^2), i.e.,

$$\gamma(h)^{(2)} = \text{Cov}(\varepsilon_t^2, \varepsilon_{t-h}^2).$$

Replacing (ε_t^2) by a function of the past values of ε^2 and of the current and past values of the innovations, we get

$$\gamma(h)^{(2)} = \text{Cov}(c + \sum_{i=1}^{\text{Max}(p,q)} (\alpha_i + \beta_i)\varepsilon_{t-i}^2 + u_t - \sum_{j=1}^{p} \beta_j u_{t-j}, \varepsilon_{t-h}^2),$$

$$\gamma(h)^{(2)} = \sum_{i=1}^{\text{Max}(p,q)} (\alpha_i + \beta_i) \text{Cov}(\varepsilon_{t-i}^2, \varepsilon_{t-h}^2) + \text{Cov}(u_t - \sum_{j=1}^{p} \beta_j u_{t-j}, \varepsilon_{t-h}^2).$$

When h is large enough, the last term of the right-hand side equals zero. Therefore, the sequence of autocovariances satisfies a linear recursive equation of order $\text{Max}(p, q)$ for h greater than $p + 1$:

$$\gamma_{(h)}^{(2)} = \sum_{i=1}^{\text{Max}(p,q)} (\alpha_i + \beta_i)\gamma(h - i)^{(2)}, \quad \forall h \geq p + 1. \tag{3.20}$$

This Yule–Walker system may be used for different purposes. First, it is useful as a tool to identify the orders $\text{Max}(p, q)$ and p, i.e., the orders p and q if $q \geq p$, or only p otherwise; second, it may also be useful to estimate the coefficients $\alpha_i + \beta_i, i = 1, \ldots, \text{Max}(p, q)$ in a consistent way. For such a purpose, we may solve the system (3.18) for $h = p + 1, \ldots, p + \text{Max}(p + q)$ after replacing the theoretical autocovariances by their empirical counterparts.

3.3 Exercises

Exercise 3.1. Consider an ARCH process of order one with a Gaussian conditional distribution. The model is written as

$$Y_t = \sqrt{a_0 + a_1 Y_{t-1}^2} \cdot \varepsilon_t,$$

where ε_t has a standard normal conditional distribution: $\varepsilon_t/\varepsilon_{t-1} \sim N(0, 1)$.

1. Determine the $2r$ order moments of the error ε and show that

$$E(Y_t^{2r}/\underline{Y_{t-1}}) = [a_0 + a_1 Y_{t-1}^2]^r \prod_{j=1}^{r}(2j - 1).$$

2. Let us introduce the vector of dimension r:

$$W_t' = (Y_t^{2r}, Y_t^{2(r-1)}, \ldots, Y_t^2).$$

By expanding the expression of the conditional moments $E(Y_t^{2r}/Y_{t-1})$, show that the conditional mean $E(W_t/W_{t-1})$ is a linear combination of W_{t-1}:

$$E(W_t/W_{t-1}) = b + A W_{t-1},$$

where A is an upper triangular matrix.

3. Verify that the stability condition: "all eigenvalues of A have modulus strictly smaller than 1" may be written as

$$a_1^r \prod_{j=1}^{r}(2j - 1) < 1.$$

4. Let us consider the particular case $r = 2$. Compute the second and fourth order moments of the process Y and show that

$$E(Y_t^2) = \frac{a_0}{1 - a_1}, \; E(Y_t^4) = \frac{3a_0^2}{(1 - a_1)^2} \frac{1 - a_1^2}{1 - 3a_1^2}$$

[see Engle (1982)].

Exercise 3.2. Let us consider a conditionally Gaussian GARCH(1,1) process defined by

$$\varepsilon_t/\varepsilon_{t-1} \sim N(0, h_t)$$

with $h_t = c + \alpha_1 \varepsilon_{t-1}^2 + \beta_1 h_{t-1}, c > 0, \alpha_1 \geq 0, \beta_1 \geq 0$.

1. Following the same approach as in exercise 3.1, show that a sufficient condition for the existence of the $(2r)^{th}$ order moment is

$$\mu(\alpha, \beta, r) = \sum_{j=0}^{r} C_r^j a_j \alpha_1^j \beta_1^{r-j} < 1,$$

with $a_0 = 1, a_j = \prod_{i=1}^{j}(2i - 1), j \geq 1$.

2. Show that the $(2r)$-th order moment may also be computed by the recursive formula

$$E(\varepsilon_t^{2r}) = a_r \left[\sum_{j=0}^{r-1} a_j^{-1} E(\varepsilon_t^{2j}) C_r^{r-j} \mu(\alpha_1, \beta_1, j) \right]$$

$$= [1 - \mu(\alpha_1, \beta_1, r)]^{-1}$$

[see Bollerslev (1986)].

Exercise 3.3. Let us consider a conditionally Gaussian ARCH model admitting moments of all orders. Show that this process is necessarily degenerated.

Exercise 3.4. Let Y be a conditionally Gaussian ARCH process:

$$Y_t/Y_{t-1} \sim N\left(0, a_0 + \sum_{i=1}^{q} a_i Y_{t-i}^2\right), \quad a_i \geq 0, \sum_{i=1}^{q} a_i < 1.$$

1. Consider the matrix ψ of dimension $(q \times q)$ defined by $\psi_{ij} = a_{i+j} + a_{i-j}$, where by convention $a_k = 0$ if $k \leq 0$ or $k > q$. Show that the fourth order moment exists if

$$3(a_1, \ldots, a_q)(Id - \Psi)^{-1} \begin{pmatrix} a_1 \\ \vdots \\ a_q \end{pmatrix} < 1.$$

2. Show that the centered second and fourth order moments are linked by

$$\mu_4 = \frac{2\mu_2^2}{1 - 3(a_1, \ldots, a_q)(Id - \Psi)^{-1}(a_1, \ldots, a_q)'}.$$

3. Verify that

$$(a_1, \ldots, a_q)(Id - \Psi)^{-1}(a_1, \ldots, a_q)' \geq 0,$$

and deduce that the marginal distribution of Y_t has fatter tails than the normal distribution [see Milhoj (1985) and Diebold (1986)].

Exercise 3.5. Let us consider a conditionally Gaussian ARCH(2) process:

$$Y_t/Y_{t-1} \sim N\left(0, a_0 + a_1 Y_{t-1}^2 + a_2 Y_{t-2}^2\right), \qquad a_1 \geq 0, a_2 \geq 0.$$

1. Verify that the fourth order moment exists if

$$a_2 + 3a_1^2 + 3a_2^2 + 3a_1^2 a_2 - 3a_2^3 < 1.$$

2. Show that the autocorrelations of Y_t^2 are such that

$$\rho_1^{(2)} = \frac{a_1}{1 - a_2}, \quad \rho_2^{(2)} = \frac{1}{1 - a_2}(a_2 + a_1^2 - a_2^2), \quad \rho_h^{(2)} = a_1 \rho_{h-1}^{(2)} + a_2 \rho_{h-2}^{(2)}.$$

3. Taking into account the various constraints on a_1, a_2, determine the variation domain of $\rho_1^{(2)}$ and $\rho_2^{(2)}$ and compare this domain with the one usually obtained for an AR(2) process [see Bollerslev (1988)].

Exercise 3.6. Consider an independent white noise (u_t) and a stationary process Z_t satisfying the ARMA representation,

$$Z_t = c + \alpha_1 Z_{t-1} + \ldots + \alpha_q Z_{t-q} + u_t + \beta_1 u_{t-1} + \ldots + \beta_p u_{t-p},$$

where the roots of the autoregressive polynomial $1 - \alpha_1 L - \ldots - \alpha_q L^q$ lie outside the unit circle.

1. Discuss the conditions to be imposed on the coefficients $c, \alpha_1, \ldots, \alpha_q, \beta_1, \ldots, \beta_p$ and on the support of the distribution of u_t to ensure that Z_t takes only positive values.

2. The conditions derived in question 1 are assumed to be satisfied. We consider a sequence of independent and identically distributed random variables such that

$$P[\delta_t = +1] = P[\delta_t = -1] = \frac{1}{2}$$

is also independent of u_t. Show that the process $\varepsilon_t = \delta_t \sqrt{Z_t}$ is stationary and admits a GARCH representation.

3. Is the model satisfied by (ε_t) compatible with the conditional normality of the process?

4

Estimation and Tests

The usual estimation and test procedures may be applied without difficulties to ARCH models. We begin by recalling the basic idea and general properties of the pseudo maximum likelihood method [hereafter referred to as PML]. In the particular case of ARCH models, the asymptotic precisions of the estimators have a closed form representation. We then compare the PML estimators to some two step least squares estimators and show that the latter ones, although intuitive and easy to implement, are usually much less precise. Finally, we discuss the construction of forecast intervals and the tests of the homoscedasticity hypothesis.

4.1 Pseudo Maximum Likelihood Estimation

4.1.1 Generalities

The statistical inference on ARCH models consists in determining the (pseudo) maximum likelihood estimator based on the normality assumption of conditional distribution. Let $l_t(y; \theta)$ denote the conditional likelihood function associated with Y_t. The likelihood function of $Y_1, \ldots, Y_T$ conditional on Y_0 is

$$L(y; \theta) = \prod_{t=1}^{T} l_t(y; \theta).$$

The estimator is then defined as a solution to the maximization problem:

$$\max_{\theta} \log L(y; \theta).$$

It is known that in general the properties of this estimator, denoted $\hat{\theta}_T$ and called pseudo maximum likelihood estimator (PML), both depend on the true underlying distribution and on the one used to compute the likelihood function (here the normal distribution). However, under standard regularity conditions (White 1981; Gouriéroux et al. 1984; Gallant 1987; Gouriéroux and Monfort 1989), this estimator is consistent even if the underlying distribution is not conditionally normal; that is, this property does not depend on the distribution that is used to build the likelihood function. Moreover, this estimator is asymptotically normal and its covariance matrix is

$$V_{as}[\sqrt{T}(\hat{\theta}_T - \theta)] = J^{-1}IJ^{-1},$$

$$J = E_0\left[-\frac{\partial^2 \log l_t(Y;\theta)}{\partial \theta \partial \theta'}\right],$$

$$I = E_0\left[\frac{\partial \log l_t(Y;\theta)}{\partial \theta} \frac{\partial \log l_t(Y;\theta)}{\partial \theta'}\right], \tag{4.1}$$

E_0 indicates that the expectation is taken with respect to the true distribution.

The two matrices I and J are generally different. They nevertheless coincide if the true distribution is compatible with the likelihood function, which in our case is conditionally normal. When $I = J$, the expression of the asymptotic precision simplifies to

$$V_{as}[\sqrt{T}(\hat{\theta}_T - \theta)] = J^{-1} = I^{-1}.$$

4.1.2   The i.i.d. case

To facilitate the understanding of the properties of the PML estimator for ARCH models, we now recall the main results on independent and identically distributed random variables. Consider such a sequence of i.i.d. variables $Y_t, t = 1, \ldots, T$, with unknown mean m and variance σ^2. The log-likelihood function based on the normality assumption is

$$\log L = -\frac{T}{2}\log \sigma^2 - \frac{T}{2}\log 2\pi - \frac{1}{2\sigma^2}\sum_{t=1}^{T}(Y_t - m)^2.$$

The first derivatives with respect to the two parameters are

$$\begin{cases} \dfrac{\partial \log L}{\partial m} = \dfrac{1}{\sigma^2}\sum_{t=1}^{T}(Y_t - m), \\[3mm] \dfrac{\partial \log L}{\sigma^2} = -\dfrac{T}{2\sigma^2} + \dfrac{1}{2\sigma^4}\sum_{t=1}^{T}(Y_t - m)^2 \end{cases}$$

The PML estimators of m and σ^2 are solutions to the likelihood equations $\frac{\partial \log L}{\partial m} = 0$ and $\frac{\partial \log L}{\partial \sigma^2} = 0$ and are given by

$$\hat{m}_T = \bar{Y}_T = \frac{1}{T} \sum_{t=1}^{T} Y_t \text{ and } \hat{\sigma}_T^2 = \frac{1}{T} \sum_{t=1}^{T} (Y_t - \bar{Y}_T)^2.$$

They simply are the empirical mean and variance of the series. This conclusion allows us to assert that these estimators are consistent, even if the true distribution of Y_t is not normal. Moreover, the asymptotic precision may be deduced from the expressions of the matrices I and J. We have

$$I = \begin{pmatrix} \frac{1}{\sigma^2} E\left(\frac{Y-m}{\sigma}\right)^2 & E\left(\frac{Y-m}{\sigma^2}\left[-\frac{1}{2\sigma^2} + \frac{1}{2\sigma^4}(Y-m)^2\right]\right) \\ \times & E\left[-\frac{1}{2\sigma^2} + \frac{1}{2\sigma^4}(Y-m)^2\right]^2 \end{pmatrix}$$

$$= \begin{pmatrix} \frac{1}{\sigma^2} & \frac{1}{2\sigma^3} Eu^3 \\ \frac{1}{2\sigma^3} Eu^3 & \frac{k-1}{4\sigma^4} \end{pmatrix},$$

where $u = \frac{Y-m}{\sigma}$ denotes the centered reduced observation, i.e., divided by the standard deviation and hence having unitary variance, and $k = \frac{Eu^4}{(Eu^2)^2} = Eu^4$, the kurtosis of the u variable. The matrix J has the usual form:

$$J = \begin{pmatrix} \frac{1}{\sigma^2} & 0 \\ 0 & \frac{1}{2\sigma^4} \end{pmatrix}.$$

We deduce that the asymptotic variance-covariance matrix is

$$V_{as}\left[\sqrt{T}\left(\begin{matrix} \hat{m}_T - m \\ \hat{\sigma}_T^2 - \sigma^2 \end{matrix}\right)\right] = \begin{bmatrix} \sigma^2 & \sigma^3 Eu^3 \\ \sigma^3 Eu^3 & (k-1)\sigma^4 \end{bmatrix}$$

$$= \begin{bmatrix} \sigma^2 & m_3 \\ m_3 & (k-1)\sigma^4 \end{bmatrix}, \tag{4.2}$$

where $m_3 = E(Y-m)^3$. When the true underlying distribution is normal, we have $m_3 = 0$ and $k = 3$. Hence, the two estimators $\hat{m}_T$ and $\hat{\sigma}_T^2$ are asymptotically uncorrelated and $V_{as}[\sqrt{T}(\hat{\sigma}_T^2 - \sigma^2)] = 2\sigma^4$.

However, these two classical properties are not satisfied in a more general case. That is, the estimators $\hat{m}_T$ and $\hat{\sigma}_T^2$ are correlated when the true distribution exhibits some asymmetries, and hence the variability of $\hat{\sigma}_T^2$ may be larger or smaller than $\frac{2\sigma^4}{T}$, depending on the value of the kurtosis; in particular, the fatter the tails, the larger the variability.

4.1.3   Regression Model with Heteroscedastic Errors

The concept of PML estimators and the analysis of their asymptotic properties may be extended directly to cover more complex regression models. In this subsection, we consider observations $Y_t, t = 1, \ldots, T$ with conditional means

$$E(Y_t/\underline{Y_{t-1}}, \underline{X_t}) = m_t(\theta) = m(\underline{Y_{t-1}}, \underline{X_t}; \theta)$$

and conditional variances

$$V(Y_t/\underline{Y_{t-1}}, \underline{X_t}) = h_t(\theta) = h(\underline{Y_{t-1}}, \underline{X_t}; \theta).$$

These two conditional moments depend on past values of the process and on current and past values of some exogenous characteristics X. As shown below, the different ARCH models introduced in section 3 may be viewed as regression models. A pseudo likelihood function is obtained by computing L as if the conditional distribution of Y_t given $\underline{Y_{t-1}}, \underline{X_t}$ were normal. This pseudo likelihood function is

$$\log L = -\frac{T}{2}\log \sigma^2 - \frac{T}{2}\log 2\pi - \frac{1}{2}\sum_{t=1}^{T} \frac{[Y_t - m_t(\theta)]^2}{h_t(\theta)}. \tag{4.3}$$

a) First Order Conditions

The first order derivative with respect to the parameter θ is

$$\frac{\partial \log L}{\partial \theta} = -\frac{1}{2}\sum_{t=1}^{T} \frac{1}{h_t(\theta)}\frac{\partial h_t(\theta)}{\partial \theta}$$

$$+ \frac{1}{2}\sum_{t=1}^{T} \frac{[Y_t - m_t(\theta)]^2}{h_t^2(\theta)}\frac{\partial h_t(\theta)}{\partial \theta} \tag{4.4}$$

$$+ \sum_{t=1}^{T} \frac{Y_t - m_t(\theta)}{h_t(\theta)}\frac{\partial m_t(\theta)}{\partial \theta}.$$

The likelihood equations $\frac{\partial \log L(\hat{\theta})}{\partial \theta} = 0$ are easily written as functions of the demeaned and divided by standard deviation residuals:

$$\hat{u}_t = \frac{Y_t - m_t(\hat{\theta})}{h_t(\hat{\theta})^{1/2}}. \tag{4.5}$$

We get

$$\frac{1}{2}\sum_{t=1}^{T}\frac{1}{h_t(\hat\theta)}\frac{\partial h_t(\hat\theta)}{\partial\theta}[\hat u_t^2-1]+\sum_{t=1}^{T}\frac{1}{h_t(\hat\theta)^{1/2}}\frac{\partial m_t(\hat\theta)}{\partial\theta}\hat u_t=0. \qquad (4.6)$$

This is an orthogonality condition between the reduced residuals, their centered squares and some other regressors, which are, respectively,

$$\frac{1}{h_t(\hat\theta)^{1/2}}\frac{\partial m_t(\hat\theta)}{\partial\theta}\quad\text{and}\quad\frac{1}{h_t(\hat\theta)}\frac{\partial h_t(\hat\theta)}{\partial\theta}.$$

Moreover, the formula (4.6) implies that it is important to plot the reduced residuals instead of the usual residuals in the heteroscedastic case. It allows for comparisons between different dates.

Note 4.7. The system of likelihood equations may be divided into two sets when the parameter vector can be partitioned as

$$\theta=\begin{pmatrix}\alpha\\\beta\end{pmatrix},$$

where α appears only in the conditional mean and β only in the conditional variance. We have

$$\left\{\begin{aligned}\frac{\partial\log L}{\partial\alpha}&=\sum_{t=1}^{T}\frac{Y_t-m_t(\alpha)}{h_t(\beta)}\frac{\partial m_t(\alpha)}{\partial\alpha}=\sum_{t=1}^{T}\frac{1}{h_t^{1/2}(\beta)}\frac{\partial m_t(\alpha)}{\partial\alpha}u_t,\\[2mm]\frac{\partial\log L}{\partial\beta}&=-\frac{1}{2}\sum_{t=1}^{T}\frac{1}{h_t(\beta)}\frac{\partial h_t(\beta)}{\partial\beta}+\frac{1}{2}\sum_{t=1}^{T}\frac{[Y_t-m_t(\alpha)]^2}{h_t^2(\beta)}\frac{\partial h_t(\beta)}{\partial\beta}\\[2mm]&=\frac{1}{2}\sum_{t=1}^{T}\frac{1}{h_t(\beta)}\frac{\partial h_t(\beta)}{\partial\beta}(u_t^2-1).\end{aligned}\right.$$

b) Asymptotic Variance–Covariance Matrix

The second order derivatives of the pseudo log-likelihood are computed in Appendix 4.1, and from their expressions one derives the matrix J by

$$J=E_0\left[\frac{1}{h_t(\theta)}\frac{\partial m_t(\theta)}{\partial\theta}\frac{\partial m_t(\theta)}{\partial\theta'}+\frac{1}{2h_t(\theta)^2}\frac{\partial h_t(\theta)}{\partial\theta}\frac{\partial h_t(\theta)}{\partial\theta'}\right]. \qquad (4.8)$$

The second matrix $I=E_0\left[\frac{\partial\log l_t}{\partial\theta}\frac{\partial\log l_t}{\partial\theta'}\right]$ depends on the conditional third order moment of Y_t

$$M_{3t}(\theta)=E[(Y_t-m_t(\theta))^3/Y_{t-1},\underline X_t]$$

and on its conditional kurtosis

$$K_t(\theta) = \frac{1}{h_t(\theta)^2} E[(Y_t - m_t(\theta))^4 / Y_{t-1}, \underline{X}_t].$$

It is given by the following expression:

$$I = E_0 \left\{ \frac{1}{4} \frac{1}{h_t(\theta)^2} \frac{\partial h_t(\theta)}{\partial \theta} \frac{\partial h_t(\theta)}{\partial \theta'} (K_t(\theta) - 1) + \frac{1}{h_t(\theta)} \frac{\partial m_t(\theta)}{\partial \theta} \frac{\partial m_t(\theta)}{\partial \theta'} \right.$$

$$\left. + \frac{1}{2h_t(\theta)^3} \left[\frac{\partial h_t(\theta)}{\partial \theta} \frac{\partial m_t(\theta)}{\partial \theta'} + \frac{\partial m_t(\theta)}{\partial \theta} \frac{\partial h_t(\theta)}{\partial \theta'} \right] M_{3t}(\theta) \right\}. \tag{4.9}$$

The formulas (4.8), (4.9) are direct extensions of the one derived in the i.i.d. case. One can easily check that the two matrices I and J coincide when the true underlying distribution is normal since $K_t(\theta) = 3$, and $M_{3t}(\theta) = 0$.

Note 4.10. When the vector of parameters is partitioned as

$$\theta = \begin{pmatrix} \alpha \\ \beta \end{pmatrix},$$

where α appears only in the mean and β only in the variance, we get

$$J = \begin{bmatrix} E_0 \left[\dfrac{1}{h_t(\beta)} \dfrac{\partial m_t(\alpha)}{\partial \alpha} \dfrac{\partial m_t(\alpha)}{\partial \alpha'} \right] & 0 \\[2ex] 0 & E_0 \left[\dfrac{1}{2h_t(\beta)^2} \dfrac{\partial h_t(\beta)}{\partial \beta} \dfrac{\partial h_t(\beta)}{\partial \beta'} \right] \end{bmatrix},$$

$$I = \begin{bmatrix} E_0 \left[\dfrac{1}{h_t(\beta)} \dfrac{\partial m_t(\alpha)}{\partial \alpha} \dfrac{\partial m_t(\alpha)}{\partial \alpha'} \right] & E_0 \left[\dfrac{1}{2h_t(\beta)^3} \dfrac{\partial m_t(\alpha)}{\partial \alpha} \dfrac{\partial h_t(\beta)}{\partial \beta'} M_{3t}(\theta) \right] \\[2ex] E_0 \left[\dfrac{1}{2h_t(\beta)^3} \dfrac{\partial h_t(\beta)}{\partial \beta} \dfrac{\partial m_t(\alpha)}{\partial \alpha'} M_{3t}(\theta) \right] & E_0 \left[\dfrac{1}{4h_t(\beta)^2} \dfrac{\partial h_t(\beta)}{\partial \beta} \dfrac{\partial h_t(\beta)}{\partial \beta} (K_t(\theta) - 1) \right] \end{bmatrix}.$$

The asymptotic variance of the estimator $\hat{\alpha}_T$ is

$$V_{as}[\sqrt{T}(\hat{\alpha}_T - \alpha)] = \left(E_0 \left[\frac{1}{h_t(\beta)} \frac{\partial m_t(\alpha)}{\partial \alpha} \frac{\partial m_t(\alpha)}{\partial \alpha'} \right] \right)^{-1},$$

and the asymptotic variance of $\hat{\beta}_T$ is

$$V_{as}[\sqrt{T}(\hat{\beta}_T - \beta)] = \left(E_0 \left[\frac{1}{2h_t(\beta)^2} \frac{\partial h_t(\beta)}{\partial \beta} \frac{\partial h_t(\beta)}{\partial \beta'} \right] \right)^{-1}$$

$$\times E_0 \left[\frac{1}{4h_t(\beta)^2} \frac{\partial h_t(\beta)}{\partial \beta} \frac{\partial h_t(\beta)}{\partial \beta'} (K_t(\theta) - 1) \right] \left(E_0 \left[\frac{1}{2h_t(\beta)^2} \frac{\partial h_t(\beta)}{\partial \beta} \frac{\partial h_t(\beta)}{\partial \beta'} \right] \right)^{-1}.$$

In practice, the matrices I and J are directly estimated by replacing the expectation E_0 with the empirical mean and the unknown parameter θ with its estimator $\hat{\theta}_T$. Such matrix approximations are, for instance,

$$
\begin{cases}
\hat{I}_T = \dfrac{1}{T} \displaystyle\sum_{t=1}^{T} \dfrac{\partial \log l_t(\hat{\theta}_T)}{\partial \theta} \dfrac{\partial \log l_t(\hat{\theta}_T)}{\partial \theta'}, \\[3mm]
\hat{J}_T = -\dfrac{1}{T} \displaystyle\sum_{t=1}^{T} \dfrac{\partial^2 \log l_t(\hat{\theta}_T)}{\partial \theta \partial \theta'},
\end{cases}
$$

and the estimated variance of $\hat{\theta}_T$ is

$$
\hat{V}_{as}[\sqrt{T}(\hat{\theta}_T - \theta)] = \hat{J}_T^{-1} \hat{I}_T \hat{J}_T^{-1}.
$$

Other consistent estimators may also be obtained from the explicit expressions of I and J. For instance, if the true underlying distribution is normal, and if the parameter vector can be partitioned as before in two subvectors where $\theta = \binom{\alpha}{\beta}$, α characterizing the mean and β the variance, we have

$$
V_{as}[\sqrt{T}(\hat{\beta}_T - \beta)] = \left(E_0 \left[\frac{1}{2h_t(\beta)^2} \frac{\partial h_t(\beta)}{\partial \beta} \frac{\partial h_t(\beta)}{\partial \beta'} \right] \right)^{-1},
$$

and this quantity may be estimated by

$$
\hat{V}_{as}[\sqrt{T}(\hat{\beta}_T - \beta)] = \left(\frac{1}{T} \sum_{t=1}^{T} \frac{1}{2h_t(\hat{\beta}_T)^2} \frac{\partial h_t(\hat{\beta}_T)}{\partial \beta} \frac{\partial h_t(\hat{\beta}_T)}{\partial \beta'} \right)^{-1}.
$$

If the true underlying conditional distribution is not normal, it is necessary to introduce an additional term to take into account the kurtosis and to estimate it by its empirical counterpart.

4.1.4 Regression Model with ARCH Errors

Let us consider a regression model with ARCH(p) errors in order to illustrate the PML estimator's properties. The observations are such that

$$
\begin{cases}
Y_t = X_t b + \varepsilon_t, \text{ where } E(\varepsilon_t / \varepsilon_{t-1}) = 0, \\
V(\varepsilon_t / \varepsilon_{t-1}) = c + a_1 \varepsilon_{t-1}^2 + \ldots + a_p \varepsilon_{t-p}^2.
\end{cases}
\tag{4.11}
$$

In this model, we have

$$
\begin{cases}
m_t(\theta) = X_t b, \\
h_t(\theta) = c + a_1(Y_{t-1} - X_{t-1}b)^2 + \ldots + a_p(Y_{t-p} - X_{t-p}b)^2,
\end{cases}
$$

with $\theta' = (b', c, a_1, \ldots, a_p) = (b', c, a')$.

Even in the simple case, we cannot estimate separately the parameters of the conditional mean and those appearing in the conditional variance. We have two vectors of parameters: $\alpha = b$ and $\beta = \binom{c}{a}$. The first set of parameters appears simultaneously in the mean and the variance, whereas the second one is specific to the variance. The first order conditions (see Appendix 4.2) are

$$\frac{\partial \log L}{\partial \alpha}(\hat{\theta}_T) = -\sum_{t=1}^{T} \frac{1}{\hat{h}_t^2}(\hat{\varepsilon}_t^2 - \hat{h}_t)\left(\sum_{j=1}^{p} \hat{a}_j x'_{t-j} \hat{\varepsilon}_{t-j}\right)$$

$$+ \sum_{t=1}^{T} \frac{\hat{\varepsilon}_t}{\hat{h}_t} x'_t = 0$$

(4.12)

$$\frac{\partial \log L}{\partial \beta}(\hat{\theta}_T) = \sum_{t=1}^{T} \frac{1}{2\hat{h}_t^2}(\hat{\varepsilon}_t^2 - \hat{h}_t)\begin{bmatrix} 1 \\ \hat{\varepsilon}_{t-1}^2 \\ \vdots \\ \hat{\varepsilon}_{t-p}^2 \end{bmatrix} = 0,$$

with $\hat{h}_t = h_t(\hat{\theta}_t)$ and $\hat{\varepsilon}_t = Y_t - X_t \hat{b}_T$.

The first subsystem is the usual set of first order conditions with exogenous heteroscedasticity. The second subsystem is easy to interpret: after having substituted the estimator $\hat{b}_T$ for the parameter b, the autoregressive equation defining the second moment may be approximated by the following:

$$\hat{\varepsilon}_t^2 \approx c + a_1 \hat{\varepsilon}_{t-1}^2 + \ldots + a_p \hat{\varepsilon}_{t-p}^2 + u_t,$$

where $V u_t = V(\varepsilon_t^2) = 2h_t^2$ (under the conditional normality assumption). It is straightforward to estimate the parameter β by weighted least squares from this approximated model, the weight being $\frac{1}{2h_t^2}$. The second subsystem defines the corresponding orthogonality conditions between the explanatory variables $1, \ldots, \hat{\varepsilon}_{t-p}^2$ and the residuals.

We have shown in the last subsection that the PML estimators of the mean and variance parameters are asymptotically correlated in the general case but uncorrelated under normality. For a regression model with ARCH errors, the parameter $\alpha = b$ appears simultaneously in the first two moments, and we may therefore expect some asymptotic correlation between $\hat{\alpha}_T$ and $\hat{\beta}_T$ even in the Gaussian model. In fact, this intuition is wrong. We can easily see that the asymptotic variance covariance matrix of the estimator is

$$V_{as}\left[\sqrt{T}\left(\begin{array}{c} \hat{\alpha}_T - \alpha \\ \hat{\beta}_T - \beta \end{array}\right)\right] = J^{-1} = \begin{bmatrix} J_{\alpha\alpha} & J_{\alpha\beta} \\ J_{\beta\alpha} & J_{\beta\beta} \end{bmatrix}^{-1},$$

with

$$J_{\alpha\alpha} = E_0\left\{\frac{1}{h_t} x'_t x_t + \frac{2}{h_t^2}\left(\sum_{j=1}^{p} a_j x'_{t-j} \varepsilon_{t-j}\right)\left(\sum_{j=1}^{p} a_j x_{t-j} \varepsilon_{t-j}\right)\right\},$$

$$J_{\beta\alpha} = -E_0\left\{\frac{1}{h_t^2}\begin{bmatrix}1\\ \varepsilon_{t-1}^2\\ \vdots\\ \varepsilon_{t-p}^2\end{bmatrix}\left(\sum_{j=1}^{p}a_j x_{t-j}\varepsilon_{t-j}\right)\right\},$$

$$J_{\beta\beta} = E_0\left\{\frac{1}{2h_t^2}\begin{bmatrix}1\\ \varepsilon_{t-1}^2\\ \vdots\\ \varepsilon_{t-p}^2\end{bmatrix}[1, \varepsilon_{t-1}^2, \ldots, \varepsilon_{t-p}^2]\right\}.$$

We can show that $J_{\beta\alpha} = 0$ by the following lemma (the proof is simple and left to the reader).

Lemma 4.13. *If $\varepsilon = (\varepsilon_t)$ admits a conditionally Gaussian ARCH representation, the transformed process ε^* defined by*

$$\varepsilon_t^* = \varepsilon_t, \quad \text{if } t \neq t_0, \quad \varepsilon_{t_0}^* = -\varepsilon_{t_0},$$

admits the same conditionally Gaussian ARCH representation.

From this property, we see directly that the expected value of a function of ε, symmetric with respect to the component ε_{t_0}, is zero:

$$\forall f, \quad f(\varepsilon_t^*) = -f(\varepsilon_t) \Rightarrow \quad Ef(\varepsilon) = 0.$$

In particular, all elements of $J_{\beta\alpha}$ are zero.

Property 4.14. *If ε has a conditionally Gaussian ARCH representation, the $\hat{\alpha}_T$ and $\hat{\beta}_T$ estimators are asymptotically uncorrelated.*

4.1.5 Application to a GARCH Model

It is well known that the ML estimation of an ARMA model is much more difficult than the estimation of a pure autoregressive model, and it is necessary to use algorithms such as the backward forecast algorithm or the Kalman filter. The same holds if an ARCH specification is replaced by a GARCH. Let us consider a conditionally Gaussian GARCH(p, q) model

$$Y_t / \underline{Y_{t-1}} \quad \sim \quad N[0; h_t],$$

where

$$h_t = c + \sum_{i=1}^{p}\alpha_i Y_{t-i}^2 + \sum_{j=1}^{q}\beta_j h_{t-j}.$$

The expression of the conditional variance in terms of parameters and observable variables is

$$h_t = \frac{1}{1 - \sum_{j=1}^{q}\beta_j L^j}\left(c + \sum_{i=1}^{p}\alpha_i Y_{t-i}^2\right),$$

where L denotes the lag-operator. Thus, $h_t(\theta)$ depends on all past values of the Y process.

Since the process is only observed during a limited time period $t = 1, \ldots, T$, it is necessary to replace $h_t(\theta)$ by its truncated approximation in which the values Y_t^2 corresponding to negative dates are set equal to zero. This is equivalent to considering the recursive equation

$$\tilde{h}_t = c + \sum_{i=1}^{p} \alpha_i \tilde{Y}_{t-i}^2 + \sum_{j=1}^{q} \beta_j \tilde{h}_{t-j}, \tag{4.15}$$

with

$$\tilde{Y}_t = 0, \quad \text{if } t \le 0; \quad \tilde{Y}_t = Y_t, \quad \text{if } t \ge 1,$$
$$\tilde{h}_t = 0, \quad \text{if } t \le 0.$$

The initial log-likelihood function is then replaced by its truncated version:

$$\log \tilde{L} = -\frac{T}{2} \log 2\pi - \frac{1}{2} \sum_{t=1}^{T} \log \tilde{h}_t(\theta) - \frac{1}{2} \sum_{t=1}^{T} \frac{Y_t^2}{\tilde{h}_t(\theta)}. \tag{4.16}$$

In practice, the optimization is carried out with numerical procedures and, for a given value θ_1 of θ, the successive conditional variances are computed through

$$\tilde{h}_t(\theta_1) = c_1 + \sum_{i=1}^{p} \alpha_{i1} \tilde{Y}_{t-i}^2 + \sum_{j=1}^{q} \beta_{j1} \tilde{h}_{t-j}(\theta_1).$$

4.1.6   Stochastic Variance Model

Let us consider the stochastic variance model (3.17), where the process (Y_t) is a white noise:

$$\begin{cases} Y_t = \theta \exp\left(\dfrac{v_t}{2}\right) e_t, \\[2mm] A(L) v_t = B(L) \eta_t, \end{cases}$$

where (ε_t), (η_t) are two independent Gaussian processes with variance 1 and σ_η^2, respectively. Note that the sign of Y_t has no informational content and hence, for estimation purposes, we can write

$$\begin{cases} Y_t^2 = \theta^2 \exp v_t \, e_t^2, \\[2mm] A(L) v_t = B(L) \eta_t, \end{cases}$$

$$\text{or} \quad \begin{cases} \log Y_t^2 = c + v_t + \left(\log e_t^2 - E \log e_t^2 \right), \\[2mm] A(L) v_t = B(L) \eta_t, \end{cases}$$

where $c = \log \theta^2 + E \log e_t^2 = \log(\theta^2) + 1.27$.

The last system is a state space model with state variable v_t and $\log Y_t^2$ as the observed variable. The equality $A(L)v_t = B(L)\eta_t$ describes the dynamics of the state variable, while $\log Y_t^2 = c + v_t + (\log e_t^2 - E \log e_t^2)$ is the measurement equation. The parameters of this state space system may be estimated consistently by the quasi-maximum likelihood method based on the normality assumption of the joint process $(\log e_t^2 - E \log e_t^2, v_t)$ using the Kalman filter. However, we may note that the assumption of normality for $\log e_t^2 - E \log e_t^2$, with a true log-gamma type distribution, results in an efficiency loss.

4.2 Two Step Estimation Procedures

4.2.1 Description of the Procedures

An ARMA–GARCH model may be interpreted as two successive ARMA applications, the first one on the process itself and the second one on the squared innovations. It is then obvious to consider two step estimation procedures that take this particular structure into account. As an illustration, let us consider a regression model with ARCH errors:

$$\begin{cases} Y_t = X_t b + \varepsilon_t, \\ V(\varepsilon_t/\varepsilon_{t-1}) = c + a_1 \varepsilon_{t-1}^2 + \ldots + a_p \varepsilon_{t-p}^2. \end{cases}$$

A consistent estimator of b is the ordinary least squares (OLS) estimator from the regression of Y_t on X_t, denoted by $\tilde{b}_T$. From this estimation, we obtain as residuals

$$\varepsilon_t = Y_t - X_t \tilde{b}_T.$$

The other parameters $c, a_1, \ldots, a_p$ appearing in the variance may also be estimated in a consistent way by regressing $\tilde{\varepsilon}_t^2$ on $1, \tilde{\varepsilon}_{t-1}^2, \ldots, \tilde{\varepsilon}_{t-p}^2$. They are denoted by $\tilde{c}_T, \tilde{a}_{1T}, \ldots, \tilde{a}_{pT}$. These two successive regressions have been estimated by OLS, that is, without accounting for the conditional heteroscedasticity. The estimator of b may be improved in the second step by applying the quasi-generalized least squares (QGLS) to a regression of Y or X using

$$\tilde{V}\varepsilon_t = \tilde{h}_t = \tilde{c}_T + \tilde{a}_{1T}\tilde{\varepsilon}_{t-1}^2 + \ldots + \tilde{a}_{pT}\tilde{\varepsilon}_{t-p}^2$$

as diagonal elements of the weighting matrix. These second step estimators are denoted by $\tilde{\tilde{b}}_T$.

Similarly, if the true distribution is conditionally Gaussian, we have

$$V(\varepsilon_t^2/\varepsilon_{t-1}) = 2h_t^2,$$

and the second step estimators of $c, a_1, \ldots, a_p$ may be improved by regressing $\tilde{\varepsilon}_t^2$ on $1, \tilde{\varepsilon}_{t-1}^2, \ldots, \tilde{\varepsilon}_{t-p}^2$ by QGLS using $V(\varepsilon_t^2/\varepsilon_{t-1}) = 2\tilde{h}_t^2$ as weights. These estimators are denoted by $\tilde{\tilde{c}}_T, \tilde{\tilde{a}}_{1T}, \ldots, \tilde{\tilde{a}}_{pT}$.

4.2.2   Comparison of the Estimation Methods under Conditional Normality

It is known that the QGLS and generalized least squares estimators have the same asymptotic properties. We can further infer that the estimator $\tilde{\tilde{b}}_T$ is asymptotically normal with an asymptotic variance-covariance matrix:

$$V_{as}[\sqrt{T}(\tilde{\tilde{b}}_T - b)] = \left[E_0 \left(\frac{x_t' x_t}{h_t(\theta)} \right) \right]^{-1}. \tag{4.17}$$

Property 4.18. *The QGLS estimator of b is asymptotically less efficient than the PML estimator.*

Proof. We have

$$V_{as}[\sqrt{T}(\hat{b}_T - b)]^{-1} = E_0 \left\{ \frac{x_t' x_t}{h_t} + \frac{2}{h_t^2} (\textstyle\sum_{j=1}^p a_j x_{t-j}' \varepsilon_{t-j})(\textstyle\sum_{j=1}^p a_j x_{t-j} \varepsilon_{t-j}) \right\}$$

$$\gg E_0 \left(\frac{x_t' x_t}{h_t} \right) = V_{as}[\sqrt{T}(\tilde{\tilde{b}}_T - b)]^{-1}.$$

Q.E.D.

Let us now consider the estimators $\tilde{\tilde{c}}_T, \tilde{\tilde{a}}_{1T}, \ldots, \tilde{\tilde{a}}_{pT}$. Under conditional normality, the information matrix is block diagonal; an estimator, which is obtained by maximizing $\log L(b_T^*, c, a_1, \ldots, a_p)$ with respect to $c, a_1, \ldots, a_p$, is then asymptotically efficient, no matter which consistent estimator b_T^* of b is used. We infer the following property:

Property 4.19. *The QGLS estimator of $c, a_1, \ldots, a_p$ is asymptotically efficient.*

Finally, we note that the asymptotic variance-covariance matrices of the two types of estimators are such that

$$\left(V_{as} \sqrt{T} \begin{bmatrix} \hat{\alpha}_T - \alpha \\ \hat{\beta}_T - \beta \end{bmatrix} \right)^{-1} = \begin{bmatrix} J_{\alpha\alpha} & 0 \\ 0 & J_{\beta\beta} \end{bmatrix},$$

$$\left(V_{as} \sqrt{T} \begin{bmatrix} \tilde{\alpha}_T - \alpha \\ \tilde{\beta}_T - \beta \end{bmatrix} \right)^{-1} = \begin{bmatrix} J_{\alpha\alpha}^* & J_{\alpha\beta}^* \\ J_{\beta\alpha}^* & J_{\beta\beta}^* \end{bmatrix}.$$

Since $\begin{pmatrix} \hat{\alpha}_T \\ \hat{\beta}_T \end{pmatrix}$ is asymptotically efficient, we have

$$\begin{bmatrix} J_{\alpha\alpha} & 0 \\ 0 & J_{\beta\beta} \end{bmatrix} - \begin{bmatrix} J_{\alpha\alpha}^* & J_{\alpha\beta}^* \\ J_{\beta\alpha}^* & J_{\beta\beta}^* \end{bmatrix} \gg 0,$$

$$\begin{bmatrix} J_{\alpha\alpha} - J_{\alpha\alpha}^* & -J_{\alpha\beta}^* \\ -J_{\beta\alpha}^* & 0 \end{bmatrix} \gg 0;$$

by applying the Cauchy–Schwarz inequality, we obtain $J_{\alpha\beta}^* = 0$.

Property 4.20. *The QGLS estimators of b and $c, a_1, \ldots, a_p$ are asymptotically uncorrelated.*

4.2.3   Efficiency Loss Analysis

The efficiency loss between $\hat{b}_T$ and $\tilde{b}_T$ may be formalized. Let us consider the model

$$Y_t = b + \varepsilon_t, \quad \text{with } \varepsilon_t/\varepsilon_{t-1} \sim N[0, c + a_1\varepsilon_{t-1}^2],$$

We have

$$V_{as}[\sqrt{T}(\tilde{b}_T - b)] = \left[E_0\left(\frac{1}{h_t}\right)\right]^{-1} = \left[E_0\left(\frac{1}{c + a_1\varepsilon_{t-1}^2}\right)\right]^{-1}$$

$$= c\left[E_0\left(\frac{1}{1 + \gamma u^2}\right)\right]^{-1},$$

with $\gamma = \frac{a_1}{1-a_1}$ and $u = \sqrt{\frac{1-a_1}{c}}\,\varepsilon$ (which may be interpreted as a reduced error). Moreover,

$$V_{as}[\sqrt{T}(\hat{b}_T - b)] = \left[E_0\left(\frac{1}{h_t} + \frac{2a_1^2\varepsilon_{t-1}^2}{h_t^2}\right)\right]^{-1}$$

$$= \left\{E_0\left(\frac{1}{c + a_1\varepsilon_{t-1}^2}\right) + E_0\left[\frac{2a_1^2\varepsilon_{t-1}^2}{(c + a_1\varepsilon_{t-1}^2)^2}\right]\right\}^{-1}$$

$$= c\left\{E_0\left(\frac{1}{1 + \gamma u^2}\right) + E_0\left(\frac{2\gamma^2}{1 + \gamma}\frac{u^2}{(1 + \gamma u^2)^2}\right)\right\}^{-1}.$$

The asymptotic relative efficiency (ARE) of $\tilde{b}_T$ with respect to $\hat{b}_T$ is

$$\text{ARE} = \frac{V_{as}[\sqrt{T}(\hat{b}_T - b)]}{V_{as}[\sqrt{T}(\tilde{b}_T - b)]}$$

$$= \frac{E_0[1/1 + \gamma u^2]}{E_0[1/1 + \gamma u^2] + 2\gamma^2/1 + \gamma\, E_0[u^2/(1 + \gamma u^2)^2]}.$$

i) According to Jensen's inequality, we have

$$E_0\left(\frac{1}{1 + \gamma u^2}\right) \geq \frac{1}{E_0(1 + \gamma u^2)} = \frac{1}{1 + \gamma};$$

we infer that

$$\text{ARE} \leq \frac{1}{1 + 2\gamma^2 E_0(u^2/(1 + \gamma u^2)^2)}.$$

Moreover, if γ tends to infinity, i.e., if a_1 tends to 1, which is compatible with the stationarity condition, we have

$$\lim_{\gamma \to \infty} \text{ARE} \leq \frac{1}{1 + 2E_0(1/u^2)},$$

and the upper bound is zero because u^2 has a chi-square conditional distribution with one degree of freedom (see exercise 4.2). Thus, the efficiency loss may be very serious if the model approaches the limit $\gamma = \infty \Leftrightarrow a_1 = 1$.

ii) On the other hand, if γ is close to zero, we have approximately

$$\text{ARE} \approx [E_0(1 - \gamma u^2 + \gamma^2 u^4)]$$
$$\times [E_0(1 - \gamma u^2 + \gamma^2 u^4) + 2\gamma^2 E_0 u^2]^{-1},$$
$$\text{ARE} \approx [1 - \gamma + \gamma^2 E_0 u^4][1 - \gamma + \gamma^2(2 + E_0 u^4)]^{-1},$$
$$\text{ARE} \approx [1 - \gamma + \gamma^2 E_0 u^4][1 + \gamma + \gamma^2(-1 - E_0 u^4)],$$
$$\text{ARE} \approx -2\gamma^2.$$

The asymptotic relative efficiency is of order γ^2, and the two estimators are close in the neighborhood of the homoscedasticity hypothesis.

4.3   Forecast Intervals

A comparison of the forecast intervals reveals the difference between ARMA and ARCH modellings. Even if these two models yield similar fitted values, the confidence interval for the predicted values is constant in the first approach and depends on the past values of Y in the second method. This allows us to find the subperiods of larger (resp. smaller) variability. To illustrate this, consider the results reported by Bollerslev (1986) on the implicit price index associated with the GNP. This variable, denoted GD_t, is first transformed to obtain stationarity, so that the models are fitted to the variable

$$\pi_t = 100 \log(GD_t / GD_{t-1}).$$

Two models have been estimated from the quarterly data covering the period 1948 to 1983: a pure autoregressive model and an autoregressive model with GARCH(1,1) errors. The results are summarized below.

Autoregressive Model

$$\pi_t = 0.240 \quad +0.552\,\pi_{t-1} \quad +0.177\,\pi_{t-2} \quad +0.232\,\pi_{t-3} \quad -0.209\,\pi_{t-4} \quad +\varepsilon_t,$$
$$\quad\; (0.080) \quad\quad (0.083) \quad\quad\quad (0.089) \quad\quad\quad (0.090) \quad\quad\quad (0.080)$$
$$h_t = 0.282.$$
$$\quad\; (0.034)$$

Autoregressive Model with GARCH(1,1) Errors

$$\pi_t = 0.141 \quad +0.433\,\pi_{t-1} \quad +0.229\,\pi_{t-2} \quad +0.349\,\pi_{t-3} \quad -0.162\,\pi_{t-4} \quad +\varepsilon_t,$$
$$\quad\; (0.060) \quad\quad (0.081) \quad\quad\quad (0.110) \quad\quad\quad (0.077) \quad\quad\quad (0.104)$$
$$h_t = 0.007 \quad +0.135\,\varepsilon_{t-1}^2 \quad +0.829\,h_{t-1}.$$
$$\quad\; (0.006) \quad\quad (0.070) \quad\quad\quad (0.068)$$

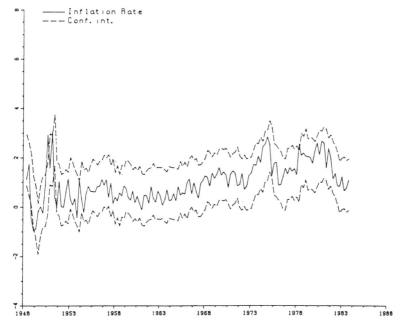

FIGURE 4.1. Forecast intervals—AR model.

Since the coefficients appearing in the conditional expectation are consistently estimated in both methods, it is of no surprise that the estimated coefficients of the expectation term are not significantly different. It implies that the fitted series obtained from the two models are alike. The h_t estimated from the autoregressive formula may be interpreted as an unconditional variance. It will then be compared to the unconditional variance resulting from the AR–GARCH estimation, which is

$$Eh_t \approx 0.007 + 0.135\, E(\varepsilon_{t-1}^2) + 0.829\, E(h_{t-1})$$
$$\Leftrightarrow Eh_t \approx \frac{0.007}{1 - 0.135 - 0.829} = 0.199.$$

Finally, the graphics displaying the forecast intervals at horizon 1 for the different dates are given in figures 4.1 and 4.2.

The important difference between the two types of prediction intervals, with and without path dependent bandwidths, also has strong implications for financial applications. As an illustration, let us consider an investor who has to reallocate his portfolio at the integer dates. Let us assume that there exist only two assets: a risk-free asset with a constant return r_f and a risky asset whose future return is predicted via a prediction interval, $(\underline{r}_t, \bar{r}_t)$ say. A natural allocation strategy may be the following. Let us assume that at the initial date $\underline{r}_0 < r_f$ and the whole portfolio is invested in the risk-free asset. Because of transaction costs, our investor may

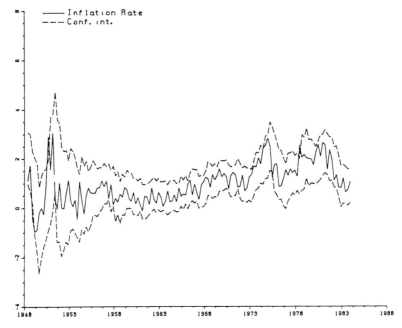

FIGURE 4.2. Forecast intervals—AR–GARCH model.

keep his portfolio unchanged until the first time $\underline{r}_t > r_f$ is observed, in which case he is (almost) sure that the risky asset is more profitable. At this date, the whole portfolio will be reinvested in the risky asset. Then this portfolio remains unchanged until the first further date at which $\bar{r}_t < r_f$, where it is completely reinvested in the risk-free asset, and so on. Under such a strategy, it is clear that the frequency of the reallocations depends heavily on the evolution of the lower and upper bounds of the prediction interval. As shown in the previous example, the bounds are more variable under ARCH modelling. From a financial point of view, the ARCH model implies more frequent tradings in order to make profits from the volatility variations.

4.4   Homoscedasticity Test

(Under the Assumption of Conditional Normality)

4.4.1   Regression Models with Heteroscedastic Errors

We assume that the parameters of the models may be partitioned into the parameter vector α, appearing in the expected value, and a vector β of parameters that are specific to the conditional variance:

$$m_t(\theta) = m_t(\alpha),\ h_t(\theta) = h_t(\alpha, \beta).$$

Moreover, it is useful in practice to have a model general enough to nest the homoscedastic case as a submodel. We assume that $\beta = \binom{\beta_0}{\beta_1}$, where β_0 is a scalar, and that the homoscedasticity hypothesis is characterized by the constraint

$$H_0 = \{\beta_1 = 0\}. \tag{4.21}$$

Under the null hypothesis, the conditional variance no longer depends on the subparameter α

$$h_t(\alpha, \beta, 0) = h(\beta_0) \text{ (say).} \tag{4.22}$$

Note 4.23. All of these conditions are satisfied in a regression model with ARCH errors. In such a case, we have

$$h_t(\alpha, \beta) = c + a_1(Y_{t-1} - X_{t-1}b)^2 + \ldots + a_p(Y_{t-p} - X_{t-p}b)^2,$$

with $\alpha = b$, $\beta_0 = c$, $\beta_1 = (a_1, \ldots, a_p)'$. The homoscedasticity hypothesis holds for $\beta_1 = 0$ and, under this hypothesis, the conditional variance depends only on $\beta_0 = c$ and not on $\alpha = b$.

The null hypothesis will be tested by a Lagrange multiplier procedure. The test statistic is

$$\xi_{\mathrm{LM}} = \sum_{t=1}^{T} z'_{1t} [\sum_{t=1}^{T} z_{1t} z'_{1t}$$

$$- \sum_{t=1}^{T} z_{1t} z'_{2t} (\sum_{t=1}^{T} z_{2t} z'_{2t})^{-1} \sum_{t=1}^{T} z_{2t} z'_{1t}]^{-1} \times \sum_{t=1}^{T} z_{1t},$$

$$\text{with} \quad z_{1t} = \frac{\partial \log l_t}{\partial \beta_1}(\hat{\alpha}^0, \hat{\beta}_0^{\,0}, 0),$$

$$z_{2t} = \frac{\partial \log l_t}{\partial \begin{pmatrix} \alpha \\ \beta_0 \end{pmatrix}}(\hat{\alpha}^0, \hat{\beta}_0^{\,0}, 0),$$

$\hat{\alpha}^0$ and $\hat{\beta}_0^{\,0}$ being the PML estimators of α and β_0 computed under the homoscedasticity hypothesis.

$$(4.24)$$

If the likelihood function is well specified, i.e., if the model is conditionally Gaussian, the Lagrange multiplier statistic has asymptotically under the null hypothesis a chi-square distribution with the number of degrees of fredom equal to the size of the vector β_1. If this size is denoted by r, the Lagrange multiplier test consists of

$$\begin{cases} \text{accepting the homoscedasticity hypothesis if } \xi_{ML} < \chi^2_{95\%}(r), \\ \text{rejecting it otherwise,} \end{cases}$$

where $\chi^2_{95\%}(r)$ is the 95% quantile of the $\chi^2(r)$.

In our case, we can give the explicit form of the components of the scores (see 4.4), noting that

$$\frac{\partial h_t}{\partial \alpha}(\alpha, \beta_0, 0) = \frac{\partial h}{\partial \alpha}(\beta_0) = 0.$$

We obtain

$$\begin{cases} \dfrac{\partial \log l_t}{\partial \alpha} = \dfrac{Y_t - m_t(\hat{\alpha}^0)}{\hat{h}_0} \dfrac{\partial m_t}{\partial \alpha}(\hat{\alpha}^0), \\[3ex] \dfrac{\partial \log l_t}{\partial \beta_0} = -\dfrac{1}{2} \dfrac{1}{\hat{h}_0} \dfrac{\partial h}{\partial \beta_0}(\hat{\beta}_0^0) + \dfrac{1}{2} \dfrac{[Y_t - m_t(\hat{\alpha}^0)]}{\hat{h}_0^2} \dfrac{\partial h}{\partial \beta_0}(\hat{\beta}_0^0), \\[3ex] \dfrac{\partial \log l_t}{\partial \beta_1} = -\dfrac{1}{2} \dfrac{1}{\hat{h}_0} \dfrac{\partial h_t}{\partial \beta_1}(\hat{\alpha}^0, \hat{\beta}_0^0, 0) + \dfrac{1}{2} \dfrac{[Y_t - m_t(\hat{\alpha}^0)]^2}{\hat{h}_0^2} \dfrac{\partial h_t}{\partial \beta_1}(\hat{\alpha}^0, \hat{\beta}_0^0, 0). \end{cases}$$

Under the null hypothesis,

$$\frac{1}{T} \sum_{t=1}^{T} \frac{\partial \log l_t}{\partial \alpha} \frac{\partial \log l_t}{\partial \beta_0} \quad \text{and} \quad \frac{1}{T} \sum_{t=1}^{T} \frac{\partial \log l_t}{\partial \alpha} \frac{\partial \log l_t}{\partial \beta_1'}$$

tend to be the expectation of odd functions of the error term ε_t. Since this latter one is conditionally normal with zero mean, these limits are zero. It is therefore possible to replace the initial Lagrange multiplier statistic by an equivalent statistic in which

$$z_{1t} = \frac{\partial \log l_t}{\partial \beta_1}(\hat{\theta}^0), \quad z_{2t} = \frac{\partial \log l_t}{\partial \beta_0}(\hat{\theta}^0).$$

Moreover, in this type of cross product,

$$\sum_{t=1}^{T} \frac{\partial \log l_t}{\partial \beta_0} \frac{\partial \log l_t}{\partial \beta_1'} = \frac{1}{4} \frac{1}{\hat{h}_0^4} \sum_{t=1}^{T} \frac{\partial h}{\partial \beta_0}(\hat{\beta}_0^0) \frac{1}{\hat{h}_0} \frac{\partial h_t}{\partial \beta_1'}(\hat{\alpha}^0, \hat{\beta}^0, 0)(\hat{\varepsilon}_t^{0^2} - \hat{h}_0)^4,$$

one can replace $(\hat{\varepsilon}_t^{0^2} - \hat{h}_0)^4$ by its estimated conditional expectation $2\hat{h}_0^2$ and obtain an asymptotically equivalent test statistic after this replacement. With these modifications, the Lagrange multiplier statistic becomes

$$\xi_{LM} = \frac{1}{2\hat{h}_0^2} \sum_{t=1}^{T} \frac{\partial h_t}{\partial \beta_1'}(\hat{\alpha}^0, \hat{\beta}_0^0, 0)(\hat{\varepsilon}_t^{0^2} - \hat{h}_0)$$

$$\times \left[\frac{1}{2\hat{h}_0^2} \sum_{t=1}^T \frac{\partial h_t}{\partial \beta_1}(\hat{\alpha}^0, \hat{\beta}_0^0, 0) \frac{\partial h_t}{\partial \beta_1'}(\hat{\alpha}^0, \hat{\beta}_0^0, 0) \right.$$

$$- \frac{1}{2\hat{h}_0^2} \sum_{t=1}^T \frac{\partial h_t}{\partial \beta_1}(\hat{\alpha}^0, \hat{\beta}_0^0, 0) \frac{\partial h}{\partial \beta_0}(\hat{\beta}_0^{\,0}) \left[\frac{1}{2\hat{h}_0^2} \sum_{t=1}^T \frac{\partial h_t^2}{\partial \beta_0}(\hat{\beta}_0^0) \right]^{-1}$$

$$\left. \times \frac{1}{2\hat{h}_0^2} \sum_{t=1}^T \frac{\partial h_t}{\partial \beta_1}(\hat{\alpha}^0, \hat{\beta}_0^0, 0) \frac{\partial h}{\partial \beta_0}(\hat{\beta}_0^{\,0}) \right]^{-1} \frac{1}{2\hat{h}_0^2} \sum_{t=1}^T \frac{\partial h_t}{\partial \beta_1}(\hat{\alpha}^0, \hat{\beta}_0^0, 0)(\hat{\varepsilon}_t^{0^2} - \hat{h}_0).$$

$$
\boxed{
\begin{aligned}
\xi_{LM} &= \frac{1}{2\hat{h}_0^2} \sum_{t=1}^T \frac{\partial h_t}{\partial \beta_1'}(\hat{\alpha}^0, \hat{\beta}_0^0, 0)(\hat{\varepsilon}_t^{0^2} - \hat{h}_0) \\
&\times \left\{ \sum_{t=1}^T \frac{\partial h_t}{\partial \beta_1}(\hat{\alpha}^0, \hat{\beta}_0^0, 0) \frac{\partial h_t}{\partial \beta_1'}(\hat{\alpha}^0, \hat{\beta}_0^0, 0) - \frac{1}{T} \left[\sum_{t=1}^T \frac{\partial h_t}{\partial \beta_1}(\hat{\alpha}^0, \hat{\beta}_0^0, 0) \right] \right. \\
&\left. \times \left[\sum_{t=1}^T \frac{\partial h_t}{\partial \beta_1'}(\hat{\alpha}^0, \hat{\beta}_0^0, 0) \right] \right\}^{-1} \\
&\times \sum_{t=1}^T \frac{\partial h_t}{\partial \beta_1}(\hat{\alpha}^0, \hat{\beta}_0^0, 0)(\hat{\varepsilon}_t^{0^2} - \hat{h}_0).
\end{aligned}
}
$$

$$(4.25)$$

4.5   The Test Statistic Interpretation

This statistic admits a simple interpretation. Indeed, the second order properties of the ε_t^2 process may be inferred from an econometric model in which the endogenous variable is the squared error term. This model is

$$\varepsilon_t^2 = h_t(\alpha, \beta_0, \beta_1) + u_t,$$

with

$$E(u_t/u_{t-1}) = 0, \qquad V(u_t/u_{t-1}) = 2h_t^2(\alpha, \beta_0, \beta_1).$$

This model can be approximated in the neighborhood of the homoscedasticity hypothesis. One may first replace the unknown variables ε_t^2 by their forecasts $(\hat{\varepsilon}_t^0)^2$ evaluated under the null hypothesis, estimate the variability of the error u_t by $2\hat{h}_0^2$, and then consider a Taylor expansion of the regression function. An approximated model is

$$(\hat{\varepsilon}_t^0)^2 \simeq h(\beta_0) + \frac{\partial h_t}{\partial \beta_1'}(\alpha, \beta_0, 0) \; \beta_1 + u_t,$$

$$E(u_t/u_{t-1}) = 0, \qquad V(u_t/u_{t-1}) = 2\hat{h}_0^2.$$

Finally, the parameters α, β_0 in the derivative $\frac{\partial h_t}{\partial \beta_1'}$ may be substituted by their constrained estimators, yielding

$$(\hat{\varepsilon}_t^0)^2 \approx h_0 + \frac{\partial h_t}{\partial \beta_1'}(\hat{\alpha}^0, \hat{\beta}_0^0, 0)\,\beta_1 + u_t,$$

$$E(u_t/\underline{u_{t-1}}) = 0, \quad V(u_t/\underline{u_{t-1}}) = 2\hat{h}_0^2. \tag{4.26}$$

One can easily see that the Lagrange multiplier statistic (4.25) equals the Lagrange multiplier statistic used to test the hypothesis $H_0 = [\beta_1 = 0]$ in this approximated linear model. It is consequently given by the equality

$$\xi_{\mathrm{LM}} = T R^2, \tag{4.27}$$

where R^2 is the square of the determination coefficient obtained from this homoscedastic regression model.

4.5.1 Application to Regression Models with ARCH or GARCH Errors

i) ARCH Errors

The econometric model for the squared error term is

$$\varepsilon_t^2 = c + \sum_{i=1}^{p} a_i \varepsilon_{t-i}^2 + u_t.$$

This model is already linear in the parameters $a_1, \ldots, a_p$, which are equal to zero under the homoscedasticity hypothesis. The test statistic therefore equals $T R^2$, where R^2 is the square of the determination coefficient corresponding to the OLS regression:

$$\hat{\varepsilon}_t^{0^2} \simeq c + \sum_{i=1}^{p} a_i \hat{\varepsilon}_{t-i}^{0^2} + u_t.$$

It may be viewed as a Portmanteau statistic on the squared residuals (see section 2.4.2).

ii) GARCH Errors

With GARCH errors, we have

$$h_t = c + \sum_{i=1}^{p} \alpha_i \varepsilon_{t-i}^2 + \sum_{j=1}^{q} \beta_j h_{t-j}.$$

The conditional variance is a function of the parameters c, α, β and b that are present in the conditional expectation term. Introducing the lag-operator, we obtain

$$\left(1 - \sum_{j=1}^{q} \beta_j L^j\right) h_t = c + \left(\sum_{i=1}^{p} \alpha_i L^i\right) \varepsilon_t^2,$$

$$h_t = \left[1 - \sum_{j=1}^{q} \beta_j L^j\right]^{-1} \left[c + \left(\sum_{i=1}^{p} \alpha_i L^i\right) \varepsilon_t^2\right].$$

In the neighborhood of the homoscedasticity hypothesis, $\alpha_i \approx 0$, $\beta_i \approx 0$, and hence this relation may be approximated by

$$h_t \approx \gamma_0 + \sum_{i=1}^{p+q} \gamma_i \varepsilon_{t-i}^2,$$

where the coefficients γ_i are functions of α_i and β_j. We infer from the last expression that a GARCH (p, q) process is locally equivalent to an ARCH $(p + q)$ model and that the test for the homoscedasticity hypothesis may be carried out using

$$\xi_{LM} = T R^2,$$

where the R^2 coefficient is computed from the regression model

$$\hat{\varepsilon}_t^{0^2} = \gamma_0 + \sum_{i=1}^{p+q} \gamma_i \hat{\varepsilon}_{t-i}^{0^2} + u_t.$$

Appendix 4.1: Matrices I and J

i) Second Order Derivatives of the Log-Likelihood Function

We have

$$\frac{\partial^2 \log L}{\partial \theta \partial \theta'} = \frac{1}{2} \sum_{t=1}^{T} \frac{1}{h_t^2} \frac{\partial h_t}{\partial \theta} \frac{\partial h_t}{\partial \theta'} - \frac{1}{2} \sum_{t=1}^{T} \frac{1}{h_t} \frac{\partial^2 h_t}{\partial \theta \partial \theta'} - \sum_{t=1}^{T} \frac{(Y_t - m_t)^2}{h_t^3} \frac{\partial h_t}{\partial \theta} \frac{\partial h_t}{\partial \theta'}$$

$$+ \frac{1}{2} \sum_{t=1}^{T} \frac{(Y_t - m_t)^2}{h_t^2} \frac{\partial^2 h_t}{\partial \theta \partial \theta'} - \sum_{t=1}^{T} \frac{\partial m_t}{\partial \theta} \frac{\partial h_t}{\partial \theta'} \frac{Y_t - m_t}{h_t^2}$$

$$+ \sum_{t=1}^{T} \frac{(Y_t - m_t)}{h_t} \frac{\partial^2 m_t}{\partial \theta \partial \theta'} - \sum_{t=1}^{T} \frac{1}{h_t} \frac{\partial m_t}{\partial \theta} \frac{\partial m_t}{\partial \theta'} - \sum_{t=1}^{T} \frac{Y_t - m_t}{h_t^2} \frac{\partial h_t}{\partial \theta} \frac{\partial m_t}{\partial \theta'}.$$

ii) Expression for Matrix J

$$J = E_0 \left[-\frac{\partial^2 \log l_t}{\partial \theta \partial \theta'} \right]$$

$$
= E_0 \left\{ -\frac{1}{2} \frac{1}{h_t^2} \frac{\partial h_t}{\partial \theta} \frac{\partial h_t}{\partial \theta'} + \frac{1}{2} \frac{1}{h_t} \frac{\partial^2 h_t}{\partial \theta \partial \theta'} + \frac{1}{h_t^2} \frac{\partial h_t}{\partial \theta} \frac{\partial h_t}{\partial \theta'} E_{t-1} u_t^2 \right.
$$

$$
-\frac{1}{2} \frac{1}{h_t^2} \frac{\partial^2 h_t}{\partial \theta \partial \theta'} E_{t-1} u_t^2 + \frac{1}{h_t^{3/2}} \frac{\partial m_t}{\partial \theta} \frac{\partial h_t}{\partial \theta'} E_{t-1} u_t + \frac{1}{h_t^{1/2}} \frac{\partial^2 m_t}{\partial \theta \partial \theta'} E_{t-1} u_t
$$

$$
\left. + \frac{1}{h_t} \frac{\partial m_t}{\partial \theta} \frac{\partial m_t}{\partial \theta'} + \frac{1}{h_t^{3/2}} E_{t-1} u_t \frac{\partial h_t}{\partial \theta} \frac{\partial m_t}{\partial \theta'} \right\},
$$

where E_{t-1} denotes the conditional expectation given the past values computed with respect to the true distribution, and where $u_t = \frac{(Y_t - m_t)}{h_t^{1/2}(\theta)}$. As $E_{t-1} u_t = 0$ and $E_{t-1} u_t^2 = 1$, we obtain

$$
J = E_0 \left[\frac{1}{2} \frac{1}{h_t^2} \frac{\partial h_t}{\partial \theta} \frac{\partial h_t}{\partial \theta'} + \frac{1}{h_t} \frac{\partial m_t}{\partial \theta} \frac{\partial m_t}{\partial \theta'} \right].
$$

iii) Expression for Matrix I

We get

$$
I = E_0 \left[\frac{\partial \log l_t}{\partial \theta} \frac{\partial \log l_t}{\partial \theta'} \right]
$$

$$
= E_0 \left\{ \left[-\frac{1}{2} \frac{1}{h_t} \frac{\partial h_t}{\partial \theta} + \frac{1}{2} \frac{1}{h_t} \frac{\partial h_t}{\partial \theta} u_t^2 + \frac{1}{h_t^{1/2}} \frac{\partial m_t}{\partial \theta} u_t \right] \right.
$$

$$
\left. \times \left[-\frac{1}{2} \frac{1}{h_t} \frac{\partial h_t}{\partial \theta'} + \frac{1}{2} \frac{1}{h_t} \frac{\partial h_t}{\partial \theta'} u_t^2 + \frac{1}{h_t^{1/2}} \frac{\partial m_t}{\partial \theta'} u_t \right] \right\}
$$

$$
= E_0 \left\{ \left[\frac{1}{4} \frac{1}{h_t^2} \frac{\partial h_t}{\partial \theta} \frac{\partial h_t}{\partial \theta'} + \frac{1}{4} \frac{1}{h_t^2} \frac{\partial h_t}{\partial \theta} \frac{\partial h_t}{\partial \theta'} E_{t-1} u_t^4 + \frac{1}{h_t} \frac{\partial m_t}{\partial \theta} \frac{\partial m_t}{\partial \theta'} \right. \right.
$$

$$
\left. \left. -\frac{1}{2} \frac{1}{h_t^2} \frac{\partial h_t}{\partial \theta} \frac{\partial h_t}{\partial \theta'} + \frac{1}{2} \frac{1}{h_t^{3/2}} \left[\frac{\partial h_t}{\partial \theta} \frac{\partial m_t}{\partial \theta'} + \frac{\partial m_t}{\partial \theta} \frac{\partial h_t}{\partial \theta'} \right] E_{t-1} u_t^3 \right\}
$$

$$
= E_0 \left\{ \left[\frac{1}{4} \frac{1}{h_t^2} \frac{\partial h_t}{\partial \theta} \frac{\partial h_t}{\partial \theta'} [K_t(\theta) - 1] + \frac{1}{h_t} \frac{\partial m_t}{\partial \theta} \frac{\partial m_t}{\partial \theta'} \right. \right.
$$

$$
\left. \left. + \frac{1}{2} \frac{1}{h_t^3} \left[\frac{\partial h_t}{\partial \theta} \frac{\partial m_t}{\partial \theta'} + \frac{\partial m_t}{\partial \theta} \frac{\partial h_t}{\partial \theta'} \right] M_{3t} \right\}.
$$

Appendix 4.2: Derivatives of the Log-Likelihood Function and Information Matrix for a Regression Model with ARCH Errors

i) First Order Derivatives
From formula (4.7) we deduce

$$
\frac{\partial \log L}{\partial \alpha} = -\frac{1}{2} \sum_{t=1}^{T} \frac{1}{h_t} \left(-2 \sum_{j=1}^{p} a_j x'_{t-j}(y_{t-j} - x_{t-j} b) \right) + \frac{1}{2} \sum_{t=1}^{T} \frac{(y_t - m_t)^2}{h_t^2}
$$

$$\times \left(-2 \sum_{j=1}^{p} a_j x'_{t-j} (y_{t-j} - x_{t-j} b) \right) + \sum_{t=1}^{T} \frac{y_t - m_t}{h_t} x'_t$$

$$= -\sum_{t=1}^{T} \frac{1}{h_t^2} (\varepsilon_t^2 - h_t) \sum_{j=1}^{p} a_j x'_{t-j} \varepsilon_{t-j} + \sum_{t=1}^{T} \frac{\varepsilon_t}{h_t} x'_t,$$

$$\frac{\partial \log L}{\partial \beta} = -\frac{1}{2} \sum_{t=1}^{T} \frac{1}{h_t} \begin{bmatrix} 1 \\ \varepsilon_{t-1}^2 \\ \vdots \\ \varepsilon_{t-p}^2 \end{bmatrix} + \frac{1}{2} \sum_{t=1}^{T} \frac{\varepsilon_t^2}{h_t^2} \begin{bmatrix} 1 \\ \varepsilon_{t-1}^2 \\ \vdots \\ \varepsilon_{t-p}^2 \end{bmatrix}$$

$$= \sum_{t=1}^{T} \frac{1}{2h_t^2} (\varepsilon_t^2 - h_t) \begin{bmatrix} 1 \\ \varepsilon_{t-1}^2 \\ \vdots \\ \varepsilon_{t-p}^2 \end{bmatrix}.$$

ii) Components of matrix J

From formula (4.8) we deduce

$$J_{\alpha\alpha} = E_0 \left\{ \frac{1}{h_t} x'_t x_t + \frac{2}{h_t^2} \left(\sum_{j=1}^{p} a_j x'_{t-j} \varepsilon_{t-j} \right) \left(\sum_{j=1}^{p} a_j x_{t-j} \varepsilon_{t-j} \right) \right\},$$

$$J_{\beta\alpha} = -E_0 \left\{ \frac{1}{h_t^2} \begin{bmatrix} 1 \\ \varepsilon_{t-1}^2 \\ \vdots \\ \varepsilon_{t-p}^2 \end{bmatrix} \left(\sum_{j=1}^{p} a_j x_{t-j} \varepsilon_{t-j} \right) \right\},$$

$$J_{\beta\beta} = E_0 \left\{ \frac{1}{2h_t^2} \begin{bmatrix} 1 \\ \varepsilon_{t-1}^2 \\ \vdots \\ \varepsilon_{t-p}^2 \end{bmatrix} [1, \varepsilon_{t-1}^2, \dots, \varepsilon_{t-p}^2] \right\}.$$

4.6   Exercises

Exercise 4.1. Let us consider a regression model with heteroscedastic error. We assume that

$$m_t(\theta) = m_t(\alpha), \ h_t(\theta) = \beta_0 \, h(z_t \beta_1),$$

where h is a given function satisfying $h(0) = 1$. Deduce from the expression of the Lagrange multiplier statistic and from its interpretation in the approximated linear model case that this statistic is independent of the function h.

Exercise 4.2. A positive variable X follows a continuous gamma distribution $\gamma(\nu)$, $\nu > 0$, with the density function

$$f(x) = \frac{\exp(-x) x^{\nu-1}}{\Gamma(\nu)}, \quad x > 0,$$

where $\Gamma(\nu) = \int_0^\infty \exp(-x)x^{\nu-1}\,dx$.

i) Discuss the existence of moments of the type

$$E(X^r), \ r \in \mathbb{R}.$$

ii) Consider a variable U following a standard normal distribution and the square of this variable $Y = U^2$. By definition, the distribution of Y is a chi-square with one degree of freedom. Show that $\frac{1}{2}Y$ follows the $\gamma(\frac{1}{2})$ distribution. Derive the existence conditions for the moments $E(Y^r), \ r \in \mathbb{R}$.

Exercise 4.3. (Bera and Lee 1988) Let us consider the autoregressive model

$$\varepsilon_t = \sum_{j=1}^{p} \varphi_{jt}\varepsilon_{t-j} + u_t,$$

where (u_t) is a Gaussian white noise and where the coefficients (φ_{jt}) are random, time independent, independent of the process u and such that

$$[\varphi_{1t}, \ldots, \varphi_{pt}]' \sim N(0, \Omega).$$

i) Determine the conditional distribution of ε_t given $\underline{\varepsilon_{t-1}}$ by integrating out the random coefficients (φ_{jt}). Show that this model leads to an ARCH formulation.

ii) Find a test for absence of heterogeneity; it is called the "information matrix test" [see Chesher (1984)].

iii) Compare this test with the test for the homoscedasticity hypothesis directly based on the ARCH model.

5

Some Applications of Univariate ARCH Models

In this chapter, we present several applications of ARCH models proposed in the literature. The discussion covers the modelling aspects (sections 1, 4, 5), the random walk hypothesis tests (section 3) and the interpretation of ARCH models as discrete approximations of continuous time models (section 2). We emphasize the particular importance of these different questions in financial econometrics.

5.1 Leptokurtic Aspects of Financial Series and Aggregation

5.1.1 The Normality Assumption

Just like the ARMA specifications, the ARCH models have the advantage of being very flexible in their application, under assumptions that essentially concern the first and second order moments. However, it has sometimes appeared useful to introduce the assumption of normally distributed innovations. For instance, we have described the properties of pseudo maximum likelihood estimators under the normality assumption. We have seen that these estimators are consistent even if this normality assumption is not satisfied. For this reason, one could expect that this assumption is not very stringent. Nevertheless, if the innovations are not normally distributed, these estimators may be less efficient. It is then useful to examine whether this assumption is relevant.

If the innovations are Gaussian and the series satisfies a usual ARMA model, we know that the series is itself Gaussian. If the innovations are Gaussian and the series

TABLE 5.1. Kurtosis Coefficients

Securities	Period	k
Alcoa	1966–1976	7.2
AM. Can.	–	5.7
AT and T	–	6.3
Anaconda	–	11.1
Chrysler	–	6.9
Dupont	–	4.8
Kodak	–	6.3
G.Electric	–	5.1
G.Foods	–	5.7
G.Motors	–	7.2
Harvester	–	5.7
Metals		
Gold	1975–82	11.4
Silver	1970–74	11.4
Copper	1966–81	9.9
Lead	1970–81	9.6
Tin	–	9.9
Zinc	–	15.0
Currency		
£/$	1974–82	8.4

satisfies an ARCH formulation, we also know that the series must admit a kurtosis that is greater than one of normal distribution. In the case of Gaussian innovations, it is then natural to begin the empirical study by computing the kurtosis coefficient to find out whether the instantaneous variability of the model to be adjusted depends on the past.

In order to illustrate the problem, we present the kurtosis coefficients corresponding to the return series of several spot prices (Taylor 1985). Let us recall that the empirical kurtosis is conventionally:

$$ k = \frac{1}{T} \sum_{t=1}^{T} (Y_t - \bar{Y})^4 \Bigg/ \left[\frac{1}{T} \sum_{t=1}^{T} (Y_t - \bar{Y})^2 \right]^2 . $$

It should be close to 3 in the case of a Gaussian series Y. The fact that it is greater than 3 indicates an instantaneous past dependent variability.

It is worth noting that these return series show a significant leptokurticity, which suggests a rejection of the normality of the series but not necessarily of the corresponding innovations. The same kind of results are obtained from French data. For instance, Thomas (1989) studied the price evolution of 140 securities traded on the Paris stock exchange from January 1969 to January 1982. These securities have been classified into ten homogeneous portfolios with respect to decreasing risk, each of the portfolios being composed of 14 securities. The following table shows the historical kurtosis of each of the portfolios and the ratio of the historical variabilities corresponding to the third and first subperiods. The last coefficient shows heteroscedasticity. Finally, we also present the skewness coefficient, often considered as a nonlinearity indicator.

portfolio	kurtosis	variance ratio	skewness coefficient
1	9.0	2.4	0.3
2	11.4	1.8	0.4
3	2.1	2.5	0.3
4	3.0	1.9	0.5
5	123.0	0.2	8.7
6	150.0	0.3	8.6
7	8.7	2.5	0.7
8	4.8	2.0	0.6
9	7.2	2.7	0.4
10	4.8	2.3	0.2

5.1.2   The Choice of a Time Unit

This leptokurtic aspect is not incompatible with an ARCH formulation (see chapter 3). Still, one may ask whether normality has to be assumed on the innovations corresponding to the available dates or on some innovations that are constructed using an alternative time unit. Thus, if weekly series are available, do we fit the Gaussian ARCH model to this series or, for example, to the unobserved underlying daily process?

A natural way to proceed is to estimate a conditionally Gaussian ARCH model on the raw series itself and to compute the residuals. Then, we evaluate the kurtosis coefficient corresponding to the residuals. Two main cases are to be distinguished: if the kurtosis is close to 3, the Gaussian assumption is not rejected; if it is significantly larger than 3, one may prefer to modify the conditional variance specification or retain an ARCH model on a smaller time unit. A kurtosis significantly lower than 3 seems to occur rarely in practice. Two questions have to be answered:

- Is it possible to get an idea, even approximately, of the underlying time unit?

- How can we estimate an ARCH model corresponding to a time unit smaller than that of the observations?

The second point will be discussed in section 2. We now investigate the first question by means of a simple example.

Let us consider the process defined by

$$Y_\tau = \sqrt{a_0 + a_1 Y_{\tau-1}^2} \, \varepsilon_\tau,$$

where (ε_τ) is a standard Gaussian white noise. We assume that the duration between observations is h times the time unit used to define the underlying process. Hence we need to study the properties of the observed series,

$$\tilde{Y}_t = Y_{th}, \quad t \in \mathbb{Z},$$

and, in particular, the conditional distribution of the current value $\tilde{Y}_t$ given the lagged one $\tilde{Y}_{t-1}$. This requires that we first forecast the latent process Y at horizon h. For example, let us show how the second and fourth order moments can be computed.

Following the procedure in exercise 3.1, we obtain

$$E(Y_t^2/Y_{t-1}) = (a_0 + a_1 Y_{t-1}^2),$$
$$E(Y_t^4/Y_{t-1}) = (a_0 + a_1 Y_{t-1}^2)^2 E \varepsilon_t^4$$
$$= 3a_0^2 + 6a_0 a_1 Y_{t-1}^2 + 3a_1^2 Y_{t-1}^4.$$

In a vector notation, the equalities are written as

$$\left[\begin{array}{c} E(Y_t^2/Y_{t-1}) \\ E(Y_t^4/Y_{t-1}) \end{array} \right] = \left[\begin{array}{c} a_0 \\ 3a_0^2 \end{array} \right] + \left[\begin{array}{cc} a_1 & 0 \\ 6a_0 a_1 & 3a_1^2 \end{array} \right] \left[\begin{array}{c} Y_{t-1}^2 \\ Y_{t-1}^4 \end{array} \right]$$

or

$$\left[\begin{array}{c} E(Y_t^2 - m_2/Y_{t-1}) \\ E(Y_t^4 - m_4/Y_{t-1}) \end{array} \right] = \left[\begin{array}{cc} a_1 & 0 \\ 6a_0 a_1 & 3a_1^2 \end{array} \right] \left[\begin{array}{c} Y_{t-1}^2 - m_2 \\ Y_{t-1}^4 - m_4 \end{array} \right],$$

with

$$m_2 = \frac{a_0}{1 - a_1}, \quad m_4 = \frac{3a_0^2}{(1 - a_1)^2} \frac{1 - a_1^2}{1 - 3a_1^2}.$$

By the law of iterated expectation, we have

$$\left[\begin{array}{c} E(Y_t^2 - m_2/Y_{t-h}) \\ E(Y_t^4 - m_4/Y_{t-h}) \end{array} \right] = \left[\begin{array}{cc} a_1 & 0 \\ 6a_0 a_1 & 3a_1^2 \end{array} \right]^h \left[\begin{array}{c} Y_{t-h}^2 - m_2 \\ Y_{t-h}^4 - m_4 \end{array} \right].$$

This shows that the process $\tilde{Y}$ is such that

$$\begin{cases} E(\tilde{Y}_t^2/\tilde{Y}_{t-1}) = c_{1h} + a_1^h \tilde{Y}_{t-1}^2, \\ E(\tilde{Y}_t^4/\tilde{Y}_{t-1}) = c_{2h} + c_{3h} \tilde{Y}_{t-1}^2 + 3^h a_1^{2h} \tilde{Y}_{t-1}^4, \end{cases}$$

where c_{1h}, c_{2h}, c_{3h} are functions of h, a_0, a_1. It is then an ARCH(1) process.

These formulas provide an easy method of empirically determining the order h. It consists in regressing $\tilde{Y}_t^2$ on $\tilde{Y}_{t-1}^2$ as well as $\tilde{Y}_t^4$ on $\tilde{Y}_{t-1}^2$ and $\tilde{Y}_{t-1}^4$. Let us denote by α_1 the coefficient of $\tilde{Y}_{t-1}^2$ in the first regression, and by α_2 the coefficient of $\tilde{Y}_{t-1}^4$ in the second one. If the conditionally Gaussian ARCH model is well specified, a consistent estimator of h is

$$\hat{h} = \text{Log}\, \alpha_2 - 2\,\text{Log}\, \alpha_1 - \text{Log}\, 3.$$

This method is of a rather empirical interest. It does not guarantee an integer value estimator and is likely not very precise. Nevertheless, the approximate value obtained may be useful for applying the simulated methods described in section 5.2.

5.2   ARCH Processes as an Approximation of Continuous Time Processes

In a deterministic framework, it is common to study jointly the recursive equations and the differential equations to see the analogies and differences between discrete and continuous time analyses. The same approach may also be followed in a stochastic framework, provided that we have a precise definition of the notion of stochastic differential equations.

5.2.1   Stochastic Integrals

As usual, differentials and integrals are considered jointly, and we first define the notion of integral as a limit of the Riemann sum.

Two types of stochastic integrals may be defined: integrals of random functions with respect to deterministic measures, and integrals of random functions with respect to random measures. This last case is more difficult and requires several constraints, both on the random measure to be retained and the function to be integrated.

i) Integral of a Random Function with Respect to a Deterministic Measure

Let us denote by $A(t)$, $t \in \mathbb{R}^+$, a family of random variables indexed by time and consider integration with respect to the Lebesgue measure. A natural definition is

$$\int_0^t A(s)\,ds = \lim_{n \to \infty} \sum_{i=1}^n A(t_i)(t_{i+1} - t_i),$$

(5.1)

where in the limit the step of the subdivision $0 = t_1 < t_2 \cdots < t_n = t$ tends to zero. In this form, the definition is clearly incomplete. We must first specify the type of convergence to the limit. If the two terms on the right-hand side of the equality are random, one of the usual notions of stochastic limit has to be chosen. One usually retains a limit in quadratic mean (qm).

In addition, we need a condition ensuring that the qm limit exists and does not depend on the selected partition. Such a condition is

$$\int_0^t E[A(s)^2]\,ds < +\infty.$$

(5.2)

ii) Integral of a Random Function with Respect to a Random Measure

The idea is similar to the one used to build the integral with respect to a deterministic measure. Let us denote by $B(t)$ the random function to be integrated and $W(t)$ the random measure with respect to which we integrate. We wish to write formally

$$\int_0^t B(s)\,dW(s) = \lim_{n\to\infty} \sum_{i=1}^n B(t_i)[W(t_{i+1}) - W(t_i)], \tag{5.3}$$

where the qm limit is evaluated when the step of the subdivision $0 = t_1 < t_2 \cdots < t_n = t$ tends to zero.

The study of the convergence in quadratic mean is difficult without a few additional assumptions that allow for a simple computation of the variance of $\sum_{i=1}^n B(t_i)[W(t_{i+1}) - W(t_i)]$.

We first note that it is always possible to suppose that the variable $W(t)$ has zero mean. Indeed, in the contrary case, we would add the mean $\sum_{i=1}^n B(t_i)[EW(t_{i+1}) - EW(t_i)]$, which may be understood as an integral of a random function with respect to a deterministic measure. This case was discussed in the last section.

Moreover, the increments $W(t_{i+1}) - W(t_i)$ may be normalized by an appropriate multiplicative factor which is then incorporated into the function to be integrated. The factor is generally chosen such that on average it again yields the Lebesgue measure

$$V[W(t_{i+1}) - W(t_i)] = t_{i+1} - t_i. \tag{5.4}$$

Other assumptions allow us to compute the variance of $\sum_{i=1}^n B(t_i)[W(t_{i+1}) - W(t_i)]$ as a sum of variances. The first one is

(A1) *The process* $[B(t)]$ *is subordinate to the process* $[W(t)]$, i.e., $B(t)$ is a function of the current and past values of W but not of the future ones. For example, we now can write

$$E[B(t_i)[W(t_{i+1}) - W(t_i)]^2 / \underline{W(t_i)}] = B(t_i)^2 E([W(t_{i+1}) - W(t_i)]^2 / \underline{W(t_i)}).$$

The second assumption allows easy computation of the conditional variance.

(A2) *The process* $[W(t)]$ *has independent increments, i.e.,* $W(t) - W(s)$ *is independent of* $[W(u),\ u \le s]$ *for every value* $t \ge s$.

The different constraints on the stochastic measure are particularly satisfied if for W we substitute a Brownian motion.

Definition 5.5. *A Brownian motion (or Wiener process) is a process* $(W(t),\ t \in \mathbb{R}^+)$ *with Gaussian distribution with zero mean* $EW(t) = 0$, $\forall t$, *and covariance* $\mathrm{Cov}[W(t), W(s)] = \mathrm{Min}(s, t)$, $\forall s, t$.

We verify that $\mathrm{Cov}[W(t) - W(s), W(u)] = u - u = 0$, if $u \le s \le t$. The variables being uncorrelated and Gaussian imply the independence of the increments (A2). Moreover, the process is normalized since

$$V[W(t_{i+1}) - W(t_i)] = VW(t_{i+1}) - VW(t_i) - 2\,\mathrm{Cov}[W(t_i), W(t_{i+1})]$$

$$= t_{i+1} - t_i - 2t_i = t_{i+1} - t_i.$$

According to the definition, we find that $W(0) = 0$.

5.2.2 Stochastic Differential Equations

i) Definitions

We now simultaneously define the stochastic differential equation and its solutions.

Definition 5.6. *Let* $[W(t), t \in \mathbb{R}^+]$ *be a Brownian motion and* $A(t, y)$, $B(t, y)$ *two functions defined on* $\mathbb{R}^+ \times \mathbb{R}$. *A process* $[Y(t), t \in \mathbb{R}^+]$ *is a solution of the stochastic differential equation (or diffusion equation)*

$$dY(t) = A(t, Y(t))dt + B(t, Y(t))dW(t)$$

if and only if it is subordinate to the process $[W(t), t \in R^+]$ *and such that*

$$Y(t) = Y(0) + \int_0^t A(s, Y(s))\, ds + \int_0^t B(s, Y(s))\, dW(s).$$

We do not discuss the conditions of existence for the solutions of stochastic differential equations. Instead, we try to point out their properties heuristically. As usual, the infinitesimal element $dY(t)$ may be assigned to $Y(t+dt) - Y(t)$ for small dt so that the equation may be written as

$$Y(t+dt) - Y(t) \approx A(t, Y(t))dt + B(t, Y(t))(W(t+dt) - W(t)).$$

We see that the increment is, conditionally to $W(t)$, roughly normal, with conditional mean $A(t, Y(t))dt$ and conditional variance $B^2(t, Y(t))dt$. Consequently, the model implies that the conditional mean and variance are of the same order. This result may be formularized in another way. The increment $Y(t+dt) - Y(t)$ is, conditionally on $W(t)$, a sum of the deterministic term of order dt, e.g., $A(t, Y(t))dt$, and of the random term with zero mean and order $(dt)^{1/2}$ corresponding to the standard deviation of $B(t, Y(t))[W(t+dt) - W(t)]$.

ii) Ito's Formula

The previous interpretation allows us to understand easily how to carry out a change of variables technique in the framework of stochastic differential equations. Indeed, let us consider a function of time and of $Y(t)$ being the solution of the equation, denoted $f[t, Y(t)]$. We assume that this function is twice differentiable with respect to its components. A second order Taylor expansion yields

$$df(t, Y(t)) \approx \frac{\partial f}{\partial t}(t, Y(t))dt + \frac{\partial f}{\partial y}(t, Y(t))dY(t)$$
$$+ \frac{1}{2}\left\{ \frac{\partial^2 f}{\partial t^2}(t, Y(t))(dt)^2 + 2\frac{\partial^2 f}{\partial t \partial y}(t, Y(t))dt\, dY(t) + \frac{\partial^2 f}{\partial y^2}(t, Y(t))(dY(t))^2 \right\}.$$

Keeping only the deterministic and random terms of order $(dt)^{1/2}$ or (dt), we obtain

$$df(t, Y(t)) \approx \left[\frac{\partial f}{\partial t}(t, Y(t)) + \frac{\partial f}{\partial y}(t, Y(t))A(t, Y(t)) \right] dt$$

$$+ \frac{\partial f}{\partial y}(t, Y(t))B(t, Y(t))dW(t)$$

$$+ \frac{1}{2}\frac{\partial^2 f}{\partial^2 y}(t, Y(t))B^2(t, Y(t))(dW(t))^2.$$

The distribution of $dW(t)$ is approximately normal with zero mean and variance dt. We infer that $\frac{[dW(t)]^2}{dt}$ has approximately a chi-square distribution with one degree of freedom; it is therefore a sum of the deterministic term equal to 1 (mean of this chi-square distribution) and of a centered random term that is of order smaller than the order of the expansion. Finally, the approximation yields Ito's formula.

Ito's Formula 5.7.

$$df(t, Y(t)) = \left\{ \frac{\partial f}{\partial t}(t, Y(t)) \right.$$

$$+ \frac{\partial f}{\partial y}(t, Y(t))A(t, Y(t)) + \frac{1}{2}\frac{\partial^2 f}{\partial y^2}(t, Y(t))B^2(t, Y(t)) \Bigg\} dt$$

$$+ \frac{\partial f}{\partial y}(t, Y(t))B(t, Y(t))dW(t).$$

The transformed process $[f(t, Y(t))]$ also satisfies a stochastic differential equation. Compared to the change of variables formula in the deterministic framework

$$df(t, Y(t)) = \frac{\partial f}{\partial t}(t, Y(t))dt + \frac{\partial f}{\partial y}(t, Y(t))dY(t),$$

the additional term $\frac{1}{2}\frac{\partial^2 f}{\partial y^2}B^2(t, Y(t))]dt$ must generally be introduced, which accounts for the stochastic aspect.

5.2.3   Some Equations and Their Solutions

As in the deterministic case, the solutions of stochastic differential equations do not generally have closed forms. Nevertheless, it is useful to examine equations for which closed form solutions are available and to develop methods that allow us to simplify the task in other more general cases.

i) Equations with Deterministic Coefficients, Independent of Y

The equations

$$dY(t) = A(t)dt + B(t)dW(t)$$

may be solved explicitly. According to the definition, the solutions are

$$Y(t) = Y(0) + \int_0^t A(s)\,ds + \int_0^t B(s)\,dW(s).$$

The integral $\int_0^t B(s) \, dW(s)$ being a limit of Riemann sums, which are linear combinations of Gaussian variables, implies that the solution is itself a Gaussian process for a deterministic initial condition $Y(0)$. The mean of $Y(t)$ is $\int_0^t A(s) \, ds$, and its variance is $\int_0^t B^2(s) \, ds$. Thus the solution process can be second order stationary only in the degenerate case: $A(t) = B(t) = 0, \forall t$.

ii) Equations that can Easily be Reduced to Equations with Coefficients Independent of Y

Let us consider a stochastic differential equation of the type

$$dY(t) = H(t, Y(t)) \left\{ dW(t) + C(t)dt + \frac{1}{2} \frac{\partial H}{\partial y}(t, Y(t))dt \right\}, \qquad (5.8)$$

where H and C are two functions to be defined later.

The form of the equation suggests that we rewrite it as

$$\frac{1}{H(t, Y(t))} dY(t) = dW(t) + C(t)dt + \frac{1}{2} \frac{\partial H}{\partial y}(t, Y(t))dt$$

and introduce the transformed variable

$$Z(t) = \mathcal{K}(t, Y(t)), \qquad (5.9)$$

where $\mathcal{K}(t, z) = \int_0^z \frac{1}{H(t,u)} \, du$. By applying Ito's formula (5.7), we get

$$dZ(t) = \frac{\partial \mathcal{K}}{\partial y}(t, Y(t))dY(t) + \frac{1}{2} \frac{\partial^2 \mathcal{K}}{\partial^2 y}(t, Y(t))H^2(t, Y(t))dt$$

$$= \frac{1}{H(t, Y(t))} dY(t) - \frac{1}{2} \frac{\partial H(t, Y(t))}{\partial y} dt$$

$$= dW(t) + C(t)dt.$$

We find the solutions such that

$$\mathcal{K}(t, Y(t)) = \mathcal{K}(0, Y(0)) + W(t) + \int_0^t C(s) \, ds. \qquad (5.10)$$

Note 5.11. If the function $H(t, Y(t))$ is strictly positive (or strictly negative), the function $\mathcal{K}(t, Y(t))$ is invertible and provides by means of a simple inversion the solution of the initial equation. The same technique may also be applied locally if the function H has no constant sign but is continuous, and if we start from an initial value such that $H(0, Y(0)) > 0$ (resp. < 0).

Example 5.12. Let us consider the following equation:

$$dY(t) = Y(t)[A(t)dt + B(t)dW(t)].$$

It may also be written as

$$\frac{1}{Y(t)}dY(t) = A(t)dt + B(t)dW(t).$$

Let us write $Z(t) = \log Y(t)$ (restraining to the positive values of Y). We have

$$d\log Y(t) = A(t)dt + B(t)dW(t) - \frac{1}{2}B^2(t)dt.$$

It leads to

$$\log Y(t) - \log Y(0) = \int_0^t \left[A(s) - \frac{B^2(s)}{2}\right]ds + \int_0^t B(s)dW(s).$$

Therefore, the marginal distribution of $Y(t)$ is (for $\log Y(0) = 0$) a log-normal distribution with parameters

$$LN\left[\int_0^t \left[A(s) - \frac{B^2(s)}{2}\right]ds, \int_0^t B^2(s)ds\right].$$

In particular, its mean is equal to

$$EY(t) = \exp\left[\int_0^t \left[A(s) - \frac{B^2(s)}{2}\right]ds + \frac{1}{2}\int_0^t B^2(s)ds\right]$$

$$= \exp\int_0^t A(s)ds,$$

and its variance is

$$VY(t) = \exp\left[2\int_0^t \left[A(s) - \frac{B^2(s)}{2}\right]ds + \int_0^t B^2(s)ds\right]\left[\exp\int_0^t B^2(s)ds - 1\right]$$

$$= \exp\left[2\int_0^t A(s)ds\right]\left[\exp\int_0^t B^2(s)ds - 1\right].$$

5.2.4   Continuous and Discrete Time

Continuous time models have been largely used in theoretical finance, mainly because Ito's calculus often allows us to analyze problems in a stylish and relatively simple way. However, several empirical difficulties arise when the available data are observed at discrete times. The distribution of a sequence of observations $Y_t, Y_{t+1}, Y_{t+2}, \cdots$ should then be derived from the stochastic differential equations defining the model. This is easy to do only if the equation has a closed form solution, i.e., in rather rare cases like the classical examples shown in section 5.2.3. An alternative approach consists in replacing the differential equation by a recursive equation and in finding the likelihood function for this approximated model.

Before discussing the technical details concerning such approximations, it is worth making two simple remarks. On the one hand, we notice that a number of recursive equations may be considered as good approximations of a given differential equation. This is due to the fact that various recursive equations may have common closed form solutions. On the other hand, if the models considered in discrete time are stationary ARCH, the diffusion models that approximate them must also satisfy a stationarity condition. Consequently, one cannot expect to find some of the models solved in section 5.2.3 as continuous approximations of ARCH models, since they admit nonstationary solutions.

In order to formularize the problem more rigorously, we introduce a sequence of multivariate processes in discrete time, indexed by the time unit h between two successive observations. Such processes may easily be extended to the continuous time setup by supposing that they remain constant between two successive observation times. The h-th process is of the form

$$Y_t^{(h)} = Y_{kh}^{(h)}, \quad \text{if } kh \le t \le h(k+1), \ k \in \mathbb{N}.$$

The distribution of this process is characterized by the distribution of the discrete time variables $[Y_{kh}, k \in \mathbb{N}]$ and may be described by the sequence of conditional distributions. Since we wish to obtain the limiting differential equation of order one, it is natural to impose constraints on the distribution of the discrete process. We assume that this process is Markov of order one, i.e., the value $Y_{(k+1)h}^{(h)}$ depends on the past values $Y_{kh}^{(h)}, Y_{(k-1)h}^{(h)}, \cdots$ only through the most recent one. The distribution of this process is then characterized by the initial distribution γ_h and by the conditional distribution given the last observed value:

$$\Pi_h(y, A) = P[Y_{kh}^{(h)} \in A / Y_{(k-1)h}^{(h)} = y].$$

We now need to impose coherency conditions between the various Π_h's and the initial distribution to ensure that, when the time unit tends to zero, the distribution of the process $Y^{(h)}$ tends to the distribution of a process that satisfies a diffusion equation. Precise regularity conditions are stated in Stroock and Varadhan (1979) and Nelson (1990). We present here only the main ones, which will allow us to find easily the form of the limiting stochastic differential equation. The simple idea is to ensure the convergence of the drift and volatility by the time unit when h tends to zero. The drift is

$$b_h(y) = \frac{1}{h} E[Y_{kh}^{(h)} - Y_{(k-1)h}^{(h)} / Y_{(k-1)h}^{(h)} = y], \tag{5.13}$$

and the volatility is

$$a_h(y) = \frac{1}{h} E\left\{ [Y_{kh}^{(h)} - Y_{(k-1)h}^{(h)}][Y_{kh}^{(h)} - Y_{(k-1)h}^{(h)}]' / Y_{(k-1)h}^{(h)} = y \right\}. \tag{5.14}$$

The following theorem holds under a few additional technical conditions.

Theorem 5.15. *If the initial measures γ_h tend to a limiting distribution γ_0, and if $b_h(y)$ and $a_h(y)$ tend to limits $b(y)$ and $a(y)$, where $a(y)$ is positive definite, then the sequence in processes $Y^{(h)}$ converges in distribution to a process Y solution of*

$$Y(t) = Y_0 + \int_0^t b(Y_s)\,ds + \int_0^t \sigma(Y_s)\,dW(s),$$

where $\sigma(y)$ is a positive definite matrix such that $a(y) = \sigma(y)\sigma(y)'$, and W is a standard Brownian motion with the same dimension as Y and independent of Y_0, where Y_0 has the distribution γ_0.

5.2.5 Examples

i) Euler Approximation of a Diffusion

Let us consider a diffusion equation

$$dY_t = b(Y_t)dt + \sigma(Y_t)dW_t. \tag{5.16}$$

A natural time discretization consists in replacing the differential elements by the increments. An approximate equation is

$$Y_{(k+1)h}^{(h)} = Y_{kh}^{(h)} + hb(Y_{kh}^{(h)}) + \sqrt{h}\sigma(Y_{kh}^{(h)})\varepsilon_k^{(h)}, \tag{5.17}$$

where the sequence $(\varepsilon_k^{(h)}, k$ varying) is a Gaussian standard white noise.
We have

$$b_h(y) = \frac{1}{h}E[Y_{(k)h}^{(h)} - Y_{(k-1)h}^{(h)} / Y_{(k-1)h}^{(h)} = y]$$

$$= \frac{1}{h}hb(y) = b(y),$$

and

$$a_h(y) = \frac{1}{h}E\left\{[Y_{kh}^{(h)} - Y_{(k-1)h}^{(h)}]^2 / Y_{(k-1)h}^{(h)} = y\right\},$$

$$= \frac{1}{h}h\sigma^2(y) = \sigma^2(y).$$

Therefore, for small h, the recursive equation (5.17) constitutes a good approximation of the differential equation (5.16).

ii) Approximation of a GARCH-M Model

The general theorem (5.15) may also be used to find the continuous approximations of models defined in discrete time. In some cases, this provides information on the invariant distribution of the initial model. The following example has been studied by Nelson (1990). Let us consider a GARCH-M(1,1) model in discrete time defined by

$$\begin{cases} Y_t = Y_{t-1} + f(\sigma_t^2) + \sigma_t \varepsilon_t, \\ \sigma_{t+1}^2 = w + \sigma_t^2(\beta + \alpha \varepsilon_t), \end{cases} \tag{5.18}$$

where $(\varepsilon_t, t \in \mathbf{Z})$ is a sequence of independent standard normal variables.

In order to find a continuous approximation, the model must be replaced by a sequence of models that are indexed by h, and such that the coefficients ω, β, α are appropriately chosen with respect to h. Such a sequence of models is

$$\begin{cases} Y_{kh} = Y_{(k-1)h} + f(\sigma_{(k-1)h}^2)h + \sqrt{h}\sigma_{(k-1)h}\varepsilon_k^{(h)}, \\ \sigma_{kh}^2 = w_h + \sigma_{(k-1)h}^2(\beta_h + h\alpha_h \varepsilon_k^{(h)2}). \end{cases}$$

The last system defines a bivariate latent process with components Y and the conditional variance process. It is then natural to end up with a diffusion equation that is also bivariate. We now have to choose the parameters α_h, β_h, w_h to ensure the convergence of the drifts and variabilities when h tends towards zero. We have

$$b_{1h}(y) = E\left[\frac{1}{h}(Y_{kh} - Y_{(k-1)h})/Y_{(k-1)h} = y_1, \sigma_{(k-1)h}^2 = y_2\right] = f(y_2),$$

$$b_{2h}(y) = E\left[\frac{1}{h}(\sigma_{kh}^2 - \sigma_{(k-1)h}^2)/Y_{(k-1)h} = y_1, \sigma_{(k-1)h}^2 = y_2\right]$$

$$= \frac{w_h}{h} + y_2\frac{1}{h}(\beta_h - 1 + h\alpha_h).$$

These drifts tend to limits if $\frac{w_h}{h}$ and $\frac{1}{h}(\beta_h - 1 + h\alpha_h)$ converge.

Let us now consider the second order moments. We have

$$a_{11h}(y) = E\left[\frac{1}{h}(Y_{kh} - Y_{(k-1)h})^2/Y_{(k-1)h} = y_1, \sigma_{(k-1)h}^2 = y_2\right]$$

$$= hf^2(y_2) + y_2,$$

$$a_{12h}(y) = E\left[\frac{1}{h}(Y_{kh} - Y_{(k-1)h})(\sigma_{kh}^2 - \sigma_{(k-1)h}^2)/Y_{(k-1)h} = y_1, \sigma_{(k-1)h}^2 = y_2\right]$$

$$= w_h f(y_2) + y_2 f(y_2)(\beta_h - 1 + h\alpha_h),$$

$$a_{22h}(y) = E\left[\frac{1}{h}(\sigma_{kh}^2 - \sigma_{(k-1)h}^2)^2/Y_{(k-1)h} = y_1, \sigma_{(k-1)h}^2 = y_2\right]$$

$$= \frac{w_h^2}{h} + 2\frac{w_h}{h}(\beta_h - 1 + h\alpha_h)y_2 + \frac{1}{h}(\beta_h - 1 + h\alpha_h)^2 y_2^2 + 2h\alpha_h^2 y_2^2.$$

In addition to the previous conditions on α_h, β_h, w_h, the convergence of $h\alpha_h^2$ has to be assumed. For instance, let us suppose that

$$\lim_{h\to\infty}\frac{w_h}{h} = w, \quad \lim_{h\to\infty}\frac{1}{h}(\beta_h - 1 + h\alpha_h) = \theta, \quad \lim_{h\to\infty} 2h\alpha_h^2 = \alpha^2. \tag{5.19}$$

The limits of the drifts and variabilities are

$$
\begin{cases}
b_1 & = f(y_2), \\
b_2 & = w - \theta y_2
\end{cases}
\qquad
\begin{cases}
a_{11}(y) & = y_2, \\
a_{12}(y) & = 0, \\
a_{22}(y) & = \alpha^2 y_2^2.
\end{cases}
$$

The associated diffusion equation is

$$
\begin{cases}
dY_t = f(\sigma_t^2)dt + \sigma_t dW_{1t}, \\
d\sigma_t^2 = (w - \theta\sigma_t^2)dt + \alpha\sigma_t dW_{2t},
\end{cases}
\tag{5.20}
$$

where (W_{1t}), (W_{2t}) are two independent standard Brownian motions.

This last system has a recursive form: the second equation describes the evolution of the conditional variability, and the evolution of the entire series is then defined by the first equation. Such bivariate models are called **stochastic volatility models**.

The second equation may be analyzed directly. In particular, it has an invariant marginal distribution such that the process of conditional precision $\left(\frac{1}{\sigma_t^2}\right)$ follows a Gamma distribution $\gamma\left(1 + \frac{2\theta}{\alpha^2}, \frac{2w}{\alpha^2}\right)$ $\left(\text{if } \frac{2\theta}{\alpha^2} > -1\right)$ (Nelson 1989). This distribution also provides a good approximation of the marginal distribution of the inverse of the volatilities, which is defined by the GARCH-M model in discrete time.

iii) A Class of Approximations

We have seen how to approximate a univariate diffusion equation by the Euler method. A similar approach may be followed in the multivariate case and consists in replacing the independent components of the Brownian motion W_{1t}, W_{2t}, ... by discrete approximations which are also independent. But, we have seen in the last example that discrete approximations can be obtained using a smaller number of independent white noises. The idea involves introducing this noise both linearly [ε_t in the first equation of (5.17)] and nonlinearly [ε_t^2 in the second equation of (5.17)]. Here we intend to extend such a procedure. It is based on the property that, when the variable ε is standard normal, the variables ε and $\frac{|\varepsilon| - (2/\pi)^{1/2}}{(1 - 2/\pi)^{1/2}}$ are both zero mean, have variance 1 and are uncorrelated (see exercise 5.6). Let us now consider a bivariate diffusion equation

$$
\begin{cases}
dY_t = A_1(\sigma_t^2, Y_t, t)dt + G_1(\sigma_t^2, Y_t, t)dW_{1t}, \\
d\sigma_t^2 = A_2(\sigma_t^2, Y_t, t)dt + G_2(\sigma_t^2, Y_t, t)dW_{2t},
\end{cases}
\tag{5.21}
$$

where (W_{1t}), (W_{2t}) are two independent Brownian motions.

A discrete approximation is

$$
\begin{cases}
Y_{(k+1)h} = Y_{kh} + A_1(\sigma_{kh}^2, Y_{kh}, kh)h + G_1(\sigma_{kh}^2, Y_{kh}, kh)\sqrt{h}\varepsilon_k, \\
\sigma_{(k+1)h}^2 = \sigma_{kh}^2 + A_2(\sigma_{kh}^2, Y_{kh}, kh)h + G_2(\sigma_{kh}^2, Y_{kh}, kh)\sqrt{h}\,\dfrac{|\varepsilon_k| - (2/\pi)^{1/2}}{(1 - 2/\pi)^{1/2}},
\end{cases}
\tag{5.22}
$$

where (ε_k) is a Gaussian standard white noise. We leave it to the reader to verify that the conditions of theorem 5.15 hold.

In fact, the last approach provides a large number of discrete approximations. Indeed, the initial system (5.21) may be transformed into another equivalent one by Ito's formula if we consider the evolution of two functions of Y and σ^2. In particular, the approximation (5.22) is not necessarily compatible with the nonnegativity of the volatility, but another type of discrete time approximation may be derived by applying the approach to the log-volatility instead of the volatility itself.

We derive a class of models called **exponential GARCH** (EGARCH) (Nelson 1990) with the dynamics described by

$$\begin{cases} Y_t = \sigma_t \varepsilon_t, \\ \log \sigma_t^2 = c + \sum_{i=1}^{p} \alpha_i \log \sigma_{t-i}^2 + \sum_{j=1}^{p} \beta_j \{\theta \varepsilon_{t-j} + \gamma(|\varepsilon_{t-j}| - (2/\pi)^{1/2})\}, \end{cases}$$

where the combination of ε_t and $|\varepsilon_t| - (2/\pi)^{1/2}$ may arise because of the bidimensionality of the underlying system.

5.2.6 Simulated Estimation Methods

In order to eliminate the leptokurtic effect (see section 5.1) as well as to employ good approximations of continuous time dynamic equations, we consider recursive equations with a time unit smaller than the period of the observations. More precisely, let us consider a dynamic system

$$Y_t = H(Y_{t-1}, \varepsilon_t; \theta) \Leftrightarrow \varepsilon_t = G(Y_t, Y_{t-1}; \theta), \tag{5.23}$$

where (ε_t) is a standard Gaussian white noise. Suppose that the observations on the process are available only every two periods. One may easily write explicitly the distribution of the observed process; indeed, the conditional density function of $\tilde{Y}_t = Y_{2t}$ given $\tilde{Y}_{t-1} = Y_{2(t-1)}$ is

$$\tilde{l}(\tilde{y}_t/\tilde{y}_{t-1}; \theta) = \int l(\tilde{y}_t/y_{2t-1}; \theta) l(y_{2t-1}/\tilde{y}_{t-1}; \theta) \, dy_{2t-1}$$

$$\frac{1}{2\pi} \int \frac{\partial G}{\partial \tilde{y}_t}(\tilde{y}_t; y; \theta) \frac{\partial G}{\partial y}(y; \tilde{y}_{t-1}; \theta) \varphi[G(\tilde{y}_t, y; \theta)] \varphi[G(y, \tilde{y}_{t-1}; \theta)] \, dy,$$

where φ denotes the pdf of the standard normal distribution.

One may then wish to estimate the parameter θ by maximum likelihood. The log-likelihood function

$$\tilde{L}(\theta) = \sum_{t=1}^{T} \log \tilde{l}(\tilde{y}_t/\tilde{y}_{t-1}; \theta) \tag{5.24}$$

$$= \sum_{t=1}^{T} \log \left[\int l(\tilde{y}_t/y; \theta) l(y/\tilde{y}_{t-1}; \theta) \, dy \right]$$

will nevertheless be difficult to handle because of the integral, which in general cannot be computed analytically. A natural way to overcome this difficulty is by simulating the missing values y_{2t-1} before carrying out the estimation.

i) Simulated Maximum Likelihood

One may apply the maximum likelihood approach after replacing the integral in the expression of the log-likelihood function by a Monte-Carlo approximation. Let $\varepsilon^s_{2t-1,h}$, $h = 1, \ldots, H$, t varying, be independent drawings from the $N(0, 1)$ distribution, and let $y^s_{2t-1,h}(\theta) = H(y_{2t-2}, \varepsilon^s_{2t-1,h}; \theta)$ $h = 1, \ldots, H$, t varying, be the associated simulated missing values. The log-likelihood function is approximated by

$$L^s(\theta) = \sum_{t=1}^{T} \log \left\{ \frac{1}{H} \sum_{h=1}^{H} l(\tilde{y}_t, y^s_{2t-1,h}(\theta); \theta) \, l(y^s_{2t-1,h}(\theta), \tilde{y}_{t-1}; \theta) \right\}. \quad (5.25)$$

The **simulated maximum likelihood estimator** is then defined as the solution of the maximization problem.

If the number of replications H and the number of obervations T tend to infinity, one can show that the simulated maximum likelihood estimator (SMLE) is consistent. In practice, good approximations of the maximum likelihood estimator are obtained even if the number of replications H is quite low (about ten).

ii) Method of Simulated Moments (MSM)

Under the previous procedure, the simulations must be replicated. It seems easier to use a method requiring only the simulation of a single path. This is possible if the maximum likelihood method is replaced by the generalized method of moments (GMM). We describe this method through an example, where θ is one dimensional. The conditional expectation of $\tilde{y}_t$ given $\tilde{y}_{t-1}$ is

$$E(\tilde{y}_t / \tilde{y}_{t-1}; \theta) = m(\tilde{y}_{t-1}, \theta)$$
$$= \int \tilde{y}_t l(\tilde{y}_t / y_{2t-1}; \theta) l(y_{2t-1} / \tilde{y}_{t-1}; \theta) \, dy_{2t-1}.$$

The nonlinear least squares estimator of θ is the solution of

$$\min_{\theta} \sum_{t=1}^{T} [\tilde{y}_t - m(\tilde{y}_{t-1}; \theta)]^2. \quad (5.26)$$

As before, the optimization would require the computation of the integral analytically or by simulations.

However, the least squares approach may easily be transformed by replacing the equality between the conditional moments $E(\tilde{Y}_t / \tilde{Y}_{t-1}; \theta) = m(\tilde{Y}_{t-1}, \theta)$ by the equality between the marginal moments $E(\tilde{Y}_t) = Em(\tilde{Y}_{t-1}, \theta)$.

A GMM estimator based on this idea would be defined as a solution of

$$\frac{1}{T}\sum_{t=1}^{T}\tilde{y}_t = \frac{1}{T}\sum_{t=1}^{T}m(\tilde{y}_{t-1},\theta). \qquad (5.27)$$

The estimator is obtained by matching the mean of the observations with the mean of their forecasts computed from the model. These forecasts are optimal, i.e., defined as conditional expectations. Yet, one may think about finding their values by simulation. Let us consider independent drawings of ε_t^s, t varying from a standard normal distribution and determine a path corresponding to this simulated noise by the equation

$$\begin{cases} Y_0^s \text{ given,} \\ y_t^s = H(y_{t-1}^s(\theta),\varepsilon_t^s,\theta). \end{cases}$$

One may introduce the **simulated moments estimator (SME)** solution of

$$\min_{\theta}\left[\frac{1}{T}\sum_{t=1}^{T}\tilde{y}_t - \frac{1}{T}\sum_{t=1}^{T}\tilde{y}_t^s(\theta)\right]^2 = \min_{\theta}\left[\frac{1}{T}\sum_{t=1}^{T}y_{2t} - \frac{1}{T}\sum_{t=1}^{T}y_{2t}^s(\theta)\right]^2. \qquad (5.28)$$

This estimator is consistent (Duffie and Singleton 1989; Gouriéroux and Monfort 1996) and simple to compute. Nevertheless, only a few things are known about its asymptotic efficiency, which depends heavily on the moments retained for calibration.

Note 5.29. The approach leads to a number of simulated paths of the process $y_t^s(\theta)$ equal to the number of values of parameter θ used for the numerical optimization of (5.26) but only to one simulated path of the noise. Among these simulated paths of the process, only one, $y_t^s(\tilde{\theta})$, where $(\tilde{\theta})$ is the simulated estimator, yields an interpretation.

Note 5.30. The knowledge of the values of the process at dates 2t is not exploited in the simulation; hence, $y_{2t}^s(\tilde{\theta})$ is generally different from y_{2t}.

5.3   The Random Walk Hypothesis

5.3.1   Description of the Hypothesis

Since the works of Bachelier (1900), Fama (1965) and Samuelson (1973), the random walk hypothesis (or **martingale hypothesis**) has played an important role in the description and study of financial price series.

Definition 5.31. *A sequence (Y_t) is a martingale (or a random walk) if and only if*

$$E(Y_{t+1}/\underline{Y_t}) = Y_t, \quad \forall t.$$

Several simple interpretations of this condition are usually provided. The first one is in terms of forecasting. If the series Y is a price series, then by Definition 5.31 the best forecast of the future price at date t is the current price y_t. The market price contains in particular all of the information useful to make the best forecasts (the market is said to be **efficient**). Besides, the martingale condition may also be rewritten in terms of absolute or relative gains. It is indeed equivalent to

$$E(Y_{t+1} - Y_t / \underline{Y_t}) = 0,$$

or

$$E\left(\frac{Y_{t+1} - Y_t}{Y_t} / \underline{Y_t}\right) = 0.$$

If one buys a unit of a financial security at date t and for the price Y_t in order to resell it at date $t + 1$ for the price Y_{t+1}, the average gain is zero if the martingale condition is satisfied. This means that, under this condition, there is neither systematic profit nor systematic loss (in absence of transaction cost). These two interpretations remain valid when a longer (stochastic) horizon is considered. It is due to the following two properties.

Property 5.32. *A process (Y_t) is a martingale (or a random walk) if and only if*

$$E(Y_{t+h} / \underline{Y_t}) = Y_t, \quad \forall t,$$

for every date t and horizon h, $h \geq 0$.

Proof. The first part of the property is immediate by taking $h = 1$. The second part results from the law of iterated expectations because

$$E(Y_{t+h} / \underline{Y_t}) = E[E(Y_{t+h} / \underline{Y_{t+h-1}}) / \underline{Y_t}]$$
$$= E(Y_{t+h-1} / \underline{Y_t});$$

the property is then derived for any h by iteration.   Q.E.D.

In order to present the next property, we must first explain the notion of random horizon. To do this, we consider the second interpretation and assume that we are buying an asset at date t and selling it at a future date, possibly randomly chosen, s.t. $v \geq t$. The decision to sell or to keep the owned asset depends on the current and past stock prices at the moment of the decision. The random variable v should then be selected such that

$$\forall h \geq 0, \quad (v > t + h) \in \underline{Y_{t+h}}. \tag{5.33}$$

The decision to keep the security $(v > t + h)$ depends on $Y_{t+h}, Y_{t+h-1}, \ldots$. The integer valued variable v, which satisfies the last condition, is called **a stopping time**.

Property 5.34. *A process (Y_t) is a martingale (or a random walk) if and only if*

$$E(Y_v / \underline{Y_t}) = Y_t, \quad \forall t,$$

for every date t and stopping time v larger than or equal to t.

Proof. The sufficient part of the property being immediate, we just prove the necessary part. We have

$$E(Y_v/\underline{Y_t}) = E(\sum_{h=0}^{\infty} Y_v \mathbb{I}_{v=t+h}/\underline{Y_t})$$

$$= \sum_{h=0}^{\infty} E(Y_v \mathbb{I}_{v=t+h}/\underline{Y_t})$$

$$= \sum_{h=0}^{\infty} E(Y_{t+h} \mathbb{I}_{v=t+h}/\underline{Y_t})$$

$$= \sum_{h=0}^{\infty} E(Y_{t+h}[\mathbb{I}_{v>t+h-1} - \mathbb{I}_{v>t+h}]/\underline{Y_t})$$

$$= \sum_{h=0}^{\infty} E[(Y_{t+h+1} - Y_{t+h})\mathbb{I}_{v>t+h}/\underline{Y_t}] + Y_t$$

$$= \sum_{h=0}^{\infty} E\ [E(Y_{t+h+1} - Y_{t+h})\mathbb{I}_{v>t+h}/\underline{Y_{t+h}})/\underline{Y_t}] + Y_t$$

$$= \sum_{h=0}^{\infty} E\ [\mathbb{I}_{v>t+h} E((Y_{t+h+1} - Y_{t+h})/\underline{Y_{t+h}})/\underline{Y_t}] + Y_t$$

$$= \sum_{h=0}^{\infty} E[\mathbb{I}_{v>t+h}\ \ 0/\underline{Y_t}] + Y_t = Y_t. \qquad \text{Q.E.D.}$$

Therefore, no matter the degree of sophistication of the retained sell technique, the average gain is always zero. The importance of the random walk hypothesis is now obvious. Picking up the asset with prices following a random walk allows us to identify the assets for which the systematic profit (resp. loss) is not expected.

5.3.2   The Classical Test Procedure of the Random Walk Hypothesis

In order to test the random walk hypothesis for the price series (Y_t), one generally makes use of a test for white noise applied either to the differentiated series $Y_t - Y_{t-1}$ or to the return series $\frac{Y_t - Y_{t-1}}{Y_{t-1}}$ (which is approximately equivalent to the log-differences $\log Y_t - \log Y_{t-1}$). Denoting this series by (ε_t), the correlations for the nondemeaned series are

$$\hat{\rho}(h) = \sum_{t=1}^{T-h} \varepsilon_t \varepsilon_{t-h} / \sum_{t=1}^{T} \varepsilon_t^2,$$

or, after centering, the correlations

$$\hat{\rho}(h) = \sum_{t=1}^{T-h} (\varepsilon_t - \bar{\varepsilon})(\varepsilon_{t-h} - \bar{\varepsilon}) / \sum_{t=1}^{T} (\varepsilon_t - \bar{\varepsilon})^2,$$

with $\bar{\varepsilon} = \sum_{t=1}^{T} \varepsilon_t$. Next, we compute the Portmanteau statistic

$$Q_H = T \sum_{h=1}^{H} \hat{\rho}(h)^2, \tag{5.35}$$

which is asymptotically chi-square distributed with H degrees of freedom if (ε_t) is an independent white noise. The test consists in accepting the random walk hypothesis if $Q_H < \chi^2_{95\%}(H)$, where $\chi^2_{95\%}(H)$ is the 95% quantile of the $\chi^2(H)$ distribution, or rejecting it otherwise.

As an illustration, we present the test results corresponding to spot price series for the period January 1966–December 1976 [Daily Stock Record's data; see Taylor(1985)]. A direct analysis of these numbers leads to a rejection of the random walk hypothesis in 60% of the cases and to an acceptance in the remaining cases. The Portmanteau statistic, which symmetrically takes into account the correlations of any order, would be insufficient to indicate the best way to handle the securities presenting a positive average profit. It would be interesting to extend the study and examine precisely the estimated autocorrelation function.

	Q_{10}	Q_{30}	Q_{50}
Spot Series			
Allied	23.55	54.20	70.50
Alcoa	102.91	124.40	145.30
Am. Can.	58.30	85.40	99.53
AT and T	40.89	64.56	77.21
Am. Brands	44.65	63.24	76.96
Anaconda	14.81	23.07	34.78
Bethlehem	45.63	61.40	88.49
Chrysler	26.78	51.05	71.43
Dupont	52.04	66.15	75.90
Kodak	19.91	37.37	54.56
G. Electric	38.98	59.61	70.54
G. Foods	46.13	67.32	87.00
G. Motors	25.89	51.00	60.01
G. Telephone	20.04	40.36	49.02
Harvester	24.67	42.17	68.94
FT30	20.31	39.93	49.04
Gold	29.31	63.26	88.20
Silver	34.03	49.30	68.64
Lead	10.33	36.75	66.84
Tin	15.96	29.29	48.47
Zinc	8.41	23.11	50.22
£/$	35.28	80.60	125.69

Futures Series			
Corn(12)	15.51	36.34	61.09
Corn(6)	22.04	38.64	51.78
Corn(3)	27.15	36.07	42.74
Cocoa(12)	41.57	83.18	92.76
Cocoa(6)	36.25	72.99	85.16
Cocoa(3)	46.43	65.33	72.56
Coffee(12)	66.60	84.14	100.54
Coffee(6)	76.36	88.02	101.32
Coffee(3)	71.27	83.92	91.85
Sugar(12)	73.17	105.59	122.70
Sugar(6)	85.01	109.70	132.63
Sugar(3)	92.94	114.51	121.00
Wool(12)	19.96	42.31	64.64
£/$ (6)	16.67	32.70	41.54
DM/$ (6)	29.76	56.79	64.08
SF/$ (6)	13.24	42.17	53.28
T-Bond	11.39	23.72	38.44
Critical point	18.31	43.77	67.50

5.3.3   Limitations of the Portmanteau Tests

The Portmanteau test has two limitations. The first one is that the implicit null hypotheses of these tests are hypotheses of serial uncorrelation, weaker than the martingale's property. Indeed, the null concerns the hypothesis of orthogonality between $Y_t - Y_{t-1}$ and the linear functions of $Y_{t-1} - Y_{t-2}$, $Y_{t-2} - Y_{t-3}$, ..., and not the orthogonality with the linear and nonlinear functions of these last differences. Thus, the hypothesis that is actually tested is a direct consequence of the martingale hypothesis. If the test leads to a rejection, it is natural to infer the rejection of the martingale hypothesis. On the other hand, the test may lead to an acceptance, whereas the martingale hypothesis should be rejected.

In addition, the critical value of the test is determined under the hypothesis that the process $\varepsilon = (\varepsilon_t)$ is an independent white noise. As mentioned earlier in empirical work, the test may a priori be applied to the price changes $Y_t - Y_{t-1}$ or to the series of gross returns $\frac{Y_t - Y_{t-1}}{Y_{t-1}}$. It is obvious that the strong white noise hypothesis cannot hold simultaneously for both series. Namely, if $Y_t - Y_{t-1}$ satisfies that white noise condition, the series of gross returns $\frac{Y_t - Y_{t-1}}{Y_{t-1}}$ has a conditional variance $\frac{\sigma^2}{Y_{t-1}^2}$ that features conditional heteroscedasticity. One may wish to investigate whether the critical value or the statistic itself should not be modified to accommodate this heteroscedasticity. We now set up to study this problem.

5.3.4 Portmanteau Tests with Heteroscedasticity

The Portmanteau test is based on the second order cross moments

$$\hat{\gamma}(h) = \frac{1}{T} \sum_{t=1}^{T-h} \varepsilon_t \varepsilon_{t-h}, \quad h = 1, \ldots, H.$$

To derive the statistic, one usually studies the asymptotic properties of these co-variances and shows that, if ε_t is an independent white noise, the vector

$$\sqrt{T}[\hat{\gamma}(1), \ldots, \hat{\gamma}(H)]'$$

is asymptotically normal with zero mean and a scalar variance $\sigma^4 Id$, where $\sigma^2 = V\varepsilon_t$. The associated quadratic form, with σ^2 replaced by its empirical counterpart $\frac{1}{T} \sum_{t=1}^{T} \varepsilon_t^2$, provides the Portmanteau statistic (5.35).

To study the properties of the statistic Q_H in the case where the process ε is a conditionally heteroscedastic white noise, we must again derive the asymptotic properties of the empirical covariances. These last ones are easily found since we know that $T[\hat{\gamma}(1), \ldots, \hat{\gamma}(H)]'$ is directly related to the OLS estimators of the parameters $a_1, \ldots, a_H$ in the regression model:

$$\varepsilon_t = a_1 \varepsilon_{t-1} + \ldots + a_H \varepsilon_{t-H} + u_t, \quad t = 1, \ldots, T - H. \tag{5.36}$$

We have

$$\begin{pmatrix} \hat{a}_1 \\ \vdots \\ \hat{a}_H \end{pmatrix} = \begin{pmatrix} \sum \varepsilon_{t-1}^2 & \sum \varepsilon_{t-1}\varepsilon_{t-2} \cdots & \sum \varepsilon_{t-1}\varepsilon_{t-H} \\ \vdots & & \vdots \\ \sum \varepsilon_{t-1}\varepsilon_{t-H} & \cdots & \sum \varepsilon_{t-H}^2 \end{pmatrix}^{-1}$$

$$\times \begin{pmatrix} \sum \varepsilon_t \varepsilon_{t-1} \\ \vdots \\ \sum \varepsilon_t \varepsilon_{t-H} \end{pmatrix}$$

$$= \begin{pmatrix} \sum \varepsilon_{t-1}^2 & \sum \varepsilon_{t-1}\varepsilon_{t-2} \cdots & \sum \varepsilon_{t-1}\varepsilon_{t-H} \\ \vdots & & \vdots \\ \sum \varepsilon_{t-1}\varepsilon_{t-H} & \cdots & \sum \varepsilon_{t-H}^2 \end{pmatrix}^{-1} T$$

$$\times \begin{pmatrix} \hat{\gamma}(1) \\ \vdots \\ \hat{\gamma}(H) \end{pmatrix}.$$

Let us denote $h_t = V(\varepsilon_t/\varepsilon_{t-1}) = V(u_t/\varepsilon_{t-1})$. From the asymptotic properties of the OLS estimators under heteroscedasticity, we directly see that, under the hypothesis $a_1 = 0, \ldots, a_H = 0$,

$$\begin{bmatrix} \hat{\gamma}(1) \\ \vdots \\ \hat{\gamma}(H) \end{bmatrix} \xrightarrow{d} N(0, \Omega),$$

with

$$\Omega = \lim_{T \to \infty} \frac{1}{T - H} \sum_{t=1}^{T-H} \begin{bmatrix} \varepsilon_{t-1} \\ \vdots \\ \varepsilon_{t-H} \end{bmatrix} h_t[\varepsilon_{t-1}, \ldots, \varepsilon_{t-H}]$$

$$= E\left(\begin{bmatrix} \varepsilon_{t-1} \\ \vdots \\ \varepsilon_{t-H} \end{bmatrix} h_t[\varepsilon_{t-1}, \ldots, \varepsilon_{t-H}] \right)$$

$$= E\left(\begin{bmatrix} \varepsilon_{t-1} \\ \vdots \\ \varepsilon_{t-H} \end{bmatrix} E(\varepsilon_t^2/\underline{\varepsilon_{t-1}})[\varepsilon_{t-1}, \ldots, \varepsilon_{t-H}] \right)$$

$$= \lim_{T \to \infty} \frac{1}{T - H} \sum_{t=1}^{T-H} \begin{bmatrix} \varepsilon_{t-1} \\ \vdots \\ \varepsilon_{t-H} \end{bmatrix} \varepsilon_t^2[\varepsilon_{t-1}, \ldots, \varepsilon_{t-H}].$$

If the white noise is conditionally homoscedastic, we find the classical result used to build the Q_H statistic:

$$\Omega = E\left(\begin{bmatrix} \varepsilon_{t-1} \\ \vdots \\ \varepsilon_{t-H} \end{bmatrix} E(\varepsilon_t^2/\underline{\varepsilon_{t-1}})[\varepsilon_{t-1}, \ldots, \varepsilon_{t-H}] \right)$$

$$= \sigma^2 E\left(\begin{bmatrix} \varepsilon_{t-1} \\ \vdots \\ \varepsilon_{t-H} \end{bmatrix} [\varepsilon_{t-1}, \ldots, \varepsilon_{t-H}] \right)$$

$$= \sigma^2 \sigma^2 Id_H = \sigma^4 Id_H.$$

Nevertheless, as soon as there is conditional heteroscedasticity, this formula of the variance-covariance matrix is no longer valid, and the standard critical value of the Portmanteau statistic is erroneous. For instance, let us consider the case where $H = 1$. The usual test consists in comparing $\sqrt{T}|\hat{\rho}(1)|$ with $2 \simeq 1.96$, the 97.5% quantile of the standard normal distribution, or the asymptotic equivalent of comparing $\sqrt{T}|\hat{\gamma}(1)|$ with $2V\varepsilon_t$. In fact, the comparison should be based on a critical value corresponding to the corrected expression of the asymptotic variance covariance matrix, that is

$$2\sqrt{E(\varepsilon_t^2 \varepsilon_{t-1}^2)}.$$

Note that the two aforementioned critical values are different. In fact, their ratio is

$$\frac{\sqrt{E(\varepsilon_t^2 \varepsilon_{t-1}^2)}}{E(\varepsilon_t^2)},$$

and may a priori take several values, as the following example shows.

Example 5.37. In order to provide a simple and general example, we consider an independent white noise $u = (u_t)$, a nonlinear function g and the moving average process of order one:

$$\varepsilon_t = g(u_{t-1}) + u_t.$$

The process ε is derived from the noise u through a time independent transformation. Since u is strongly stationary, (ε_t) and (ε_t^2) are both weakly stationary. One assumes in what follows that the function g and the distribution of u_t are such that $Eg(u_t) = 0$ and $E[u_t g(u_t)] = 0$.

Under these constraints, the process ε has zero mean and zero serial correlations $\rho(h)$, $h \geq 1$. Therefore, it is a weak white noise which might be identified by a Portmanteau test. In this example, we have

$$E\varepsilon_t^2 = Eu^2 + Eg^2(u),$$

$$E(\varepsilon_t^2 \varepsilon_{t-1}^2) = E[(u_t + g(u_{t-1}))^2 (u_{t-1} + g(u_{t-2}))^2]$$
$$= [Eg^2(u)]^2 + E[u^2 g^2(u)] + Eu^2 Eg^2(u) + (Eu^2)^2,$$

and

$$\frac{E(\varepsilon_t^2 \varepsilon_{t-1}^2)}{E(\varepsilon_t^2)^2} - 1 = \frac{\text{Cov}(u^2, g^2(u))}{(Eu^2 + Eg^2(u))^2}.$$

In the heteroscedastic case, the structure of the asymptotic variance-covariance Ω provides a simple hint about how to correct the initial Portmanteau statistic. This correction for heteroscedasticity is the one proposed by White. We have

$$\tilde{Q} = T[\hat{\gamma}(1) \ldots \hat{\gamma}(H)] \left(\frac{1}{T} \begin{bmatrix} \sum \varepsilon_{t-1}^2 \varepsilon_t^2 & \cdots & \sum \varepsilon_{t-1} \varepsilon_{t-H} \varepsilon_t^2 \\ \vdots & & \vdots \\ \sum \varepsilon_{t-1} \varepsilon_{t-H} \varepsilon_t^2 & \cdots & \sum \varepsilon_{t-H}^2 \varepsilon_t^2 \end{bmatrix} \right)^{-1}$$

$$\times \begin{pmatrix} \hat{\gamma}(1) \\ \vdots \\ \hat{\gamma}(H) \end{pmatrix},$$

which asymptotically follows a $\chi^2(H)$ distribution. The random walk test is then performed in the usual way, comparing the value of the $\tilde{Q}_H$ statistic with the $\chi^2_{95\%}(H)$ quantile.

5.4   Threshold Models

5.4.1   Definition and Stationarity Conditions

ARCH(1) models are built using a specific form of conditional variance, i.e., a quadratic function of the past observations. Other functional forms may be retained that lead to new parameter interpretations and models. For instance, it may seem natural to conjecture that the heteroscedasticity effect varies depending on whether the error is positive or negative. This leads us to the Threshold ARCH models

[TARCH; Rabemananjara and Zakoian (1993), Zakoian (1994)]. The TARCH of order one is defined by

$$Y_t = (\varphi_0 + \varphi_1 Y_{t-1} \mathbb{I}_{Y_{t-1}>0} - \varphi_2 Y_{t-1} \mathbb{I}_{Y_{t-1}<0}) u_t, \tag{5.38}$$

where φ_0, φ_1 and φ_2 are positive real numbers, and u_t is a standard Gaussian white noise. The dynamics reflects the behavior of the underlying processes $Y_{t-1} \mathbb{I}_{Y_{t-1}>0}$, $Y_{t-1} \mathbb{I}_{Y_{t-1}<0}$ which has to be examined further to find out if the Y process is second order stationary. We have $E(Y_t/Y_{t-1}) = 0$, and the process (Y_t) is centered and uncorrelated. We now need to study the variance. To do this, let us distinguish the positive and negative components of Y_t and take the squares subsequently:

$$\begin{cases} Y_t \mathbb{I}_{Y_t>0} = (\varphi_0 + \varphi_1 Y_{t-1} \mathbb{I}_{Y_{t-1}>0} - \varphi_2 Y_{t-1} \mathbb{I}_{Y_{t-1}<0}) u_t \mathbb{I}_{u_t>0}, \\ Y_t \mathbb{I}_{Y_t<0} = (\varphi_0 + \varphi_1 Y_{t-1} \mathbb{I}_{Y_{t-1}>0} - \varphi_2 Y_{t-1} \mathbb{I}_{Y_{t-1}<0}) u_t \mathbb{I}_{u_t<0}, \\ Y_t^2 \mathbb{I}_{Y_t>0} = (\varphi_0^2 + \varphi_1^2 Y_{t-1}^2 \mathbb{I}_{Y_{t-1}>0} - \varphi_1^2 Y_{t-1}^2 \mathbb{I}_{Y_{t-1}<0} \\ \qquad + 2\varphi_0\varphi_1 Y_{t-1} \mathbb{I}_{Y_{t-1}>0} - 2\varphi_0\varphi_2 Y_{t-1} \mathbb{I}_{Y_{t-1}<0}) u_t^2 \mathbb{I}_{u_t>0}, \\ Y_t^2 \mathbb{I}_{Y_t<0} = (\varphi_0^2 + \varphi_1^2 Y_{t-1}^2 \mathbb{I}_{Y_{t-1}>0} + \varphi_2^2 Y_{t-1}^2 \mathbb{I}_{Y_{t-1}<0} \\ \qquad + 2\varphi_0\varphi_1 Y_{t-1} \mathbb{I}_{Y_{t-1}>0} - 2\varphi_0\varphi_2 Y_{t-1} \mathbb{I}_{Y_{t-1}<0} u_t^2 \mathbb{I}_{u_t<0}. \end{cases}$$

Since u_t is standard normal, we have

$$\begin{cases} E[u_t \mathbb{I}_{u_t>0}] & = -E[u_t \mathbb{I}_{u_t<0}] = \dfrac{1}{\sqrt{2\pi}}, \\ \\ E[u_t^2 \mathbb{I}_{u_t>0}] & = -E[u_t^2 \mathbb{I}_{u_t<0}] = \dfrac{1}{2}. \end{cases}$$

Let us denote by m_t the vector with components

$$E(Y_t \mathbb{I}_{Y_t>0}), \; E(Y_t \mathbb{I}_{Y_t<0}), \; E(Y_t^2 \mathbb{I}_{Y_t>0}), \; E(Y_t^2 \mathbb{I}_{Y_t<0}).$$

The sequence m_t satisfies the linear recursive equation

$$m_t = \begin{bmatrix} \varphi_0/\sqrt{2\pi} \\ -\varphi_0/\sqrt{2\pi} \\ \varphi_0^2/2 \\ \varphi_0^2/2 \end{bmatrix} + \begin{bmatrix} \varphi_1/\sqrt{2\pi} & -\varphi_2/\sqrt{2\pi} & 0 & 0 \\ -\varphi_1/\sqrt{2\pi} & \varphi_2/\sqrt{2\pi} & 0 & 0 \\ \varphi_0\varphi_1 & -\varphi_0\varphi_2 & \varphi_1^2/2 & \varphi_2^2/2 \\ \varphi_0\varphi_1 & -\varphi_0\varphi_2 & \varphi_1^2/2 & \varphi_2^2/2 \end{bmatrix} m_{t-1}.$$

The eigenvalues of the matrix factor of m_{t-1} are

$$0, 0, (\varphi_1 + \varphi_2)/\sqrt{2\pi}, (\varphi_1^2 + \varphi_2^2)/2.$$

Therefore, the equation is stable if

$$(\varphi_1 + \varphi_2) < \sqrt{2\pi} \text{ and } \varphi_1^2 + \varphi_2^2 < 2,$$

that is, if

$$\varphi_1^2 + \varphi_2^2 < 2. \tag{5.39}$$

As soon as this condition is satisfied, the sequence m_t tends towards a limit such that

$$\begin{cases} E[Y_t \mathbb{I}_{Y_t > 0}] = -E[Y_t \mathbb{I}_{Y_t < 0}] = \varphi_0 / \sqrt{2\pi} + (\varphi_1 + \varphi_2)/\sqrt{2\pi}\, E(Y_t \mathbb{I}_{Y_t > 0}), \\ \\ E[Y_t^2 \mathbb{I}_{Y_t > 0}] = E[Y_t^2 \mathbb{I}_{Y_t < 0}] = \varphi_0^2/2 + \varphi_0(\varphi_1 + \varphi_2)E(Y_t \mathbb{I}_{Y_t > 0}) + \dfrac{1}{2}(\varphi_1^2 + \varphi_2^2)E(Y_t^2 \mathbb{I}_{Y_t > 0}) \end{cases}$$

or equivalently

$$\begin{cases} E[Y_t \mathbb{I}_{Y_t > 0}] &= \dfrac{\varphi_0}{\sqrt{2\pi} - (\varphi_1 + \varphi_2)}, \\ \\ E[Y_t^2 \mathbb{I}_{Y_t > 0}] &= \dfrac{\varphi_0^2}{2 - (\varphi_1^2 + \varphi_2^2)} \dfrac{\sqrt{2\pi} + \varphi_1 + \varphi_2}{\sqrt{2\pi} - (\varphi_1 + \varphi_2)}. \end{cases} \tag{5.40}$$

We infer the marginal variance of the process Y_t:

$$V(Y_t / Y_{t-1}) = \dfrac{2\varphi_0^2}{2 - (\varphi_1^2 + \varphi_2^2)} \dfrac{\sqrt{2\pi} + \varphi_1 + \varphi_2}{\sqrt{2\pi} - (\varphi_1 + \varphi_2)}.$$

Example 5.41. If $\varphi_2 = \varphi_1$, the model becomes $Y_t = (\varphi_0 + \varphi_1|Y_{t-1}|)u_t$, and the conditional variance takes the form $V(Y_t / Y_{t-1}) = (\varphi_0 + \varphi_1|Y_{t-1}|)^2$. The stationarity condition is $\varphi_1 < 1$, and the unconditional variance is defined by the following expression:

$$V Y_t = \dfrac{\varphi_0^2}{1 - \varphi_1^2} \dfrac{\sqrt{2\pi} + 2\varphi_1}{\sqrt{2\pi} - 2\varphi_1}.$$

Remark 5.42. *There are many other formulas of the conditional variance to which this approach can be applied (see exercises 5.1 and 5.2).*

5.4.2 Homoscedasticity Test

The log-likelihood function conditional on the first observation is

$$\log L(y; \varphi) = -\dfrac{T}{2}\log 2\pi - \sum_{t=1}^{T} \log(\varphi_0 + \varphi_1 Y_{t-1}\mathbb{I}_{Y_{t-1}>0} - \varphi_2 Y_{t-1}\mathbb{I}_{Y_{t-1}<0})$$

$$-\dfrac{1}{2}\sum_{t=1}^{T} \dfrac{Y_t^2}{(\varphi_0 + \varphi_1 Y_{t-1}\mathbb{I}_{Y_{t-1}>0} - \varphi_2 Y_{t-1}\mathbb{I}_{Y_{t-1}<0})^2}.$$

We may partition the set of observations into two subsets:

$$\mathcal{J}_1 = \{t : Y_{t-1} > 0\}, \quad \mathcal{J}_0 = \{t : Y_{t-1} < 0\}.$$

With this distinction, we have

$$\log L(y; \varphi) = -\dfrac{T}{2}\log 2\pi - \sum_{t \in \mathcal{J}_1} \log(\varphi_0 + \varphi_1 Y_{t-1}) - \sum_{t \in \mathcal{J}_0} \log(\varphi_0 - \varphi_2 Y_{t-1})$$

$$-\dfrac{1}{2}\sum_{t \in \mathcal{J}_1} \dfrac{Y_t^2}{(\varphi_0 + \varphi_1 Y_{t-1})^2} - \dfrac{1}{2}\sum_{t \in \mathcal{J}_0} \dfrac{Y_t^2}{(\varphi_0 - \varphi_2 Y_{t-1})^2}.$$

In order to find a score test for the null hypothesis of conditional homoscedasticity, $H_0 = \{\varphi_1 = \varphi_2 = 0\}$, we compute the scores corresponding to φ_1 and φ_2, and evaluate under the null hypothesis. We have

$$\left[\frac{\partial \log l(y; \varphi)}{\partial \varphi_1}\right]_{H_0} = -\sum_{\mathcal{J}_1} \frac{Y_{t-1}}{\varphi_0} + \sum_{\mathcal{J}_1} \frac{Y_t^2 Y_{t-1}}{\varphi_0^3},$$

$$\left[\frac{\partial \log l(y; \varphi)}{\partial \varphi_2}\right]_{H_0} = \sum_{\mathcal{J}_0} \frac{Y_{t-1}}{\varphi_0} - \sum_{\mathcal{J}_0} \frac{Y_t^2 Y_{t-1}}{\varphi_0^3}.$$

Under the null hypothesis, the parameter φ_0 may be estimated:

$$\hat{\varphi}_0 = \frac{1}{T} \sum_{t=1}^{T} Y_t^2.$$

The test based on the scores is equivalent to testing whether the covariances between Y_t^2 and $Y_{t-1} \mathbb{I}_{Y_{t-1} < 0}$ and between Y_t^2 and $Y_{t-1} \mathbb{I}_{Y_{t-1} > 0}$ are close to zero.

5.4.3   Qualitative ARCH Models

Other types of threshold models may be considered. Gouriéroux and Monfort (1989) proposed the following specification:

$$Y_t = \sum_{i=1}^{p} \alpha_i \mathbb{I}_{Y_{t-1} \in A_i} + \left(\sum_{i=1}^{p} \beta_i \mathbb{I}_{Y_{t-1} \in A_i}\right) u_t, \tag{5.43}$$

where u_t is a standard strong white noise and $(A_1, \ldots, A_p)$ is a given partition of the real line. In this model, the influence of the past is a function of the state A_i occupied by Y_{t-1}. In the i-th state, the conditional expectation is α_i and the conditional standard error is β_i. Such a model is based on the qualitative state variables

$$Z_t = (\mathbb{I}_{Y_t \in A_1}, \ldots, \mathbb{I}_{Y_t \in A_p}),$$

which associate observations to the states. The process (Z_t) is a homogenous Markov chain, and the stationarity properties of the observed process Y follow (see exercise 5.1). The pseudo maximum likelihood estimators of the parameters are

$$\begin{cases} \hat{\alpha}_i &= \dfrac{\sum_t Y_t \mathbb{I}_{Y_{t-1} \in A_i}}{\sum_t \mathbb{I}_{Y_{t-1} \in A_i}}, \\[2ex] \hat{\beta}_i &= \dfrac{\sum_t Y_t^2 \mathbb{I}_{Y_{t-1} \in A_i}}{\sum_t \mathbb{I}_{Y_{t-1} \in A_i}} - \hat{\alpha}_i^2. \end{cases}$$

They simply correspond to the empirical means and variances computed state by state. It is important to note that these means do not concern consecutive dates as usual, but in fact endogenous subsets of dates $\mathcal{T}_i = (t : Y_{t-1} \in A_i)$.

In practice, the elements of the partition $(A_1, \ldots, A_p)$ may be chosen according to several criteria. We may introduce states that separate the behavior of the series in

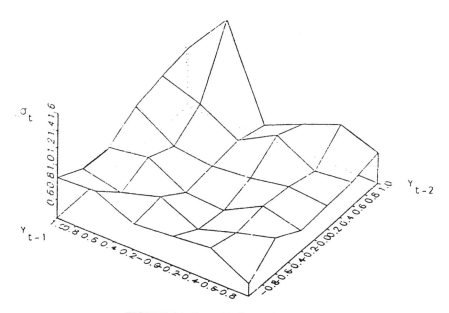

FIGURE 5.1. Franc–Dollar exchange rates.

phases of increasing and decreasing prices, in phases of weak and strong deviation from the mean, etc.

We may also choose a sufficiently fine partition, which allows us to consider the functions

$$\sum_{i=1}^{p} \alpha_i \mathbb{I}_{Y_{t-1} \in A_i}, \quad \sum_{i=1}^{p} \beta_i \mathbb{I}_{Y_{t-1} \in A_i},$$

as approximations of more complicated functions (see section 5.4.4).

According to this point of view, we provide in figure 5.1 estimations performed using data on increments of Franc–Dollar exchange rates. The retained partition corresponds to the following limits:

$$-0.8; -0.6; -0.4; -0.2; 0; 0.2; 0.4; 0.6; 0.8.$$

The model includes two lags:

$$Y_t = \sum_i \sum_j \alpha_{ij} \mathbb{I}_{Y_{t-1} \in A_i} \mathbb{I}_{Y_{t-2} \in A_j} + \left(\sum_i \sum_j \beta_{ij} \mathbb{I}_{Y_{t-1} \in A_i} \mathbb{I}_{Y_{t-2} \in A_j} \right) u_t.$$

The coefficients α_{ij} are not significant, which implies the acceptance of the (weak) random walk hypothesis for the considered exchange rate. We display the estimated values $\hat{\beta}_{ij}$ as functions of the lagged values of Y_{t-1} and Y_{t-2}.

The type of dependence of the conditional variance on the past differs to a large extent from that modelled in the usual ARCH. In that case, we would have, for

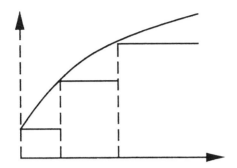

FIGURE 5.2. Approximation by a stepwise function.

instance,

$$Y_t \approx (a_0 + a_1 Y_{t-1}^2 + a_2 Y_{t-2}^2 + a_3 Y_{t-1} Y_{t-2})^{\frac{1}{2}} u_t,$$

and a parabolic form of the variance as a function of Y_{t-1}, Y_{t-2}. The estimation results from the exchange rate series show that such a form is not acceptable, especially because of the strong asymmetries in the response of the variance to positive and negative lagged values (the so-called **leverage effect**) (Black 1976).

5.4.4   Nonparametric Approaches

If the number of states becomes large, the threshold models, based either on piecewise linear or on qualitative approximations (see sections 5.4.1, 5.4.2 and 5.4.3), can be interpreted as nonparametric approaches. For instance, the autoregressive model of order one in a general setup can be written

$$Y_t = g(Y_{t-1}) + h(Y_{t-1}) u_t,$$

where u_t is a reduced white noise. The function $g(Y_{t-1})$ may be interpreted as the conditional expectation of Y_t given the past and $h(Y_{t-1})$ as the conditional standard error. These functions g and h may be approximated by piecewise linear functions, yielding the threshold models (TARCH) (see figure 5.2), or by stepwise functions, yielding the qualitative models (QTARCH) (see figure 5.3).

Nevertheless, there exist other nonparametric methods that apply to the estimation of the conditional variance and allow smoothing of the estimated conditional moments. Among these approaches, we may mention the kernel methods (Pagan-Schwert 1990; Hafner 1996) the Fourier flexible form (Gallant 1981) or the polynomial approximations (Gallant and Tauchen 1989; Gallant et al. 1990). As an example, we describe the most commonly used kernel method. To estimate the conditional expectation at a point y, that is $g(y) = E(Y_t / Y_{t-1} = y)$, we use a weighted average of Y_t values, putting larger weights on values, of Y_{t-1} close to y. More precisely, we introduce a kernel, i.e., a function defined on $\mathbb{R}$ that is generally nonnegative with a unitary mass: $\int x K(x) dx = 1$.

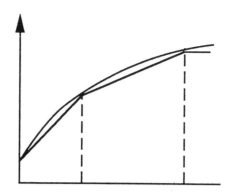

FIGURE 5.3. Piecewise linear approximation.

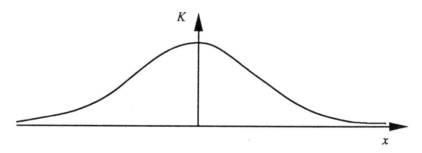

FIGURE 5.4. Kernel.

A classical example of such a function is the Gaussian kernel defined by

$$K(x) = \frac{1}{\sqrt{2\pi}} \exp - \left(\frac{x^2}{2}\right).$$

$K(.)$ has the form given in figure 5.4. This kernel is useful to determine the weights

$$\omega_t = \frac{1}{H} K \left(\frac{Y_{t-1} - y}{H}\right) / \frac{1}{H} \sum_{t=1}^{T} K \left(\frac{Y_{t-1} - y}{H}\right), H \geq 0.$$

The kernel estimator of $g(y)$ is then defined by

$$\hat{g}(y) = \sum_{t=1}^{T} \omega_t Y_t = \frac{\sum_{t=1}^{T} Y_t K \left(\frac{Y_{t-1} - y}{H}\right)}{\sum_{t=1}^{T} K \left(\frac{Y_{t-1} - y}{H}\right)}. \tag{5.44}$$

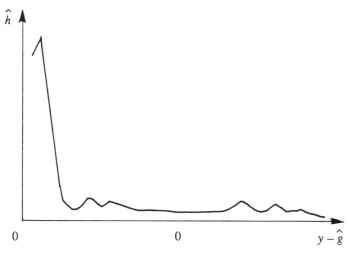

FIGURE 5.5. Estimated volatility.

Thus, to each observation a weight is assigned, which decreases when the gap between Y_{t-1} and y increases. Such an estimator depends on the choice of the constant H (called bandwidth). The larger H, the more important is the smoothing phenomenon. There are several practices for choosing H that will not be described here.

The last method is easily applied to the estimation of the conditional variance that arises as a function of the conditional expectations of Y_t^2 and Y_t. Thus, a kernel estimator of the function h is

$$\hat{h}(y) = \sum_{t=1}^{T} \omega_t Y_t^2 - \left(\sum_{t=1}^{T} \omega_t Y_t \right)^2 = \frac{\sum_{t=1}^{T} Y_t^2 K(Y_{t-1} - y/H)}{\sum_{t=1}^{T} K(Y_{t-1} - y/H)} \qquad (5.45)$$
$$- \left[\frac{\sum_{t=1}^{T} Y_t K(Y_{t-1} - y/H)}{\sum_{t=1}^{T} K(Y_{t-1} - y/H)} \right]^2 .$$

We display in figure 5.5 a kernel based estimation of the return volatility reported by Pagan and Schwert (1990). It is worth noting that the nonparametric procedures, which are very useful from a descriptive point of view, are difficult to handle when we are interested in studying structural problems like those discussed in chapter 8.

5.5   Integrated Models

5.5.1   The IGARCH(1,1) Model

In the usual framework of ARMA processes, the stationarity condition is characterized by the roots of the autoregressive polynomial, with the modulus required
to be strictly larger than one. It is then interesting to investigate the limiting case
where some roots may have a modulus one. These are nonstationary processes
called ARIMA processes (I for integrated), which generalize the notion of random
walk. The same reasoning holds for the GARCH processes but yields quite different results. In order to simplify the presentation, we consider the case of integrated
GARCH(1,1) or [IGARCH(1,1)] processes (Nelson 1990). Under the assumption
of conditional normality, the process is

$$\left\{\varepsilon_t/\underline{\varepsilon_{t-1}} \sim N[0, h_t], \quad \text{with } h_t = c + \beta h_{t-1} + \alpha \varepsilon_{t-1}^2, \ \alpha \geq 0, \beta \geq 0. \quad (5.46)\right.$$

The forecasts of conditional variances at different horizons take the following
form:

$$E(h_{t+k}/\underline{\varepsilon_t}) = (\alpha + \beta)^k h_t + c\left[\sum_{i=0}^{k-1}(\alpha + \beta)^i\right].$$

If $\alpha + \beta < 1$, the process (ε_t) is second order stationary, and a shock to the
conditional variance h_t has a decaying impact on h_{t+k} when k increases, and is
asymptotically negligible.

If $\alpha + \beta \geq 1$, the effect on h_{t+k} does not die out asymptotically. This property is
called **persistence** in the literature. So, in the particular case

$$\alpha + \beta = 1 \text{ (IGARCH(1,1) case)}, \quad (5.47)$$

we have

$$E[h_{t+k}/\underline{\varepsilon_t}] = h_t + kc.$$

The forecast properties of h correspond to those of a random walk with or
without drift depending on whether c is equal to or different from zero. To carry
out a precise study of such processes, we introduce the standard Gaussian process
defined by $Z_t h_t^{1/2} = \varepsilon_t$. The conditional variance becomes

$$h_t = c + \beta h_{t-1} + \alpha h_{t-1} Z_{t-1}^2,$$

$$h_t = c + (\beta + \alpha Z_{t-1}^2) h_{t-1}.$$

By recursions starting from an initial date 0, we derive the explicit expression

$$h_t = h_0 \prod_{i=1}^{t}(\beta + \alpha Z_{t-i}^2) + c\left[1 + \sum_{k=1}^{t-1}\prod_{i=1}^{t}(\beta + \alpha Z_{t-i}^2)\right]. \quad (5.48)$$

5.5.2   The Persistence Effect

At this stage, it is interesting to revise the persistence effect. Let us consider the IGARCH(1,1) model constrained by $\alpha + \beta = 1$. We have

$$E\left(\prod_{i=1}^{t}(\beta + \alpha Z_{t-i}^2)\right) = \prod_{i=1}^{t} E(\beta + \alpha Z_{t-i}^2), \quad \text{because of the independence,}$$

$$= \prod_{i=1}^{t}(\alpha + \beta), \quad \text{since } Z_t \text{ has unitary variance and zero mean,}$$

$$= 1.$$

Therefore, expectation has a persistent pattern. However, one may also write

$$\prod_{i=1}^{t}(\beta + \alpha Z_{t-i}^2) = \exp \sum_{i=1}^{t} \log(\beta + \alpha Z_{t-i}^2)$$

But, according to the convexity inequality:

$$E \log(\beta + \alpha Z_{t-i}^2) < \log E(\beta + \alpha Z_{t-i}^2) = 0.$$

Applying the law of large numbers, we find that $\frac{1}{t}\sum_{i=1}^{t} \log(\beta + \alpha Z_{t-i}^2)$ tends almost surely (a.s.) to the strictly negative real number $E \log(\beta + \alpha Z_{t-i}^2)$, and consequently the factor $\prod_{i=1}^{t}(\beta + \alpha Z_{t-i}^2)$ tends a.s. to zero. Thus, the persistence disappears in terms of the past of the process but not in terms of expectation.

Property 5.49. *The IGARCH(1,1) model shows a persistence property in expected values but not path by path.*

The property may also be easily extended by relaxing the constraint $\alpha + \beta = 1$. The parameter space can be divided into three regions.

i) If $\alpha + \beta < 1$, there is persistence neither in expectation nor path by path (region 1).

ii) If $1 \le \alpha + \beta$ and $\log(\beta + \alpha Z_{t-i}^2) < 0$, there is persistence of expectation but not path by path (region 2).

iii) If $E \log (\beta + \alpha Z_{t-i}^2) \ge 0$, there is persistence both in expectation and path by path (region 3).

Furthermore, if the variable Z_t follows a standard normal distribution, it has been shown that (Nelson 1990)

$$E \log(\beta + \alpha Z_t^2) = \log 2\alpha + \psi(1/2)$$
$$+ [2\Pi\beta/\alpha]^{1/2} F_1(1/2; 3/2; \beta/2\alpha) - \beta/\alpha F_2(1, 1; 2, 3/2; \beta/2\alpha),$$

where ψ denotes the Euler Psi function, F_1 the hypergeometric function and F_2 the generalized hypergeometric function. The shapes of the different regions are given in figure 5.6.

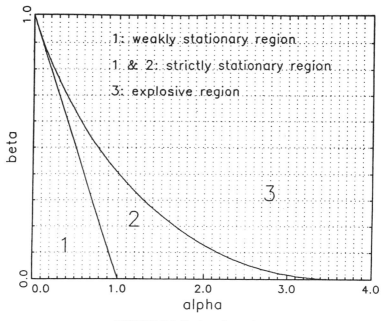

FIGURE 5.6. Stationarity regions.

5.5.3   Weak and Strong Stationarity

Much more precise results concerning strict stationarity can be derived. If $E \log(\beta + \alpha Z_t^2) < 0$ (regions 1 and 2), we have

$$h_t \approx h_t^* = c[1 + \sum_{k=0}^{\infty} \prod_{i=1}^{k} (\beta + \alpha Z_{t-i}^2)] \text{ and } \varepsilon_t \approx \varepsilon_t^* = h_t^{*1/2} Z_t.$$

The following property, presented without proof, was established by Nelson (1990).

Property 5.50. *The process* (h_t^*, ε_t^*) *is strictly stationary if and only if* $E \log(\beta + \alpha Z_t^2) < 0$.

Thus, region 1 arises as the region where (h_t) is (asymptotically) weakly stationary and region $1 \cup 2$ as that where (h_t) is (asymptotically) strongly stationary. In this example, the weak stationarity implies the strong stationarity. The result is obviously explained by the nonexistence of the expected conditional variance in region 2. Therefore, the IGARCH(1,1) process, located on the frontier between regions 1 and 2, is stationary with marginal distributions featuring fat tails.

5.5.4 Example

The discussion above is only of interest if, in practice, the estimation of GARCH models yields values in the region of nonexistence of the moments. This seems to occur frequently in practice. French et al. (1987) estimated a GARCH model using data on the return R_t of a Standard and Poor's composite portfolio deflated by a risk-free rate (30 day Treasury Bill). The model has the form

$$R_t = a + \varepsilon_t - \theta\varepsilon_{t-1},$$

with

$$V(\varepsilon_t/\varepsilon_{t-1}) = h_t$$
$$h_t = c + \beta h_{t-1} + \alpha_1\varepsilon_{t-1}^2 + \alpha_2\varepsilon_{t-2}^2.$$

The estimated values on various subperiods are the following:

Subperiod	β	α_1	α_2
January 1928	0.92	0.12	-0.04
December 1984	(0.002)	(0.007)	(0.007)
January 1928	0.90	0.10	-0.01
December 1952	(0.004)	(0.009)	(0.009)
January 1953	0.92	0.13	-0.06
December 1984	(0.004)	(0.01)	(0.01)

Without taking into account the estimated standard deviation, we note that the sum $\beta + \alpha_1 + \alpha_2$ equals $1.00, 0.99, 0.99$, respectively, which is close to 1, i.e., to the limit case we were interested in.

5.6 Exercises

Exercise 5.1. Qualitative ARCH model (Gouriéroux and Monfort 1991). Let us consider the threshold model defined by

$$Y_t = \left(\sum_{j=1}^{p}\alpha_j \mathbb{I}_{Y_{t-1}\in A_j}\right)u_t,$$

where (u_t) is a standard Gaussian white noise, $\alpha_1, \ldots, \alpha_p$ are positive coefficients and $A_1, \ldots, A_p$ is a given partition of the real line.

1) Verify that the underlying process $Z_t = (\mathbb{I}_{Y_t\in A_1}, \ldots, \mathbb{I}_{Y_{t-1}\in A_p})$ is a homogeneous Markov chain. Find the ergodicity conditions of the case $p = 2$.

2) Derive the expressions of the maximum likelihood estimators for the coefficients $\alpha_1, \ldots, \alpha_p$.

3) Determine their asymptotic variances under the null hypothesis of homoscedasticity $H_0 = \{\alpha_1 = \alpha_2 = \ldots = \alpha_p\}$. Build a test of this hypothesis. How does this test differ from the usual Chow test for time varying variances?

Exercise 5.2. Let us consider the threshold model defined by

$$Y_t = \left(\varphi_0 + \varphi_1 Y_{t-1}^2 \mathbb{I}_{Y_{t-1}>0} + \varphi_2 Y_{t-1}^2 \mathbb{I}_{Y_{t-1}<0} \right)^{1/2} u_t,$$

where $(\varphi_0, \varphi_1, \varphi_2)$ are positive coefficients and u is a standard Gaussian noise.

1) Find sufficient conditions on φ_0, φ_1, φ_2 for the Y process to be second order stationary.

2) Verify that the last model nests the ARCH(1) model and propose a test for this submodel.

Exercise 5.3. For a strong standard white noise (Y_t), the correlations

$$\hat{\rho}(h) = \frac{\sum_t Y_t Y_{t-h}}{\sum_t Y_t^2}, h = 1, \ldots, H$$

are asymptotically normal, uncorrelated, with zero mean and variance $\frac{1}{T}$.

1) What is the asymptotic distribution of the statistic

$$\xi = \sqrt{T} \max_{1 \geq h \geq H} |\hat{\rho}(h)|?$$

2) Propose a test for the white noise hypothesis based on the largest observed correlation and compare it to the Portmanteau test.

Exercise 5.4. Propose a continuous time approximation of the threshold ARCH model

$$Y_t = \left(\varphi_0 + \varphi_1 Y_{t-1} \mathbb{I}_{Y_{t-1}>0} - \varphi_2 Y_{t-1} \mathbb{I}_{Y_{t-1}<0} \right) u_t.$$

Exercise 5.5. Let us consider the threshold model

$$Y_t = \left(\varphi_0 + \varphi_1 Y_{t-1} \mathbb{I}_{Y_{t-1}>0} - \varphi_2 Y_{t-1} \mathbb{I}_{Y_{t-1}<0} \right) u_t.$$

1) Find the stationarity conditions for Y_t up to the fourth order.

2) What is the value of $E Y^4$?

3) Show how the kurtosis depends on the parameters φ_0, φ_1, φ_2. When does it attain its minimum?

Exercise 5.6. Let ε be a standard Gaussian variable.

1) Compute $E|\varepsilon|$.

2) Show that the variable $\frac{|\varepsilon|-(2/\pi)^{1/2}}{1-(2/\pi)^{1/2}}$ is centered, reduced and uncorrelated with ε.

Exercise 5.7. (Drost and Nijman 1993). Let us consider a GARCH(1,1) model

$$E(Y_t/Y_{t-1}) = 0,$$
$$E(Y_t^2/Y_{t-1}) = h_t = \Psi + \beta h_{t-1}^2 + \alpha Y_{t-1}^2.$$

1) After having rewritten the GARCH condition of the form

$$Y_t^2 = \Psi + (\beta + \alpha)Y_{t-1}^2 + \eta_t - \beta\eta_{t-1},$$

where η is a weak white noise, show by substitution that

$$Y_t^2 = \Psi(1 + \beta + \alpha) + (\beta + \alpha)^2 Y_{t-2}^2 + u_t,$$

with $u_t = \eta_t + \alpha\eta_{t-1} - \beta(\beta + \alpha)\eta_{t-2}$. Verify that $E(u_t u_{t-2k}) = 0, \forall k > 1$.

2) Let λ be the root of the equation below lying between 0 and 1:

$$\lambda(1 + \lambda^2)^{-1} = \beta(\beta + \alpha)[1 + \alpha^2 + \beta^2(\beta + \alpha)^2]^{-1}.$$

    i) Study the properties of the process

$$\omega_t = (1 - \lambda L^2)^{-1} u_t.$$

    ii) Show that

$$E[Y_t^2 / Y_{t-2}, Y_{t-4}, \ldots] - \lambda E[Y_{t-2}^2 / Y_{t-4}, Y_{t-6}, \ldots]$$
$$= \Psi[1 + \beta + \alpha] + [(\beta + \alpha)^2 - \lambda]Y_{t-2}.$$

    iii) Does the process $\tilde{Y}_t = (Y_{2t})$ admit a GARCH representation?

Exercise 5.8. Compare the dynamic properties of the following ARCH type models introduced to take into account the asymmetric relationship between returns and volatility:

i) Quadratic GARCH (QGARCH) model:

$$\sigma_t^2 = \alpha_0 + \sum_{i=1}^{p} \beta_i \sigma_{t-i}^2 + \sum_{j=1}^{q} \gamma_j y_{t-j}^2 + \sum_{k=1}^{r} \sum_{l=1}^{r} \delta_{kl} Y_{t-k} y_{t-l}.$$

ii) Asymmetric GARCH (AGARCH) model:

$$\sigma_t^2 = \alpha_0 + \sum_{i=1}^{p} \beta_i \sigma_{t-i}^2 + \sum_{j=1}^{q} \left(\alpha_j |Y_{t-j}|^\theta + \gamma_j Y_{t-j}\right).$$

iii) Box–Cox transformed GARCH:

$$\sigma_t^2 = \left\{\alpha_0^\delta + \sum_{i=1}^{p} \beta_i (\sigma_{t-i}^2)^\delta + \sum_{j=1}^{q} \gamma_j (Y_{t-j}^2)^\delta\right\}^{1/\delta}.$$

6

Multivariate ARCH Models

6.1 Unconstrained Models

6.1.1 Multivariate GARCH Models

In chapter 3, we studied univariate processes $\epsilon = (\epsilon_t)$ satisfying GARCH (p, q) representations. The conditional expectations and variances were defined by

$$
\begin{cases}
E(\varepsilon_t/\underline{\varepsilon_{t-1}}) = 0, \\
V(\varepsilon_t/\underline{\varepsilon_{t-1}}) = h_t = c + \displaystyle\sum_{i=1}^{q} \alpha_i \varepsilon_{t-i}^2 + \sum_{j=1}^{p} \beta_j h_{t-j}.
\end{cases}
$$

In theory, if the process ϵ is multivariate with n components, all of the elements of the conditional variance–covariance matrix can be specified in the same way. If the components of the process are denoted by $(\epsilon_{lt}, l = 1, \ldots, n)$, and if $H_t = V(\epsilon_t/\underline{\epsilon_{t-1}})$ has elements h_{klt}, we can write

$$
\begin{cases}
E(\varepsilon_t/\underline{\varepsilon_{t-1}}) = 0, \ V(\varepsilon_t/\underline{\varepsilon_{t-1}}) = H_t, \\
h_{klt} = c_{kl} + \displaystyle\sum_{i=1}^{q} \Big[\sum_{k',l'} \alpha_{klk'l'i} \, \varepsilon_{k',t-i} \, \varepsilon_{l',t-i} \Big] \\
+ \displaystyle\sum_{i=1}^{p} \Big[\sum_{k',l'} \beta_{klk'l'i} \, h_{k',l',t-i} \Big].
\end{cases}
\tag{6.1}
$$

The different coefficients c, α, β occurring in this formula may obviously be constrained without loss of generality, noting that the matrices H_{t-i} and $\epsilon_{t-i}\epsilon'_{t-i}$

are symmetric. These constraints are

$$
\begin{cases}
c_{kl} = c_{lk}, \\
\alpha_{klk'l'i} = \alpha_{lkk'l'i}, \quad \alpha_{klk'l'i} = \alpha_{lkl'k'i}, \\
\beta_{klk'l'i} = \beta_{lkk'l'i}, \quad \beta_{klk'l'i} = \beta_{kll'k'i}.
\end{cases}
$$

Under these restrictions, the number of independent parameters in model (6.1) is

$$
\frac{n(n+1)}{2} + (p+q)\left[\frac{n(n+1)}{2}\right]^2.
$$

Thus, in an ARCH(1) model, this number of parameters equals $1 + \frac{n(n+1)}{2}$ for each equation. These parameter numbers are listed in the following table:

n	1	2	3	4
$1 + \dfrac{n(n+1)}{2}$	2	4	7	11
Total number of parameters	2	12	42	110

The definition (6.1) may be written in a compact form using matrix notation.

i) For instance, one may rewrite the condition (6.1)

$$
\operatorname{vec} h(H_t) = \operatorname{vec} hC + \sum_{i=1}^{q} \underline{A_i} \operatorname{vec} h(\varepsilon_{t-i}\varepsilon'_{t-i}) + \sum_{i=1}^{p} \underline{B_i} \operatorname{vec} h(H_{t-i}), \quad (6.2)
$$

where $\operatorname{vec} h(H)$ denotes the operator representing the lower part of the symmetric matrix H in a vectorized form and where A_i, $\underline{B_i}$ are the appropriate matrices, with elements being functions of α and $\overline{\beta}$, respectively.

ii) Another representation may be obtained without vectorizing the covariance matrix H_t. Let us introduce the matrices A_{kli}, B_{kli} with elements

$$
\begin{aligned}
\alpha_{klk'l'i}, \quad k' = 1, \ldots, n, \ l' = 1, \ldots, n, \\
\beta_{klk'l'i}, \quad k' = 1, \ldots, n, \ l' = 1, \ldots, n,
\end{aligned}
$$

respectively, and the matrices A_i and B_i of dimension $n^2 \times n^2$ containing the block elements A_{kli}, B_{kli}. We obtain

$$
h_{kl,t} = C_{kl} + \sum_{i=1}^{q} \varepsilon'_{t-i} A_{kli} \varepsilon_{t-i}
$$

$$
+ \sum_{i=1}^{p} E[\varepsilon'_{t-i} B_{kli} \varepsilon_{t-i} / \varepsilon_{t-i-1}].
$$

Let us introduce the Kronecker product of matrices $\otimes$. The Kronecker product of the two matrices C and D is the matrix $C \otimes D$ with block elements

$C_{ij}D$. We have

$$H_t = C + \sum_{i=1}^{q}(Id_n \otimes \varepsilon'_{t-i})A_i(Id_n \otimes \varepsilon_{t-i}) \qquad (6.3)$$

$$+ \sum_{i=1}^{p} E[(Id_n \otimes \varepsilon'_{t-i})B_i(Id_n \otimes \varepsilon_{t-i})/\underline{\varepsilon_{t-i-1}}].$$

6.1.2 Positivity Constraints

We have just defined the covariance matrix by means of a recursive equation yielding a symmetric solution. Still, the matrix H_t must also be positive semi-definite. According to (6.4), we easily see that sufficient conditions for the positivity are that the matrices

$$C, A_i, i = 1, \ldots, q, B_i, i = 1, \ldots, p \qquad (6.4)$$

be symmetric positive semi-definite.

6.1.3 Stability Conditions

Finally, other restrictions on the coefficients originate from the stability conditions. Following the same procedure as in chapter 3, we consider the vector of innovations of the squared process

$$u_t = \text{vec}\, h(\epsilon_t \epsilon'_t) - \text{vec}\, h(H_t).$$

Replacing vec $h H_t$ in equation (6.2) by its expression in terms of the innovations yields

$$\text{vec}\, h(\epsilon_t \epsilon'_t) = \text{vec}\, hC + \sum_{i=1}^{\text{Max}(p,q)} (\underline{A_i} + \underline{B_i})\,\text{vec}\, h(\epsilon_{t-i}\epsilon'_{t-i})$$

$$+ u_t - \sum_{i=1}^{p} B_i u_{t-i}.$$

The process (ϵ_t) is centered and uncorrelated since $E(\varepsilon_t/\underline{\varepsilon_{t-1}}) = 0$. It is also second order stationary if the variance can be considered time independent. From the preceding recursive equation, we have

$$E \,\text{vec}\, h(\epsilon_t \epsilon'_t) = \text{vec}\, hC + \sum_{i=1}^{\text{Max}(p,q)} (\underline{A_i} + \underline{B_i})E \,\text{vec}\, h(\epsilon_{t-i}\epsilon'_{t-i}).$$

The solutions of this equation tend towards a constant limit if the roots of the determinantal equation

$$\det[Id - \sum_{i=1}^{\text{Max}(p,q)} (\underline{A_i} + \underline{B_i})z^i] = 0 \qquad (6.5)$$

lie strictly outside the unit circle.

This condition is obviously sufficient but not necessary. It does not seem to admit a simplified form that takes into account the positivity constraint as in the univariate case.

The unconditional covariance matrix is then

$$\operatorname{vec} h E(\epsilon_t \epsilon_t') = \left[Id - \sum_{i=1}^{\operatorname{Max}(p,q)} (\underline{A_i} + \underline{B_i}) \right]^{-1} \operatorname{vec} h C. \tag{6.6}$$

6.1.4 An Example

In order to illustrate the different specifications of the multivariate GARCH models and the various constraints on the parameters, we examine a bidimensional ARCH(1) model. We have three distinct elements of the covariance matrix:

$$h_{11,t} = E(\varepsilon_{1,t}^2/\varepsilon_{t-1}), \quad h_{12,t} = E(\varepsilon_{1,t}\varepsilon_{2,t}/\varepsilon_{t-1}),$$
$$h_{22,t} = E(\varepsilon_{2,t}^2/\varepsilon_{t-1}).$$

Equation (6.2) can be rewritten

$$\begin{bmatrix} h_{11,t} \\ h_{12,t} \\ h_{22,t} \end{bmatrix} = \begin{bmatrix} c_{11} \\ c_{12} \\ c_{22} \end{bmatrix} + \begin{bmatrix} a_{11} & a_{12} & a_{13} \\ a_{21} & a_{22} & a_{23} \\ a_{31} & a_{32} & a_{33} \end{bmatrix} \begin{bmatrix} \varepsilon_{1,t-1}^2 \\ \varepsilon_{1,t-1}\varepsilon_{2,t-1} \\ \varepsilon_{2,t-1}^2 \end{bmatrix}.$$

It implies the following relations (6.1), written component by component:

$$\begin{cases} h_{11,t} = c_{11} + a_{11}\varepsilon_{1,t-1}^2 + a_{12}\varepsilon_{1,t-1}\varepsilon_{2,t-1} + a_{13}\varepsilon_{2,t-1}^2, \\ h_{21,t} = c_{21} + a_{21}\varepsilon_{1,t-1}^2 + a_{22}\varepsilon_{1,t-1}\varepsilon_{2,t-1} + a_{23}\varepsilon_{2,t-1}^2, \\ h_{31,t} = c_{31} + a_{21}\varepsilon_{1,t-1}^2 + a_{32}\varepsilon_{1,t-1}\varepsilon_{2,t-1} + a_{33}\varepsilon_{2,t-1}^2. \end{cases}$$

Finally, this system may be rewritten in matrix form. We have

$$\begin{cases} h_{11,t} = c_{11} + (\varepsilon_{1,t-1}, \varepsilon_{2,t-1}) \begin{pmatrix} a_{11} & \dfrac{a_{12}}{2} \\ \dfrac{a_{12}}{2} & a_{13} \end{pmatrix} \begin{pmatrix} \varepsilon_{1,t-1} \\ \varepsilon_{2,t-1} \end{pmatrix}, \\[3em] h_{12,t} = c_{12} + (\varepsilon_{1,t-1}, \varepsilon_{2,t-1}) \begin{pmatrix} a_{21} & \dfrac{a_{22}}{2} \\ \dfrac{a_{22}}{2} & a_{23} \end{pmatrix} \begin{pmatrix} \varepsilon_{1,t-1} \\ \varepsilon_{2,t-1} \end{pmatrix}, \\[3em] h_{22,t} = c_{22} + (\varepsilon_{1,t-1}, \varepsilon_{2,t-1}) \begin{pmatrix} a_{31} & \dfrac{a_{32}}{2} \\ \dfrac{a_{32}}{2} & a_{33} \end{pmatrix} \begin{pmatrix} \varepsilon_{1,t-1} \\ \varepsilon_{2,t-1} \end{pmatrix}. \end{cases}$$

Using the Kronecker product, we get

$$H_t = C + \begin{pmatrix} \varepsilon_{1,t-1} & \varepsilon_{2,t-1} & 0 & 0 \\ 0 & 0 & \varepsilon_{1,t-1} & \varepsilon_{2,t-1} \end{pmatrix} \begin{pmatrix} a_{11} & \dfrac{a_{12}}{2} & a_{21} & \dfrac{a_{22}}{2} \\ \dfrac{a_{12}}{2} & a_{13} & \dfrac{a_{22}}{2} & a_{23} \\ a_{21} & \dfrac{a_{22}}{2} & a_{31} & \dfrac{a_{32}}{2} \\ \dfrac{a_{22}}{2} & a_{23} & \dfrac{a_{32}}{2} & a_{33} \end{pmatrix}$$

$$\begin{pmatrix} \varepsilon_{1,t-1} & 0 \\ \varepsilon_{2,t-1} & 0 \\ 0 & \varepsilon_{1,t-1} \\ 0 & \varepsilon_{2,t-1} \end{pmatrix}.$$

If the two matrices C and $\underline{A_1}$ appearing in the last expression are symmetric positive semi-definite, the matrix H_t shares this property.

6.1.5   Spectral Decompositions

A convenient tool for any multivariate model analysis is the spectral decomposition. Such decompositions also exist for the multivariate GARCH models.

i) One may first infer from (6.3) that the conditional covariance matrix is the sum of several symmetric positive semi-definite matrices, which are constant or depend on lagged values ε_{t-i} or H_{t-i}:

$$H_t = C + \sum_{i=1}^{q} A_i(\varepsilon_{t-i}) + \sum_{i=1}^{p} B_i(H_{t-i}).$$

Every matrix appearing in this sum may be written in terms of its eigenvalues and eigenvectors; thus, we have, for example,

$$A_i(\varepsilon_{t-i}) = \sum_{j=1}^{n} \lambda_{ij}(\varepsilon_{t-i}) f_{ij}(\varepsilon_{t-i}) f_{ij}'(\varepsilon_{t-i}),$$

where $\lambda_{ij}(\varepsilon_{t-i})$, $j = 1, \ldots, n$ are the eigenvalues of $A_i(\varepsilon_{t-i})$, and $f_{ij}(\varepsilon_{t-i})$, $j = 1, \ldots, n$ is an orthonormal basis of associated eigenvectors. Hence the decomposition of H_t is

$$H_t = \sum_{j=1}^{n} v_j h_j h_j' + \sum_{i=1}^{q} \sum_{j=1}^{n} \lambda_{ij}(\varepsilon_{t-i}) f_{ij}(\varepsilon_{t-i}) f_{ij}'(\varepsilon_{t-i}) \qquad (6.7)$$

$$+ \sum_{i=1}^{q} \sum_{j=1}^{n} \mu_{ij}(H_{t-i}) g_{ij}(H_{t-i}) g_{ij}'(H_{t-i}),$$

with clear notations for the spectral decompositions of C and $B_i(H_{t-i})$. A simplification arises when some eigenvalues are zero or when the eigenvalues (or the eigenvectors) are time independent. This justifies some of the constraints that are usually imposed on the multivariate ARCH models.

ii) An alternative decomposition may also be derived from the formula (6.3). Let us introduce the spectral decompositions of the matrices A_i and B_i:

$$A_i = \sum_{j=1}^{n^2} \lambda_{ij} \begin{bmatrix} a_{ij1} \\ \vdots \\ a_{ijn} \end{bmatrix} [a'_{ij1}, \ldots, a'_{ijn}],$$

$$B_i = \sum_{j=1}^{n^2} \mu_{ij} \begin{bmatrix} b_{ij1} \\ \vdots \\ b_{ijn} \end{bmatrix} [b'_{ij1}, \ldots, b'_{ijn}],$$

where the vectors a_{ijk}, b_{ijk} have dimension n. We have

$$(Id_n \otimes \varepsilon'_{t-i}) A_i (Id_n \otimes \varepsilon_{t-i}) = \sum_{j=1}^{n^2} \lambda_{ij} (Id_n \otimes \varepsilon'_{t-i}) \begin{bmatrix} a_{ij1} \\ \vdots \\ a_{ijn} \end{bmatrix}$$

$$[a'_{ij1}, \ldots, a'_{ijn}] (Id_n \otimes \varepsilon_{t-i})$$

$$= \sum_{j=1}^{n^2} \lambda_{ij} \begin{bmatrix} \varepsilon'_{t-i} a_{ij1} \\ \vdots \\ \varepsilon'_{t-i} a_{ijn} \end{bmatrix} [a'_{ij1} \varepsilon_{t-i}, \ldots, a'_{ijn} \varepsilon_{t-i}]$$

$$= \sum_{j=1}^{n^2} \lambda_{ij} \begin{bmatrix} a'_{ij1} \varepsilon_{t-i} \\ \vdots \\ a'_{ijn} \varepsilon_{t-i} \end{bmatrix} \begin{bmatrix} a'_{ij1} \varepsilon_{t-i} \\ \vdots \\ a'_{ijn} \varepsilon_{t-i} \end{bmatrix}'$$

$$= \sum_{j=1}^{n^2} \lambda_{ij} \begin{bmatrix} a'_{ij1} \\ \vdots \\ a'_{ijn} \end{bmatrix} \varepsilon_{t-i} \varepsilon'_{t-i} \begin{bmatrix} a'_{ij1} \\ \vdots \\ a'_{ijn} \end{bmatrix}'$$

$$= \sum_{j=1}^{n^2} \lambda_{ij} \bar{A}_{ij} \varepsilon_{t-i} \varepsilon'_{t-i} \bar{A}'_{ij},$$

with $\bar{A}_{ij} = \begin{bmatrix} a'_{ij1} \\ \vdots \\ a'_{ijn} \end{bmatrix}$. The same approach may also be applied to the matrices in B. If $\bar{B}_{ij} = \begin{bmatrix} b'_{ij1} \\ \vdots \\ b'_{ijn} \end{bmatrix}$, we get

$$E[(Id_n \otimes \varepsilon'_{t-i}) B_i (Id_n \otimes \varepsilon_{t-i}) / \underline{\varepsilon_{t-i-1}}] = \sum_{j=1}^{n^2} \mu_{ij} E[\bar{B}_{ij} \varepsilon_{t-i} \varepsilon'_{t-i} \bar{B}'_{ij} / \underline{\varepsilon_{t-i-1}}]$$

$$= \sum_{j=1}^{n^2} \mu_{ij} \, \bar{B}_{ij} \, H_{t-i} \, \bar{B}'_{ij}.$$

Finally, we see that the GARCH relation may be rewritten

$$H_t = C + \sum_{i=1}^{q} \left[\sum_{j=1}^{n^2} \lambda_{ij} \, \bar{A}_{ij} \, \varepsilon_{t-i} \, \varepsilon'_{t-i} \, \bar{A}'_{ij} \right] \tag{6.8}$$

$$+ \sum_{i=1}^{p} \left[\sum_{j=1}^{n^2} \mu_{ij} \, \bar{B}_{ij} \, H_{t-i} \, \bar{B}'_{ij} \right],$$

where λ_{ij}, μ_{ij} are positive real numbers and $\bar{A}_{ij}, \bar{B}_{ij}$ are (n, n) matrices. This second decomposition was proposed by Baba et al. (1987). In addition, one may establish the existence of a decomposition of the same kind with $\frac{n(n+1)}{2}$ instead of n^2 terms inside the brackets (see exercise 6.1).

6.2   Constrained Models

As noted before, the direct extension of GARCH models to the multivariate case leads to a proliferation of parameters and makes these models difficult for empirical work without additional constraints. In this section, we present several restrictions that have been proposed in empirical studies. These constraints yield simple interpretations, have to be compatible with the positivity conditions and must lead to tractable estimation procedures.

6.2.1   Diagonal Models

To begin, we assume that the (k, l) term of the conditional variance–covariance matrix depends only on the lagged theoretical or empirical terms with the same index, i.e., $h_{kl,t-i}, \epsilon_{k,t-i}\epsilon_{l,t-i}$. This constraint is equivalent to the diagonality of the matrices:

$$\underline{A}_i \text{ and } \underline{B}_i \text{ are diagonal.} \tag{6.9}$$

Such a formulation has several drawbacks.

i) The constraint is not invariant with respect to the portfolio composition. Let us suppose that the observed series are the gains from several assets and consider a bidimensional diagonal model of the type

$$\begin{cases} h_{11,t} = c_{11} + b_{11} h_{11,t-1}, \\ h_{12,t} = c_{12} + b_{12} h_{12,t-1}, \\ h_{22,t} = c_{22} + b_{22} h_{22,t-1}. \end{cases}$$

For a portfolio constituted of α_1 shares of the first asset and α_2 shares of the second one, the variance is

$$
\begin{aligned}
h_{\alpha,t} &= \alpha_1^2 h_{11,t} + \alpha_2^2 h_{22,t} + 2\alpha_1\alpha_2 h_{12,t} \\
&= \alpha_1^2 c_{11} + \alpha_2^2 c_{22} + 2\alpha_1\alpha_2 c_{12} \\
&\quad + \alpha_1^2 b_{11} h_{11,t-1} + \alpha_2^2 b_{22} h_{22,t-1} + 2\alpha_1\alpha_2 b_{12} h_{12,t-1},
\end{aligned}
$$

which cannot be written in a diagonal form:

$$
h_{\alpha,t} = c_\alpha + b_\alpha h_{\alpha,t-1}.
$$

ii) A second drawback is the fact that the proposed model does not take into account risk substitutions among the assets. Thus, the risk premium on the first asset, which in the usual setup is a function of the conditional variance $h_{11,t}$ (see section 8.1), is independent of the evolution of the conditional variance of the second asset. The fact that the return on this second asset is more volatile ($h_{22,t}$, $h_{22,t-1}$ ... larger) does not modify the expected return on security 1.

iii) Finally, the condition "A_i, B_i diagonal" is not coherent with the positivity constraint. For instance, let us consider the following diagonal model

$$
H_t = C + \begin{pmatrix} \varepsilon_{1,t-1} & \varepsilon_{2,t-1} & 0 & 0 \\ 0 & 0 & \varepsilon_{1,t-1} & \varepsilon_{2,t-1} \end{pmatrix} \begin{pmatrix} a_{11} & 0 & 0 & \dfrac{a_{22}}{2} \\ 0 & 0 & \dfrac{a_{22}}{2} & 0 \\ 0 & \dfrac{a_{22}}{2} & 0 & 0 \\ \dfrac{a_{22}}{2} & 0 & 0 & a_{33} \end{pmatrix}
$$

$$
\begin{pmatrix} \varepsilon_{1,t-1} & 0 \\ \varepsilon_{2,t-1} & 0 \\ 0 & \varepsilon_{1,t-1} \\ 0 & \varepsilon_{2,t-1} \end{pmatrix},
$$

that is,

$$
\begin{cases}
h_{11,t} = c_{11} + a_{11}\varepsilon_{1,t-1}^2, \\
h_{21,t} = c_{12} + a_{22}\varepsilon_{1,t-1}\varepsilon_{2,t-1}, \\
h_{22,t} = c_{22} + a_{33}\varepsilon_{2,t-1}^2.
\end{cases}
$$

The positivity constraint is satisfied if the principal minors of the matrix are positive:

$$
a_{11} \geq 0, \quad -a_{11}\frac{a_{22}^2}{2} \geq 0, \quad \left(\frac{a_{22}}{2}\right)^4 - a_{11}a_{33}\frac{a_{22}^2}{2} \geq 0.
$$

As soon as a_{11} or a_{33} is strictly positive, we have $a_{22} = 0$. Thus, it is impossible to model simultaneously a dynamic for the variance and covariance while satisfying the positivity requirement.

Diagonal specifications have also been proposed for the multivariate stochastic variance models (Harvey et al. 1994), and a similar discussion may be presented.

6.2.2 Models with Constant Conditional Correlations

These models (Bollerslev 1987) are built by assuming that the conditional correlations are time independent. So, if the autoregressive and moving average orders equal one, the second order moments are defined by

$$
\begin{cases}
h_{ii,t} = c_{ii} + a_{ii}\varepsilon_{i,t-1}^2 + b_{ii}h_{ii,t-1}, \\[2mm]
h_{ij,t} = \rho_{ij}\, h_{ii,t}^{1/2}\, h_{jj,t}^{1/2}, \, i \neq j.
\end{cases}
\tag{6.10}
$$

The conditional variance–covariance matrix may be written as

$$
H_t = \mathrm{diag}(h_{ii,t}^{1/2})\, R\, \mathrm{diag}(h_{ii,t}^{1/2}),
$$

where R is the correlation matrix. One may also normalize the preceding decomposition by introducing the quantities $d_{i,it} = h_{i,it}/c_{ii}$ and the matrix Γ with a general term $\gamma_{ij} = \rho_{ij}\, c_{ii}^{1/2} c_{jj}^{1/2}$:

$$
\begin{aligned}
H_t &= \mathrm{diag}(d_{i,it}^{1/2})\, \Gamma\, \mathrm{diag}(d_{i,it}^{1/2}) \\[2mm]
&= D_t\, \Gamma\, D_t, \text{ according to the definition.}
\end{aligned}
\tag{6.11}
$$

This specification suggests a conditional variance decomposition as a product of matrices depending on different parameters: ρ_{ij} and c_{ii} in Γ, and the transformed parameters a_{ii}/c_{ii}, b_{ii}/c_{ii} in D_t. This decomposition is useful from a numerical point of view. Thus, the positivity constraint may be specified separately for the two matrices: it is satisfied as soon as the variances $h_{i,it}$ (or $d_{i,it}$) are positive and the matrix R (or Γ) is positive definite. We can also see (section 6.3) that this decomposition simplifies recursive likelihood optimizations.

The model with constant correlations is also interesting as far as the interpretation is concerned. Since it accounts for the correlations between securities, it is well adapted to the risk premium analysis. Moreover, it facilitates the comparison between subperiods. One may indeed independently estimate such submodels on separate subperiods and afterwards examine whether the correlation patterns vary from one subperiod to another. For instance, this procedure has been followed in a study of the exchange rates between European currencies before and after the European Monetary System was initiated. As expected, the system results in a better coordination of the currencies' evolutions, that is it increases the correlations.

The approach presented above nevertheless has a few drawbacks. In particular, it is not invariant with respect to the portfolio composition (see exercise 6.1). In addition, it holds for the very specific factor decompositions. One may indeed write the matrix Γ in a spectral form, $\Gamma = \sum_{i=1}^{n} \lambda_i a_i a_i'$, where the a_i's are the eigenvectors associated with the eigenvalues λ_i. Substituting in the variance expression, we obtain

$$H_t = D_t \Gamma D_t = \sum_{i=1}^{n} \lambda_i (D_t a_i)(D_t a_i)'.$$

In this representation, the factors $D_t a_i$ depend on time and the weights λ_i do not.

Finally, we note that the model with constant correlation does not satisfy the GARCH definition in section 6.2.1. The usual GARCH model thus appears too restrictive, and this topic will be discussed further in the following section.

6.2.3 Models with Random Coefficients

Bera and Lee (1989) proposed an interpretation of the univariate ARCH models in terms of the autoregressive models with random coefficients. This interpretation may serve as a reference in the discussion of the multivariate models. We present this approach however for dimension one only for clarity of exposition. An autoregressive process of order p is defined by the recursive equation

$$\varepsilon_t = \sum_{i=1}^{p} \varphi_i \varepsilon_{t-i} + u_t,$$

where u_t is an independent white noise with variance σ_u^2. The autoregressive coefficients are usually assumed constant, that is, deterministic and time independent. In fact, it may appear more realistic to admit some evolution of these coefficients and to denote

$$\varepsilon_t = \sum_{i=1}^{p} \varphi_{it} \varepsilon_{t-i} + u_t. \tag{6.12}$$

Some simple assumptions on this evolution are the following.

The coefficients φ_{it} are random; the vectors $(\varphi_{1t}, \ldots, \varphi_{pt})'$ are independent from each other and from the values of the noise u. Moreover, their moments are time invariant

$$E\varphi_{it} = 0, \quad V(\varphi_{1t}, \ldots, \varphi_{pt})' = \Sigma. \tag{6.13}$$

One may then integrate out these coefficients from their joint distribution and deduce the conditional distribution of ε_t given the past $\underline{\varepsilon_{t-1}}$. The conditional moments are

$$E(\varepsilon_t / \underline{\varepsilon_{t-1}}) = E_\varphi E(\varepsilon_t / \underline{\varepsilon_{t-1}}, \varphi)$$

$$= E_\varphi [\sum_{i=1}^{p} \varphi_{it} \varepsilon_{t-i}]$$

$$= \sum_{i=1}^{p} E_\varphi(\varphi_{it}) \varepsilon_{t-i} = 0,$$

where E_φ denotes the expectation taken with respect to the distribution of the autoregressive coefficients:

$$V(\varepsilon_t / \underline{\varepsilon_{t-1}}) = V_\varphi E(\varepsilon_t / \underline{\varepsilon_{t-1}}, \varphi) + E_\varphi V(\varepsilon_t / \underline{\varepsilon_{t-1}}, \varphi)$$

$$= V_\varphi [\sum_{i=1}^{p} \varphi_{it}\, \varepsilon_{t-i}] + E_\varphi \sigma_u^2$$

$$= (\varepsilon_{t-1}, \ldots, \varepsilon_{t-p})\Sigma \begin{pmatrix} \varepsilon_{t-1} \\ \vdots \\ \varepsilon_{t-p} \end{pmatrix} + \sigma_u^2.$$

In addition to the random coefficient interpretation, the formula of the conditional variance suggests that it may be important to include in the ARCH (or GARCH) specification cross effects relative to two different lags. As a matter of fact, the previously discussed ARCH models require in particular a diagonal matrix Σ,

$$V(\varepsilon_t / \underline{\varepsilon_{t-1}}) = \sum_{i=1}^{p} \sigma_{ii} \varepsilon_{t-i}^2 + \sigma_u^2,$$

or, equivalently, that the autoregressive coefficients associated with different lags evolve in an uncorrelated manner. The introduction of cross terms $\sigma_{ij}\varepsilon_{t-i}\varepsilon_{t-j}$ may be an interesting extension of the traditional ARCH model and is analogous to the transition from ARMA to bilinear models (see chapter 2). Obviously, this extension implies an increased number of parameters.

The preceding example could lead to a wrong conclusion that models with random coefficients constitute a more general class than ARCH models. In fact, this is not true, and the two approaches are different. Let us reapply the preceding procedure assuming now

$$E\varphi_{it} = \varphi_i, \quad i = 1, \ldots, p, \quad t \text{ varying.}$$

We obtain

$$\begin{cases} E(\varepsilon_t / \underline{\varepsilon_{t-1}}) = \sum_{i=1}^{p} \varphi_i\, \varepsilon_{t-i}, \\[2em] V(\varepsilon_t / \underline{\varepsilon_{t-1}}) = (\varepsilon_{t-1}, \ldots, \varepsilon_{t-p})\Sigma \begin{pmatrix} \varepsilon_{t-1} \\ \vdots \\ \varepsilon_{t-p} \end{pmatrix} + \sigma_u^2. \end{cases}$$

We obtain an autoregressive model with heteroscedastic conditional errors, but the lags are the same for the conditional expectation and variance, and—this is essential—the conditional variance *depends on lagged values of the series itself and not on lagged values of its innovations.*

6.2.4   Model Based on a Spectral Decomposition

The spectral decomposition of the conditional variance–covariance matrix may also be used to build a multivariate ARCH model. The idea is to retain a decomposition with only a small number of terms (Baba et al. 1987; Engle and Rodriguez 1987). For instance, we have seen that the conditional variance of an ARCH(1) model can always be written

$$H_t = C + \sum_{j=1}^{n^2} \lambda_j \bar{A}_j \varepsilon_{t-1} \varepsilon'_{t-1} \bar{A}'_j.$$

The model may be constrained by keeping p terms in the sum, where p would equal, for example, 1, 2 or 3 and hence be much lower than n^2. The model is

$$H_t = C + \sum_{j=1}^{p} S_j \varepsilon_{t-1} \varepsilon'_{t-1} S_j, \qquad (6.14)$$

where S_j, $j = 1, \ldots, p$, are symmetric and C is symmetric positive definite. The positivity constraints are then satisfied.

This specification still has several drawbacks. It is hard to adjust, there are difficulties related to factor identification, and it depends on a large number of parameters equal to $\frac{n(n+1)}{2}(p + 1)$.

6.2.5   Factor ARCH Models

These models have been proposed by Diebold and Nerlove (1988, 1989) and may be considered as heteroscedasticity adjusted state variable models [see Gouriéroux and Monfort (1990, section 8.2)]. Every component of the process is expressed as a linear function of a few underlying processes (called **factors** or **state variables**) and of a noise. So, in the one factor case, the model may be written as

$$\begin{array}{cccc} \varepsilon_t & = \lambda & F_t & +e_t, \\ (n, 1) & (n, 1) & (1, 1) & (n, 1) \end{array} \qquad (6.15)$$

where λ is a vector of parameters reflecting the **sensitivity** (or **beta**) of the process **to the factor** F_t, and where (F_t) and (e_t) are two independent processes, the first one summarizing all of the heteroscedastic phenomena:

$$F_t / \underline{F_{t-1}} \sim N[0, \sigma_t^2], \text{ with } \sigma_t^2 = \alpha_0 + \sum_{i=1}^{p} \alpha_i F_{t-i}^2, \qquad (6.16)$$

and the second one defining the noise:

$$E(e_t / \underline{e_{t-1}}) = 0, \quad V(e_t / \underline{e_{t-1}}) = \Omega. \qquad (6.17)$$

The conditional variance matrix of the initial process is

$$H_t = \sigma_t^2 \lambda \lambda' + \Omega. \qquad (6.18)$$

It is easy to generalize such a formulation to accommodate several factors and processes with nonzero conditional expectation.

If $Y_t = \begin{pmatrix} Y_{1t} \\ \vdots \\ Y_{nt} \end{pmatrix}$ denotes the observed multivariate process and

$F_t = \begin{pmatrix} F_{1t} \\ \vdots \\ F_{Kt} \end{pmatrix}$ the K underlying factors, the model may be written as

$$\underset{(n,\,1)}{Y_t} = \underset{(n,\,K)}{\wedge}\quad \underset{(K,\,1)}{F_t}\quad +\underset{(n,\,1)}{e_t}, \tag{6.19}$$

with F_t and e_t two independent Gaussian processes:

$$F_t/F_{t-1} \sim N[\mu_t, \Sigma_t],$$
$$e_t/e_{t-1} \sim N[0, \Omega].$$

The process Y_t is then such that

$$Y_t/F_{t-1}, e_{t-1} \sim N[\wedge \mu_t, \wedge \Sigma_t \wedge' + \Omega].$$

However, such processes do not explain what the factors are and especially how they are linked to the process Y. In chapter 8, we will review the notion of factor models and introduce formulations linked to the theory of finance.

6.3   Estimation of Heteroscedastic Dynamic Models

6.3.1   Pseudo Maximum Likelihood Estimators

As in the univariate case, one can develop estimation procedures for the parameters of the conditional mean and the conditional variance based on the log-likelihood associated with the normal distribution. This pseudo likelihood function may then be used, whether or not the true distribution of the observations is normal. In order to present the results in a general framework, covering especially the ARCH-M models with exogenous variables, we consider two multivariate processes. The first one is endogenous, $Y_t, t = 1, 2, \ldots$, of dimension n, and the second one is exogenous, $Z_t, t = 1, 2, \ldots$ We then denote $I_{t-1} = (Z_t, Y_{t-1}, Z_{t-1}, Y_{t-2}, Z_{t-2}, \ldots, Y_1, Z_1)$ the available information at the beginning of period t; this information contains the current and past values of the exogenous variables and the lagged values of the endogenous ones. The two first conditional moments are assumed to belong to families indexed by a finite number K of parameters:

$$\begin{cases} E(Y_t/I_{t-1}) = m_t(I_{t-1}; \theta) = m_t(\theta), \\ V(Y_t/\overline{I_{t-1}}) = H_t(I_{t-1}; \theta) = H_t(\theta), \end{cases} \tag{6.20}$$

and the data generating process to be compatible with these formulations and to depend on an unknown value θ_0 of the parameters. Although the conditional distribution of Y_t given I_{t-1} is not necessarily normal, the corresponding log-likelihood function may be constructed. It is

$$\log L_T(\theta) = \sum_{i=1}^{T} \log l_t(\theta),$$

with

$$\log l_t(\theta) = -\frac{1}{2} \log \det H_t(\theta) - \frac{1}{2}[Y_t - m_t(\theta)]' H_t^{-1}(\theta)[Y_t - m_t(\theta)]$$

$$= -\frac{1}{2} \log \det H_t(\theta) - \frac{1}{2}\varepsilon_t(\theta)' H_t^{-1}(\theta)\varepsilon_t(\theta),$$

denoting by $\varepsilon_t(\theta) = Y_t(\theta) - m_t(\theta)$ the innovation term.

The pseudo maximum likelihood estimator is obtained by maximizing $\log L_T(\theta)$ or, from a practical point of view, by examining the solutions of the first order conditions:

$$\frac{\partial \log L_T(\hat{\theta}_T)}{\partial \theta} = \sum_{t=1}^{T} \frac{\partial \log l_t}{\partial \theta}(\hat{\theta}_T) = 0.$$

The explicit expressions of the scores $\frac{\partial \log l_t(\theta)}{\theta}$ are more complicated because of the multivariate aspect, and hence we begin by introducing some suitable notations. If $A(\theta)$ is an (n, m) matrix, vec $h A(\theta)$ denotes the $(nm, 1)$ vector obtained by writing the columns of the matrix $A(\theta)$ underneath each other.

If θ_i is the i-th component of the vector θ, $i = 1, \ldots, p$, $\frac{\partial A(\theta)}{\partial \theta_i}$ denotes the (n, m) matrix whose elements are the derivatives with respect to θ_i of the corresponding element of $A(\theta)$. Finally, we consider the following notation for the derivative of a matrix $A(\theta)$ with respect to θ:

$$\frac{\partial A(\theta)}{\partial \theta} = \left[\text{vec}\, h \frac{\partial A(\theta)}{\partial \theta_1}, \ldots, \text{vec}\, h \frac{\partial A(\theta)}{\partial \theta_p} \right].$$

Therefore, it is a matrix of dimension (nm, p). Using this notation, we can explicitly write the score vector corresponding to the t-th observation as

$$\frac{\partial \log l_t(\theta)}{\partial \theta} = \frac{\partial}{\partial \theta} m_t(\theta)' H_t^{-1}(\theta)\varepsilon_t(\theta) \tag{6.21}$$

$$+ \frac{1}{2} \frac{\partial}{\partial \theta} H_t(\theta)' [H_t^{-1}(\theta) \otimes H_t^{-1}(\theta)] \text{ vec } h[\varepsilon_t(\theta)\varepsilon_t(\theta)' - H_t(\theta)].$$

The first term indicates the conditional expectation and may be interpreted as the scalar product of the "explanatory variables" $\frac{\partial m_t}{\partial \theta}(\theta)$ and the errors $\varepsilon_t(\theta)$. The second term is associated with the conditional variance and is computed from the **second order residuals**, that is, a demeaned series of squared errors:

$$\varepsilon_t(\theta)\varepsilon_t(\theta)' - H_t(\theta).$$

6.3.2 Asymptotic Properties of the Pseudo Maximum Likelihood Estimator

These properties result from the sequence of scores evaluated at θ_0 viewed as a martingale difference sequence. We have

$$\begin{cases} E(\varepsilon_t(\theta_0)/I_{t-1}) = 0, \\ E([\varepsilon_t(\theta_0)\varepsilon_t(\theta_0)' - H_t(\theta_0)]/I_{t-1}) = 0, \end{cases}$$

yielding

$$E(\frac{\partial \log l_t(\theta_0)}{\partial \theta}/I_{t-1}) = 0, \quad \forall t.$$

Under additional regularity conditions, especially concerning the conditional variance of the score and the stationarity of the observed process [see, for instance, Basawa et al. (1976), Crowder (1976) and Bollerslev and Wooldridge (1988)], we claim that the pseudo maximum likelihood estimator asymptotically exists and is consistent and asymptotically normal,

$$\sqrt{T}(\hat{\theta}_T - \theta_0) \underset{d}{\to} N[0, \Omega_0],$$

with $\Omega_0 = A_0^{-1} B_0 A_0^{-1}$,

$$A_0 = E_{\theta_0}\left(-\frac{\partial^2 \log l_t(\theta_0)}{\partial\theta\,\partial\theta'}\right),$$

$$B_0 = E_{\theta_0}\left(\frac{\partial \log l_t(\theta_0)}{\partial\theta}\frac{\partial \log l_t(\theta_0)}{\partial\theta'}\right).$$

In practice, these two matrices may be estimated consistently by replacing the expectations by the empirical means and the true value of the parameter θ_0 by the estimator $\hat{\theta}_T$. These approximations are

$$\hat{A}_T = -\frac{1}{T}\sum_{t=1}^{T}\frac{\partial^2 \log l_t(\hat{\theta}_T)}{\partial\theta\,\partial\theta'},$$

$$\hat{B}_T = \frac{1}{T}\sum_{t=1}^{T}\frac{\partial \log l_t(\hat{\theta}_T)}{\partial\theta}\frac{\partial \log l_t(\hat{\theta}_T)}{\partial\theta'}.$$

Noting that

$$A_0 = E_{\theta_0}\left(-\frac{\partial^2 \log l_t(\theta_0)}{\partial\theta\,\partial\theta'}\right)$$

$$= E_{\theta_0}E_{\theta_0}\left(\frac{\partial^2 \log l_t(\theta_0)}{\partial\theta\,\partial\theta'}/I_{t-1}\right),$$

one may also propose as a consistent estimator of the matrix A_0:

$$\tilde{A}_T = \frac{1}{T}\sum_{t=1}^{T}a_t(\hat{\theta}_T), \tag{6.22}$$

where $a_t(\theta_0) = E_{\theta_0}\left(-\dfrac{\partial^2 \log l_t(\theta_0)}{\partial\theta\,\partial\theta'}/I_{t-1}\right)$. In our case, one may derive the explicit expression of the function $a_t(\theta_0)$ (see exercise 6.2). We get

$$a_t(\theta_0) = \frac{\partial m_t}{\partial\theta}(\theta_0)' H_t^{-1}(\theta_0)\frac{\partial m_t}{\partial\theta}(\theta_0) \tag{6.23}$$

$$+\frac{1}{2}\frac{\partial}{\partial\theta} H_t(\theta_0)' [H_t^{-1}(\theta_0) \otimes H_t^{-1}(\theta_0)]\frac{\partial}{\partial\theta} H_t(\theta_0).$$

This second approximation of the matrix A_0 has the advantage of being computable using the first order derivatives of the moments $\frac{\partial}{\partial\theta}m_t(\theta_0)'$ and $\frac{\partial}{\partial\theta}H_t(\theta_0)$ and does not require the computation of second order derivatives, while $\hat{A}_T$ does.

6.3.3   Model with Constant Conditional Correlations

In some models, the maximization of the pseudo likelihood function may be easy. Let us consider the model with constant conditional correlations (section 6.2.2) and a conditional expectation equal to zero. The conditional covariance matrix may be written

$$H_t(\theta) = D_t(\alpha)\Gamma D_t(\alpha), \tag{6.24}$$

where the parameters α, occurring in the diagonal matrix D_t, and the parameter elements of the matrix Γ vary independently from one another.

The log-likelihood function is given by

$$\log L_T(\theta) = -\frac{Tn}{2\pi} - \frac{1}{2}\sum_{t=1}^{T} \log \det H_t(\theta) - \frac{1}{2}\sum_{t=1}^{T} Y_t(\theta)' H_t^{-1}(\theta)Y_t(\theta)$$

$$= -\frac{Tn}{2\pi} - \frac{T}{2}\log\det\Gamma - \sum_{t=1}^{T}\log\det D_t(\alpha)$$

$$-\frac{1}{2}\sum_{t=1}^{T}(D_t^{-1}(\alpha)Y_t)'\Gamma^{-1}(D_t^{-1}(\alpha)Y_t).$$

It is worth noting that the T inversions of the matrices $H_t, t = 1,\ldots,T$ are simplified to only the inversion of the matrix Γ since the matrices D_t are diagonal. Besides, one may easily concentrate the log-likelihood with respect to the parameters occurring in Γ. The maximization with respect to these parameters yields

$$\tilde{\Gamma}(\alpha) = \frac{1}{T}\sum_{t=1}^{T}(D_t^{-1}(\alpha)Y_t)'(D_t^{-1}(\alpha)Y_t),$$

and the log-likelihood function concentrated with respect to Γ is

$$\log L_T^c(\alpha) = -\frac{Tn}{2}(1 + \log 2\pi - \log T) \tag{6.25}$$

$$-\sum_{t=1}^{T}\log\det D_t(\alpha) - \frac{T}{2}\log\det[\sum_{t=1}^{T} D_t^{-1}(\alpha)Y_t Y_t' D_t^{-1}(\alpha)].$$

The inference on parameter α may then be performed directly using this concentrated likelihood function.

6.3.4 Factor Models

Let us turn to the one factor model. The observed multivariate process (ε_t) satisfies

$$
\begin{array}{cccc}
\varepsilon_t & = \lambda & F_t & +e_t, \\
(n, 1) & (n, 1) & (1, 1) & (n, 1)
\end{array}
\tag{6.26}
$$

where the factor F_t and the noise (e_t) are two independent processes. The first one, summarizing the heteroscedasticity phenomenon, has the following distribution:

$$
F_t / \underline{F_{t-1}} \sim N[0, \alpha_0 + \alpha_1 F_{t-1}^2],
$$

and the second one is also normal:

$$
e_t / \underline{e_{t-1}} \sim N[0, \Omega].
$$

Here, in order to simplify the exposition, we have only retained an autoregressive term of order one.

i) Maximum Likelihood

The difficulty with these models arises from the unobservability of the factor. If the conditional distribution of $\varepsilon_T, F_T, \ldots, \varepsilon_1, F_1$, given an initial condition F_0, is easy to determine, it is not the case for the distribution relative to only the observed variables $\varepsilon_T, \ldots, \varepsilon_1$ (conditionally on F_0). The first set of distributions is

$$
l(\varepsilon_T, F_T, \ldots, \varepsilon_1, F_1 / F_0)
$$

$$
= \prod_{t=1}^{T} l[\varepsilon_t, F_t / \underline{\varepsilon_{t-1}}, \underline{F_{t-1}}]
$$

$$
= \prod_{t=1}^{T} l[\varepsilon_t, F_t / \varepsilon_{t-1}, F_{t-1}], \quad \text{by using the Markov property,}
$$

$$
= \prod_{t=1}^{T} l[\varepsilon_t, F_t / \varepsilon_{t-1}, F_{t-1}] \, l[F_t / \varepsilon_{t-1}, F_{t-1}]
$$

$$
= \prod_{t=1}^{T} \left\{ \frac{1}{(2\pi)^{n/2}} \frac{1}{\sqrt{\det \Omega}} \exp -\frac{1}{2} (\varepsilon_t - \lambda F_t)' \Omega^{-1} (\varepsilon_t - \lambda F_t) \right.
$$

$$
\left. \frac{1}{(2\pi)^{1/2}} \frac{1}{\sqrt{\alpha_0 + \alpha_1 F_{t-1}^2}} \exp -\frac{1}{2} \frac{F_t^2}{\alpha_0 + \alpha_1 F_{t-1}^2} \right\}.
$$

On the contrary, the second one may only be obtained by integrating out the unobserved variables:

$$
l(\varepsilon_T, \ldots, \varepsilon_1 / F_0) = \int \ldots \int l(\varepsilon_T, F_T, \ldots, \varepsilon_1, F_1 / F_0) \, dF_T \ldots dF_1.
$$

This multiple integration of order equal to the number of observations cannot be simplified further.

To avoid this difficulty, we may consider particular cases in which the computation of the likelihood function is more straightforward. Numerical methods exist in at least two cases: if the process (ε_t, F_t) is Gaussian and if the process F_t is qualitative. Although none of these conditions is satisfied in our case, one may still use this approach but must be aware of the approximation bias. Naturally, we wish to obtain not only an (approximate) value of the likelihood but also forecasts of the unknown factor values.

ii) Approximated Kalman Filter

The first idea (Diebold and Nerlove 1989) is not to rely on the exact likelihood method but rather to apply a pseudo maximum likelihood method based on the assumption of conditional normality of ε_t given ε_{t-1}. This conditional normality is obviously not satisfied by the initial model, but, as we already noted, this does not prevent us from deriving consistent estimators. We are therefore interested in computing

$$
\tilde{l}(\varepsilon_T, \ldots, \varepsilon_1, /\varepsilon_0)
$$

$$
= \prod_{t=1}^{T} \frac{1}{(2\pi)^{n/2}} \frac{1}{\sqrt{\det V(\varepsilon/\underline{\varepsilon_{t-1}})}} \exp -\frac{1}{2} [\varepsilon_t - E(\varepsilon_t/\underline{\varepsilon_{t-1}})]'(V[\varepsilon_t/\underline{\varepsilon_{t-1}}])^{-1}
$$

$$
[\varepsilon_t - E(\varepsilon_t/\underline{\varepsilon_{t-1}})]
$$

$$
= \prod_{t=1}^{T} \left\{ \frac{1}{(2\pi)^{n/2}} \frac{1}{\sqrt{\det V(\varepsilon_t/\underline{\varepsilon_{t-1}})}} \exp -\frac{1}{2} \varepsilon_t' V[\varepsilon_t/\underline{\varepsilon_{t-1}}]^{-1} \varepsilon_t, \right.
$$

that is essentially in the evaluation of $V(\varepsilon_t/\underline{\varepsilon_{t-1}})$. We have

$$
\begin{aligned}
V(\varepsilon_t/\underline{\varepsilon_{t-1}}) &= V[E(\varepsilon_t/F_{t-1}, \underline{e_{t-1}})/\underline{\varepsilon_{t-1}}] \\
&\quad + E[V(\varepsilon_t/F_{t-1}, \underline{e_{t-1}})/\underline{\varepsilon_{t-1}}] \\
&= E(\lambda\lambda'(\alpha_0 + \alpha_1 F_{t-1}^2) + \Omega/\underline{\varepsilon_{t-1}}] \\
&= \lambda\lambda'(\alpha_0 + \alpha_1 E[F_{t-1}^2/\underline{\varepsilon_{t-1}}]) + \Omega.
\end{aligned}
$$

The procedure followed by Diebold and Nerlove consists in finding first a forecast of F_t assumed to be a function of $\varepsilon_t, \underline{\varepsilon_{t-1}}, F_{t-1}$, linear in ε_t. This is easy to do, and the forecast takes the form

$$
\begin{aligned}
F_t^* &= \tilde{E}(F_t/\varepsilon_t, \underline{\varepsilon_{t-1}}, F_{t-1}) = \mathrm{Cov}(F_t, \varepsilon_t/\underline{\varepsilon_{t-1}}, F_{t-1}) V(\varepsilon_t/\underline{\varepsilon_{t-1}}, F_{t-1})^{-1} \varepsilon_t \\
&= V[F_t/\underline{\varepsilon_{t-1}}, F_{t-1}] \lambda' [\lambda\lambda'(\alpha_0 + \alpha_1 F_{t-1}^2) + \Omega]^{-1} \varepsilon_t \\
&= (\alpha_0 + \alpha_1 F_{t-1}^2) \lambda' [\lambda\lambda'(\alpha_0 + \alpha_1 F_{t-1}^2) + \Omega]^{-1} \varepsilon_t.
\end{aligned}
$$

This expression is then appproximated by

$$
F_t^* = (\alpha_0 + \alpha_1 F_{t-1}^{*2}) \lambda' [\lambda\lambda'(\alpha_0 + \alpha_1 F_{t-1}^{*2}) + \Omega]^{-1} \varepsilon_t, \tag{6.27}
$$

and the conditional variance is approximated by

$$V(\varepsilon_t / \varepsilon_{t-1}) \approx \lambda \lambda'(\alpha_0 + \alpha_1 F_{t-1}^{*2}) + \Omega. \tag{6.28}$$

This procedure is easy, since it is based on a simple recursive formula.

However, the use of several approximations may result in an estimation bias, various nonlinear features having been omitted on purpose, such as assumption of a forecast of F_t linear in ε_t, or the replacement of $E(F_{t-1}^2/\varepsilon_{t-1})$ by $[E(F_{t-1}/\varepsilon_{t-1})]^2$ and of $E(F_{t-1}/\varepsilon_{t-1}, F_{t-2})$ by $E(F_{t-1}/\varepsilon_{t-1}; F_{t-2}^*)$.

iii) Approximate Qualitative Factor

To understand the interest in a qualitative approximation of the factor, we must first explain the algorithm to compute the distribution $l(\varepsilon_t/\varepsilon_{t-1})$. This distribution will be determined jointly with the predictive distribution of the factor $l(F_t/\varepsilon_{t-1})$. Let us suppose that the latter distribution is known at date $t-1$. The steps of the algorithm are as follows.

1) Computation of the joint distribution of F_t, F_{t-1} given ε_{t-1}:

$$l(F_t, F_{t-1}/\varepsilon_{t-1}) = l(F_t/F_{t-1}, \varepsilon_{t-1}) \, l(F_{t-1}/\varepsilon_{t-1})$$
$$= l(F_t/F_{t-1}) \, l(F_{t-1}/\varepsilon_{t-1}).$$

2) Computation of the joint distribution of F_t, F_{t-1}, ε_t given ε_{t-1}:

$$l(F_t, F_{t-1}, \varepsilon_t/\varepsilon_{t-1}) = l(\varepsilon_t/F_t, F_{t-1}, \varepsilon_{t-1}) \, l(F_t, F_{t-1}/\varepsilon_{t-1})$$
$$= l(\varepsilon_t/F_{t-1}) \, l(F_t/F_{t-1}) \, l(F_{t-1}/\varepsilon_{t-1}).$$

3) Computation of the conditional distribution:

$$l(\varepsilon_t/\varepsilon_{t-1}) = \int \int l(\varepsilon_t/F_{t-1}) l(F_t/F_{t-1}) l(F_{t-1}/\varepsilon_{t-1}) \, dF_t dF_{t-1},$$

where the integration sign has a double meaning: it indicates integrals if F_t has a continuous distribution and sums if it has a discrete distribution.

4) Computation of the conditional distribution of F_t, F_{t-1} given ε_t:

$$l(F_t, F_{t-1}/\varepsilon_t) = \frac{l(F_t, F_{t-1}, \varepsilon_t/\varepsilon_{t-1})}{l(\varepsilon_t/\varepsilon_{t-1})}.$$

5) Computation of the conditional distribution of F_t given ε_t:

$$l(F_t/\varepsilon_t) = \int l(F_t, F_{t-1}/\varepsilon_t) \, dF_{t-1}$$
$$= \frac{\int l(\varepsilon_t/F_{t-1}) \, l(F_t/F_{t-1}) \, l(F_{t-1}/\varepsilon_{t-1}) \, dF_{t-1}}{\int \int l(\varepsilon_t/F_{t-1}) \, l(F_t/F_{t-1}) \, l(F_{t-1}/\varepsilon_{t-1}) \, dF_t dF_{t-1}}.$$

This algorithm requires the evaluation of as many double integrals as the number of observations in the data set and as many simple integrals as the product of the sample length and the number of all possible values of F_t. In our case, the integrals cannot be computed analytically, and thus the numerical algorithm appears to be feasible only after having transformed the variable F_t into a variable taking a finite number of values. For this purpose, one may partition the set of possible values of F_t into classes. One obtains K classes, and the conditional distribution of F_t given F_{t-1} is replaced by a transition matrix yielding approximately the values

$$p_{jk} = P[F_t \in \text{class } k / F_{t-1} \in \text{class } j].$$

The calculus of integrals is then avoided, and what remains is the calculus of finite sums corresponding to the possible values of the factor. The transition probabilities may then be approximately expressed as functions of the initial parameters. If the class k is defined by the interval (a_k, a_{k+1}), and if $F_t/F_{t-1} \sim N[0; \alpha_0 + \alpha_1 F_{t-1}^2]$, we get

$$p_{jk} = P[a_k < F_t < a_{k+1}/a_j < F_{t-1} < a_{j+1}]$$
$$\approx P\left[a_k < F_t < a_{k+1}/F_{t-1} = \frac{a_{j+1} + a_j}{2}\right]$$

(if the length of the interval is small enough)

$$= \Phi_-\left\{\frac{a_{k+1}}{\sqrt{\alpha_0 + \alpha_1 \left(a_{j+1} + a_j/2\right)^2}}\right\} - \Phi\left\{\frac{a_k}{\sqrt{\alpha_0 + \alpha_1 \left(a_{j+1} + a_j/2\right)^2}}\right\},$$

where Φ denotes the cdf of the standard normal distribution.

7
Efficient Portfolios and Hedging Portfolios

Among the major applications of ARCH models is the estimation of volatility evolving in time. This estimation allows one to compare portfolios or to build them with desired properties, for instance, those that maximize the expected utility of their return or allow one to hedge several sources of risk.

We begin by recalling the well-known theory of mean variance efficient portfolios, selected to minimize the risk subject to a given expected return. According to the mean variance criterion, the efficient portfolios consist of the risk-free security (or a proxy) and a basic efficient portfolio with composition that may be easily derived from the first and second order moments of the conditional distribution of the returns. We discuss several properties of the set of efficient portfolios, such as the efficiency frontier or aggregation across individuals. Next we describe alternative procedures for building portfolios, such as portfolios mimicking a market index, portfolios reflecting the behavior of call sellers or the hedging behavior of a firm. Finally, the last section deals with the statistical properties of the efficient allocations and their estimated performance.

7.1 Determination of an Efficient Portfolio

7.1.1 Securities and Portfolios

Suppose the existence of a finite number of securities indexed by i, $i = 1, \ldots, n$. The acquisition of a unit of the security i costs p_i, $i = 1, \ldots, n$, and $p = (p_1, \ldots, p_n)'$ denotes the vector of **acquisition costs per unit**. On the period considered, these securities generate a gain per security unit that is supposed to be random. We denote the vector of gains per security unit by $\gamma = (\gamma_1, \ldots, \gamma_n)'$. The components of γ may possibly take negative values and in such a case would correspond to a loss. The gross return on the security i over the period is $R_i = 1 + \gamma_i / p_i$, and the net return is $r_i = R_i - 1 = \gamma_i / p_i$. The random aspect of the returns $R_1, \ldots, R_n$ is summarized by the two first moments:

$$\text{expected gross returns} \quad m = E\,R,$$
$$\text{variability of the returns} \quad \Sigma = V\,R.$$

With known acquisition costs $p_i, i = 1, \ldots, n$, one finds the distribution of the gains $\gamma_i = p_i R_i - p_i$. We get

$$\text{the expected gain:} \quad E\gamma = \text{diag } p. \ m - p,$$
$$\text{the variability of the gains:} \quad V\gamma = \text{diag } p \ .\Sigma. \text{ diag } p,$$

where diag p denotes the diagonal matrix with the costs $p_1, \ldots, p_n$ on the main diagonal. A **portfolio** is described by a vector $\alpha = (\alpha_1, \ldots, \alpha_n)'$ of quantities α_i of the different securities. Often in practice, few securities are actually found in the portfolio; a **support security** is a security for which $\alpha_i \neq 0$.

Such a portfolio

$$\text{has an acquisition cost:} \quad p(\alpha) = p'\alpha,$$
$$\text{generates a random gain:} \quad \gamma(\alpha) = \gamma'\alpha,$$
$$\text{and generates a gross return:} \quad R(\alpha) = 1 + \frac{\gamma'\alpha}{p'\alpha}.$$

This return may be easily expressed as a function of the returns on the initial securities:

$$R(\alpha) = 1 + \frac{\sum_i \gamma_i \alpha_i}{\sum_i p_i \alpha_i}$$
$$= 1 + \frac{\sum_i (p_i R_i - p_i)\alpha_i}{\sum_i p_i \alpha_i}$$
$$= 1 + \sum_i \frac{p_i \alpha_i}{\sum_i p_i \alpha_i} R_i.$$

It is an average return weighted by the acquisition costs of the securities. The average gain generated by the portfolio is

$$\mu(\alpha) = E(\gamma'\alpha) = m' \text{ diag } p \ \alpha - p' \ \alpha,$$

and the variability of this gain is

$$\eta^2(\alpha) = \alpha' V \gamma \ \alpha = \alpha' \text{ diag } p \ \Sigma \text{ diag } p \ \alpha.$$

Note 7.1. Although the time aspect is not explicit in the preceding notation, it is clearly of a fundamental importance. The acquisition is carried out at date t, and the corresponding gain is relative to a period $[t, t + h]$. If this time index is taken into account, p_i is to be interpreted as the acquisition cost of the security i at date t, and R_i as the return between t and $t + h$. Therefore, we should have written $p_{i,t}$ and $R_{i,t,t+h}$, respectively. Moreover, the mean and variance are evaluated at date t given available information I_t. A more precise but heavier notation would yield the following formulas:

$$m(t, h, I) = E[R_{t,t+h}/I_t] = E_t(R_{t,t+h}),$$
$$\Sigma(t, h, I) = V[R_{t,t+h}/I_t] = V_t(R_{t,t+h}).$$

The results, which we are going to derive, implicitly depend on t, h and I, i.e., on the dates, the trading frequencies and the available information.

Note 7.2. If only two dates are considered, one may always choose the unit of the securities such that $p_{1,i} = 1$. The formulas then simplify considerably. Nevertheless, this normalization is irrelevant if the study is extended over more than two periods because it is feasible for only one date.

Note 7.3. In practice, the means to express acquisition costs and returns depends to a great extent on the securities considered. Indeed, one would have, for instance (with $h = 1$):

- For a risk-free investment such as a savings account:

$$p = 1, \quad R = 1 + i,$$

  where i is the interest rate;

- For a bond:

$$p_t \text{ and } R_t = \frac{p_{t+1} - p_t + C_t}{p_t} + 1,$$

  where p_t and C_t are the market price at t and the coupon of the bond, respectively.

- For a share:

$$p_t \text{ and } R_t = \frac{p_{t+1}/C_t - p_t + d_t + 0.5\,d_t}{p_t} + 1,$$

  where p_t and d_t are the price of the share and the dividend paid, respectively. The term $0.5 d_t$ corresponds to the tax (in the French case), and C_t is the partition coefficient of the security equal to $1/3$ if the security is divided into three new shares.

- For an investment in commodities such as coffee, cocoa, etc.:

$$p_t \text{ and } R_t = \left[p_{t+1} \frac{1}{1 + \delta} - p_t \right] \bigg/ p_t + 1,$$

where p_t is the market price and where the coefficient δ indicates the depreciation rate of the stock.

- For a forward purchase on the currency market:

$$p_t \text{ and } R_t = \frac{q_{t+1} - p_t}{p_t} + 1,$$

where, for instance, p_t is the cost in dollars at date t for the availability of one Deutschmark at date $t + 1$ (forward price) and q_t is the price in dollars of one Deutschmark immediately available (spot price, here the exchange rate).

These examples show that the general approach we are exposing covers a great number of situations that obviously have to be distinguished in concrete applications.

7.1.2   Mean Variance Criterion

Let us consider an institution or an individual who wishes to acquire securities at a global cost c_0. The buyer may retain any portfolio α such that

$$p(\alpha) = p'\alpha = c_0.$$

In order to select a portfolio among those at this cost, suppose that he relies on a criterion exclusively based on the mean $\mu(\alpha)$ and the variability $\eta^2(\alpha)$ of the gain generated by the portfolio. This criterion $v[\mu(\alpha), \eta^2(\alpha)]$ is naturally increasing in μ (preference for high expected return) and decreasing in $\eta^2(\alpha)$ (risk aversion). An optimal or **efficient portfolio** corresponding to this mean variance criterion is a solution of

$$\begin{cases} \max_{\alpha} v[\mu(\alpha), \eta^2(\alpha)], \\ \text{s.t. } p(\alpha) = p'\alpha = c_0. \end{cases} \tag{7.4}$$

Such a maximization may be performed directly or in two steps. Indeed, one may begin by fixing the expected gain at a value m_0 and maximize the objective function submitted to this additional constraint. Then in the first step we minimize the risk under two constraints, one with respect to the mean and the other one to the cost:

$$\begin{cases} \min_{\alpha} \eta^2(\alpha), \\ \text{s.t. } \mu(\alpha) = m_0, \\ p(\alpha) = c_0. \end{cases} \tag{7.5}$$

Solving this first step problem, one derives a portfolio that is a function of m_0, c_0 and is denoted $\tilde{\alpha}(m_0, c_0)$. In order to build an efficient portfolio, the appropriate value of the auxiliary parameter m_0 is to be found in the second step. This is accomplished by optimizing the objective function concentrating out the solution $\hat{m}_0(c_0)$ of the first step problem:

$$\max_{m_0} v(m_0, \eta^2[\tilde{\alpha}(m_0, c_0)]).$$

The optimal portfolio is then defined:

$$\hat{\alpha} = \tilde{\alpha}[\hat{m}_0(c_0), c_0].$$

It is obvious that an alternative two step procedure might be proposed as well. In the first step, one could fix the risk at the level η_0^2 and optimize the expected return s.t. this additional constraint. One would then obtain a portfolio $\tilde{\tilde{\alpha}}(\eta_0^2, c_0)$, which is a function of the level η_0^2. The optimal value would then be found by optimizing

$$\min_{\eta_0^2} v(\mu(\tilde{\tilde{\alpha}}(\eta_0^2, c_0), \eta_0^2).$$

This approach is the dual to the one described in (7.5) and (7.6). We conclude that the portfolio always belongs to the family $[\tilde{\alpha}(m, c_0), m$ varying$]$ or to the family $[\tilde{\tilde{\alpha}}(\eta^2, c_0), \eta^2$ varying$]$. In fact, these two families coincide, and, using the Lagrangian, we see that they also coincide with the set of solutions of

$$\begin{cases} \max_{\alpha} \mu(\alpha) - a\eta^2(\alpha), \\ \text{s.t. } p(\alpha) = p'\alpha = c_0, \end{cases} \tag{7.6}$$

with the varying positive parameter a (a may be interpreted as a Lagrange multiplier). Thus, these two families may both be derived from criteria v linear in the arguments μ and η^2.

Note 7.7. The criterion function $v[\mu(\alpha), \eta^2(\alpha)]$ does not correspond to the usual function retained in the choice theory in an uncertain environment. In this theory, the individual has preferences for portfolios that may be described by means of a utility function: $U(\gamma'\alpha)$. Since this utility level is random, the individual will maximize his expected utility s.t. the cost constraint:

$$\begin{cases} \max_{\alpha} EU(\gamma'\alpha), \\ \text{s.t.: } p'\alpha = c_0. \end{cases}$$

It is not always possible to interpret the mean variance optimization in terms of utility. It happens if $v[\mu(\alpha), \eta^2(\alpha)]$ is an increasing function of $EU(\gamma'\alpha)$ (see exercise 7.1). The problem concerning the optimization of an expected utility is discussed in Appendix 1 of this chapter.

7.1.3   Mean Variance Efficient Portfolios

i) Allocation Without a Risk-Free Security

We begin by determining the efficient portfolios when the variance matrix of the returns Σ is invertible. This condition has a very simple interpretation: saying that Σ is not invertible means that there exists a portfolio α (with cost c different from zero) such that $\alpha'\Sigma\alpha = V(\alpha'R) = 0$. This portfolio is risk-free, i.e., it has a predetermined return. Under the assumption of Σ being invertible, our search for the optimal portfolios is restricted to the linear criterion function. As was previously shown, this yields the family $[\tilde{\alpha}(m_0, c_0),\ m_0\ \text{varying}] = [\tilde{\tilde{\alpha}}(\eta_0^2, c_0),\ c_0\ \text{varying}]$. The problem to be solved is

$$\begin{cases} \underset{\alpha}{\max}\ \mu(\alpha) - a\eta^2(\alpha), \\ \text{s.t. } p(\alpha) = p'\alpha = c_0, \end{cases}$$

$$\Leftrightarrow \begin{cases} \underset{\alpha}{\max}\ m'\operatorname{diag}(p)\alpha - p'\alpha - a\alpha'\operatorname{diag}(p)\Sigma\operatorname{diag}(p)\alpha, \\ \text{s.t. } p(\alpha) = p'\alpha = c_0, \end{cases}$$

$$\Leftrightarrow \begin{cases} \underset{\alpha}{\max}\ m'\operatorname{diag}(p)\alpha - a\alpha'\operatorname{diag}(p)\Sigma\operatorname{diag}(p)\alpha, \\ \text{s.t. } p'\alpha = c_0. \end{cases}$$

Let us introduce the Lagrange multiplier λ associated with the cost constraint. The maximization of the Lagrangian

$$\mathcal{L} = m'\operatorname{diag}(p)\alpha - a\alpha'\operatorname{diag}(p)\Sigma\operatorname{diag}(p)\alpha - \lambda(p'\alpha - c_0),$$

with respect to α, λ, provides the first order conditions

$$\begin{cases} \operatorname{diag}(p)m - \lambda p - 2a\operatorname{diag}(p)\Sigma\operatorname{diag}(p)\alpha = 0, \\ p'\alpha = c_0. \end{cases} \tag{7.8}$$

From the first subsystem, we derive

$$\begin{aligned} \alpha &= \frac{1}{2a}(\operatorname{diag}(p))^{-1}\Sigma^{-1}(\operatorname{diag}(p))^{-1}[\operatorname{diag}(p)m - \lambda p] \\ &= \frac{1}{2a}(\operatorname{diag}(p))^{-1}\Sigma^{-1}m - \frac{\lambda}{2a}(\operatorname{diag}(p))^{-1}\Sigma^{-1}e, \end{aligned}$$

where e denotes the n vector whose components equal 1.
    Including the budget constraint, we find

$$p'\alpha = \frac{1}{2a}e'\Sigma^{-1}m - \frac{\lambda}{2a}e'\Sigma^{-1}e = c_0$$

and the value of the multiplier

$$\lambda = \frac{e'\Sigma^{-1}m - 2ac_0}{e'\Sigma^{-1}e}.$$

Therefore, the solution is

$$\hat{\alpha} = \frac{1}{2a}\left[(\operatorname{diag}(p))^{-1}\Sigma^{-1}m - \frac{e'\Sigma^{-1}m}{e'\Sigma^{-1}e}(\operatorname{diag}(p))^{-1}\Sigma^{-1}e\right]$$

$$+ c_0 \frac{(\mathrm{diag}(p))^{-1} \Sigma^{-1} e}{e' \Sigma^{-1} e},$$

$$
\hat{\alpha} = \frac{1}{2a} (\mathrm{diag}(p))^{-1} \left\{ \Sigma^{-1} m - \frac{e' \Sigma^{-1} m}{e' \Sigma^{-1} e} \Sigma^{-1} e \right\}
$$
$$
+ c_0 (\mathrm{diag}(p))^{-1} \frac{\Sigma^{-1} e}{e' \Sigma^{-1} e}.
$$

(7.9)

ii) Allocation with a Risk-Free Security

Let us now suppose that there exist some risk-free securities. One can easily see that these securities must all yield the same return (see exercise 7.2) and therefore may be considered identical. We denote by 1 the price of the risk-free security and by R_0 its return. We also introduce n other securities with random returns. They have mean m and an invertible variance Σ. Let α_0 denote the amount of the risk-free security in the portfolio and $\alpha = (\alpha_1, \ldots, \alpha_n)'$ the number of shares of the risky securities. The optimization problem becomes

$$
\begin{cases}
\max\limits_{\alpha_0, \alpha} m' \, \mathrm{diag}(p)\alpha + R_0 \, \alpha_0 - a \, \alpha' \, \mathrm{diag}(p) \, \Sigma \, \mathrm{diag}(p)\alpha, \\
\text{s.t.: } \alpha_0 + p'\alpha = c_0.
\end{cases}
$$

This problem may be solved easily for α after substituting out α_0 by the constraint. We deduce that $\alpha_0 = c_0 - p'\alpha$, and, by replacing this in the objective function, we obtain the new problem

$$
\max\limits_{\alpha} R_0 c_0 + (m - R_0 e)' \, \mathrm{diag}(p)\alpha - a\alpha' \, \mathrm{diag}(p) \, \Sigma \, \mathrm{diag}(p)\alpha,
$$

where e denotes a vector of ones.

The first order conditions yield the solution

$$
\hat{\alpha} = \frac{1}{2a} (\mathrm{diag}(p))^{-1} \Sigma^{-1} (m - R_0 e).
$$

(7.10)

The quantity of the risk-free security is then

$$
\hat{\alpha}_0 = c_0 - p\hat{\alpha},
$$

$$
\hat{\alpha}_0 = c_0 - \frac{1}{2a} e' \Sigma^{-1} (m - R_0 e).
$$

(7.11)

Finally, the value of the objective function at the optimum is

$$
U = R_0 c_0 + \frac{1}{2a} (m - R_0 e)' \Sigma^{-1} (m - R_0 e).
$$

It depends on the conditional distribution through the volatility Σ and the difference between the average return and the return of the risk-free security. This quantity is called the **risk premium** since it corresponds to some compensation for the risk. The quadratic form $S = (m - R_0 e)' \Sigma^{-1} (m - R_0 e)$ is called the (Sharpe) **performance of the set of n securities**.

iii) Classification of the Securities

The previous results may be used to establish a ranking of the securities from the most to the least profitable. To do this, we will in a first step consider one of these securities j and build the efficient portfolio from this security and from a risk-free one only. The characteristics of the portfolio vary with the considered security j, and it is in general less efficient than the one built with all of the securities. This partially efficient portfolio leads to an optimal value of the objective function

$$U_j = R_0 c_0 + \frac{1}{2a} \frac{(m_j - R_0)^2}{\sigma_j^2},$$

which is increasing in $\frac{m_j - R_0}{\sigma_j}$ (a being positive and m_j being greater than R_0 because of the risk premium). It is then natural to classify the securities $j = 1, \ldots, n$ by decreasing value of U_j, that is, by decreasing the value of the variation coefficient. This coefficient is called the **Sharpe performance coefficient**. It is worth noting that the purchase price has no influence on this comparison, which only depends on the date and the available information.

7.2   Properties of the Set of Efficient Portfolios

7.2.1   The Set of Efficient Portfolios

Let us consider the case where there are no risk-free securities. We may study the efficient portfolio when the cost c_0 and the criterion, that is, the parameter a, vary. As c_0 and a are positive, we immediately obtain the following result derived from (7.9).

Property 7.12. *When c_0 and a are varying, the set of efficient portfolios is a convex cone generated by the portfolios:*

$$\alpha^* = (\text{diag}(p))^{-1} \left\{ \Sigma^{-1} m - \frac{e' \Sigma^{-1} m}{e' \Sigma^{-1} e} \Sigma^{-1} e \right\},$$

$$\alpha^{**} = (\text{diag}(p))^{-1} \frac{\Sigma^{-1} e}{e' \Sigma^{-1} e}.$$

The properties of these basic portfolios are the following ones.

Property 7.13. *The cost of α^* equals zero, and the cost α^{**} equals 1.*

Proof

We have, for instance,

$$p(\alpha^*) = p'\alpha^* = p'(\text{diag}(p))^{-1}\left\{\Sigma^{-1}m - \frac{e'\Sigma^{-1}m}{e'\Sigma^{-1}e}\Sigma^{-1}e\right\}$$

$$= e'\left\{\Sigma^{-1}m - \frac{e'\Sigma^{-1}m}{e'\Sigma^{-1}e}\Sigma^{-1}e\right\} = 0.$$ Q.E.D.

Thus the basic portfolio α^* may be used in order to modify the expected return and risk without changing the cost. Such a costless portfolio is called an **arbitrage portfolio**. The statistical properties of the two basic portfolios are described as follows.

Property 7.14. *We have*

$$\mu(\alpha^*) = m'\Sigma^{-1}m - \frac{(m'\Sigma^{-1}e)^2}{e'\Sigma^{-1}e},$$

$$\mu(\alpha^{**}) = \frac{m'\Sigma^{-1}e}{e'\Sigma^{-1}e} - 1,$$

$$\eta^2(\alpha^*) = m'\Sigma^{-1}m - \frac{(m'\Sigma^{-1}e)^2}{e'\Sigma^{-1}e},$$

$$\eta^2(\alpha^{**}) = (e'\Sigma^{-1}e)^{-1}.$$

Furthermore, the returns on the two portfolios are uncorrelated.

An efficient portfolio may be written as a combination, $\frac{1}{2a}\alpha^* + c_0\alpha^{**}$. It has a cost c_0, a mean $\frac{1}{2a}\mu(\alpha^*) + c_0\mu(\alpha^{**})$ and a variance

$$\eta^2(\alpha) = \frac{1}{(2a)^2}\eta^2(\alpha^*) + c_0^2\eta^2(\alpha^{**}).$$

For a given cost c_0, the efficient portfolio with minimal variance is $\alpha^{**}c_0$. This basic portfolio is the least risky. Moreover, it helps to understand the results obtained in the case when there exists a risk-free security. The portfolio α^{**} is then naturally replaced by the risk-free security.

Furthermore, given c_0, one may draw the so-called **efficiency frontier**, which provides the expected return of an efficient portfolio as a function of its variance when a varies. This curve has the shape of a semi-parabola (see figures 7.1, 7.2).

When there exists a risk-free security, we see from the optimal composition of the portfolio [see (7.10), (7.11)] that

$$\begin{cases} \mu(\hat{\alpha}_0, \hat{\alpha}) = m'\,\text{diag}(p)\hat{\alpha} - p'\hat{\alpha} + R_0\hat{\alpha}_0 - \hat{\alpha}_0 \\[2mm] \qquad\qquad = (R_0 - 1)c_0 + \frac{1}{2a}(m - R_0e)'\Sigma^{-1}(m - R_0e), \\[2mm] \eta^2(\hat{\alpha}_0, \hat{\alpha}) = \frac{1}{(2a)^2}(m - R_0e)'\Sigma^{-1}(m - R_0e). \end{cases}$$

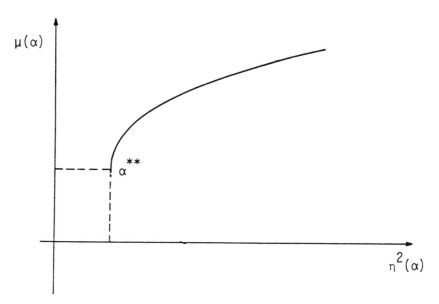

FIGURE 7.1. The efficiency frontier without a risk-free asset.

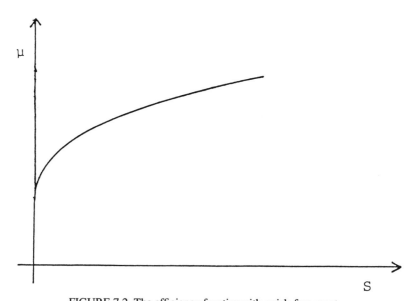

FIGURE 7.2. The efficiency frontier with a risk-free asset.

The efficiency frontier is defined by the implicit equation

$$\mu(\alpha) = (R_0 - 1)c_0 + \eta(\alpha)[(m - R_0 e)'\Sigma^{-1}(m - R_0 e)]^{\frac{1}{2}}$$
$$= (R_0 - 1)c_0 + \eta(\alpha)S^{1/2}.$$

The semi-parabola is tangent to the y axis and increases with the performance S.

7.2.2 Factors

Let us now consider a dynamic framework without risk-free securities. At each date (and without trading cost), the optimal portfolio should in general be updated because, according to (7.9):

$$\hat{\alpha}_t = \frac{1}{2a}(\text{diag}(p_t))^{-1}\left\{\Sigma_t^{-1}m_t - \frac{e'\Sigma_t^{-1}m_t}{e'\Sigma_t^{-1}e}\Sigma_t^{-1}e\right\}$$
$$+ c_0(\text{diag}(p_t))^{-1}\frac{\Sigma_t^{-1}e}{e'\Sigma_t^{-1}e}$$

depends on time. In addition, we see that the basic portfolios α^* and α^{**} also depend on time. Let us suppose that the conditional variance–covariance matrix admits a factorial decomposition

$$\Sigma_t = \sum_{i=1}^{n}\lambda_{it}\beta_i\beta_i', \tag{7.15}$$

where the factors $\beta_i, i = 1, \ldots, n$, constitute a time independent orthonormal basis of $\mathbb{R}^n$. We get

$$\Sigma_t^{-1} = \sum_{i=1}^{n}\frac{1}{\lambda_{it}}\beta_i\beta_i'.$$

One may express the efficient portfolios in terms of the uncorrelated portfolios $\beta_i, i = 1, \ldots, n$:

$$\text{diag}(p_t)\hat{\alpha}_t = \sum_{i=1}^{n}\beta_i\left\{\frac{1}{2a}\frac{1}{\lambda_{it}}\left[\beta_i'm_t - \beta_i'e\frac{\sum_j\beta_j'\,m_t\beta_j'e/\lambda_{jt}}{\sum_j(\beta_j'e)^2/\lambda_{jt}}\right]\right.$$
$$\left. + c_0\frac{1}{\lambda_{it}}\frac{\beta_i'e}{\sum_j(\beta_j'e)^2/\lambda_{jt}}\right\}.$$

Let us consider the case where some factors generate a small risk, that is, where $\lambda_{it} \approx 0$. If these factors are the $n - r$ last ones, $i = r + 1, \ldots, n$, and $\lambda_{it} \approx \lambda_i\lambda_t$, with λ_i tending to 0 for these factors, we have

$$\text{diag}(p_t)\hat{\alpha}_t = \sum_{i=1}^{r}\beta_i\left\{\frac{1}{2a}\frac{1}{\lambda_{it}}\left[\beta_i'm_t - \beta_i'e\frac{\sum_{j=r+1}^{n}\beta_j'm_t\,\beta_j'e/\lambda_j}{\sum_{j=r+1}^{n}(\beta_j'e)^2/\lambda_j}\right]\right\}$$

$$+ \sum_{i=r+1}^{n} \beta_i \left\{ \frac{1}{2a} \frac{1}{\lambda_i \lambda_t} \left[\beta_i' m_t - \beta_i' e \frac{\sum_{j=r+1}^{n} \beta_j' m_t \beta_j' e / \lambda_j}{\sum_{j=r+1}^{n} (\beta_j' e)^2 / \lambda_j} \right] \right.$$

$$\left. + c_0 \frac{1}{\lambda_i} \frac{\beta_i' e}{\sum_{j=r+1}^{n} (\beta_j' e)^2 / \lambda_j} \right\}.$$

Two cases may be distinguished:

i) Let us assume that there are at least two securities $i = r + 1, \ldots, n$ with nonzero limits:

$$\lim_{t \to \infty} \frac{1}{\lambda_i} \left[\beta_i' m_t - \beta_i' e \frac{\sum_{j=r+1}^{n} \beta_j' m_t \, \beta_j' e / \lambda_j}{\sum_{j=r+1}^{n} (\beta_j' e)^2 / \lambda_j} \right] \neq 0;$$

then some components of $\hat{\alpha}_t$ become infinite (implicitly assuming bounded prices). There exist securities that are approximately risk-free and with expected returns significantly different from one another. By arbitraging among these securities, one could reach a theoretically infinite gain (exercise 7.2).

ii) In the other limit case, where all of the asymptotically risk-free securities would have comparable returns,

$$\lim_{t \to \infty} \frac{1}{\lambda_i} \left[\beta_i' m_t - \beta_i' e \frac{\sum_{j=r+1}^{n} \beta_j' m_t \, \beta_j' e / \lambda_j}{\sum_{j=r+1}^{n} (\beta_j' e)^2 / \lambda_j} \right] = 0,$$

$\forall i = r + 1, \ldots, n$, the optimal portfolio becomes

$$\text{diag}(p_t) \hat{\alpha}_t = \sum_{i=1}^{r} \beta_i \left\{ \frac{1}{2a} \frac{1}{\lambda_{it}} \left[\beta_i' m_t - \beta_i' e \frac{\sum_{j=r+1}^{n} \beta_j' m_t \, \beta_j' e / \lambda_j}{\sum_{j=r+1}^{n} (\beta_j' e)^2 / \lambda_j} \right] \right\}$$

$$+ c_0 \sum_{i=r+1}^{n} \frac{\beta_i}{\lambda_i} \frac{\beta_i' e}{\sum_{j=r+1}^{n} (\beta_j' e)^2 / \lambda_j}.$$

It arises as a function of the $r + 1$ basic portfolios $\beta_i, i = 1, \ldots, r$, which are time invariant and of the portfolio

$$\sum_{i=r+1}^{n} \frac{\beta_i}{\lambda_i} \frac{\beta_i' e}{\sum_{j=r+1}^{n} (\beta_j' e)^2 / \lambda_j},$$

which is a combination of the "small risk" basic porfolios $\beta_i, i = r+1, \ldots, n$.

To summarize, if a factor based formulation (for instance, a factor ARCH model; see section 6.4) appears feasible, we need to determine the approximately risk-free portfolios to see if substantial profits may be obtained; in the opposite case, these securities may be replaced by only one, and the optimal portfolio is built by combining this aggregate portfolio and the securities having a significant risk.

7.3   Asymmetric Information and Aggregation

In this section, we study the impact of the available information on the choice of an efficient portfolio. We first have to review the optimization problem that describes the investor's behavior. Indeed, in this problem, the informational content is fixed so that the parameters a and η_0^2 measuring the risk aversion are considered to be constant. When the information changes, at least one of these parameters becomes modified as a function of the information. Indeed, let us assume that the behavior is described by the problem:

$$\begin{cases} \max_{\alpha} \mu(\alpha) = E[\gamma'\alpha/I], \\ \text{s.t.: } V[\gamma'\alpha/I] = \eta_0^2, \\ \qquad p'(\alpha) = c_0, \end{cases}$$

where α is chosen as a function of the information set I and η_0^2 is independent of this information. If $a(I)$ denotes the Lagrange multiplier associated with the first constraint, one obtains the equivalent problem

$$\begin{cases} \max_{\alpha} E[\gamma'\alpha/I] - a(I)\,(V[\gamma'\alpha/I] - \eta_0^2), \\ \text{s.t. } p(\alpha) = c_0, \end{cases}$$

the solution of which, $a(I)$ being known, was explained in section 7.1.

We now give the explicit form of the Lagrange multiplier $a(I)$. Constraining the variance yields

$$\frac{1}{[2a(I)]^2}\eta^2\left[\alpha^*(I)\right] + c_0^2\eta^2\left[\alpha^{**}(I)\right] = \eta_0^2$$

$$\Leftrightarrow [2a(I)]^2 = \frac{\eta^2[\alpha^*(I)]}{\eta_0^2 - c_0^2\eta^2[\alpha^{**}(I)]}.$$

Thus, while η_0^2 is information independent, $a(I)$ generally depends on it. Symmetrically, one may verify (exercise 7.5) that if the optimization problem is

$$\begin{cases} \max_{\alpha} E[\gamma'\alpha/I] - aV[\gamma'\alpha/I], \\ \text{s.t. } p(\alpha) = c_0, \end{cases}$$

with a independent of I, the variance of the optimal portfolio generally depends on the information.

7.3.1   Incoherency of the Mean Variance Approach

Following the previous discussion, we now describe the behavior of individuals facing several available information sets. For this purpose, one has to consider a family of problems indexed by the information, that is, by a family $a(I)$ [or $\eta_0^2(I)$] of parameters. Two constraints may be considered as natural: $a(I)$ independent of

I or $\eta_0^2(I)$ independent of I, resulting in different optimal portfolios as previously shown. These two constraints are not very coherent. As an example, let us consider the family of problems

$$\begin{cases} \max_{\alpha} E[\gamma'\alpha/I], \\ \text{s.t. } V[\gamma'\alpha/I] = \eta_0^2, \\ \qquad p'\alpha = c_0. \end{cases}$$

Suppose that there are two information sets I and J, one being more precise than the other: $J \supset I$. We have $V[\gamma'\alpha/I] = E(V[\gamma'\alpha/J]/I) + V[E(\gamma'\alpha/J)/I]$ by the variance analysis equation. The risk level, when the information is precise (J), increases and hence becomes strictly greater than η_0^2 when the information is I. Thus, contrary to what one may think, fixing η_0^2 independently of the information is equivalent to imposing even less stringent constraints when the information increases. This property is a consequence of the nonvalidity of the law of iterated expectations for the second order moments. A coherent approach may nevertheless be developed, provided that the dynamic behavior is based on an expected utility function (Admati 1985; Rothschild 1986).

7.3.2   Study of the Basic Portfolios

In fact, the previous argument concerns the weights with respect to the basic portfolios α^* and α^{**} but not the portfolios themselves. These portfolios also have compositions and properties depending on the information set I. Thus, we have

$$\begin{cases} \alpha^*(I) = (\text{diag } p)^{-1}\left[\Sigma(I)^{-1}m(I) - \dfrac{e'\Sigma(I)^{-1}m(I)}{e'\Sigma(I)^{-1}e}\Sigma(I)^{-1}e\right], \\ \alpha^{**}(I) = (\text{diag } p)^{-1}\dfrac{\Sigma(I)^{-1}e}{e'\Sigma(I)^{-1}e}, \end{cases}$$

with $m(I) = E[\gamma'\alpha/I]$, $\Sigma(I) = V[\gamma'\alpha/I]$. It is difficult to obtain general results on the evolution of these portfolios when, for instance, the information increases. Therefore, the property below is natural, but valid only s.t. additional assumptions.

Property 7.16. *Let J and I be two information sets, one being more precise than the other, $I \subset J$; if $V[\gamma'\alpha/I]$ and $V[\gamma'\alpha/J]$ are deterministic, then $\alpha^{**}(J)$ is less risky than $\alpha^{**}(I)$.*

Increasing the information allows one to diminish the risk of the less risky portfolio with unit cost.

Proof. We have

$$\begin{aligned} V[\gamma'\alpha/I] &= E(V[\gamma'\alpha/J]/I) + V[E(\gamma'\alpha/J)/I] \\ &\gg E(V[\gamma'\alpha/J]/I) = V(\gamma'\alpha/J). \end{aligned}$$

The risks of $\alpha^{**}(I)$ and $\alpha^{**}(J)$ are, respectively,

$$[e'V(\gamma'\alpha/I)^{-1}e]^{-1} \quad \text{and} \quad [e'V(\gamma'\alpha/J)^{-1}e]^{-1}.$$

From the ordering of the two conditional variance–covariance matrices, one deduces that

$$[e'V(\gamma'\alpha/I)^{-1}e]^{-1} \geq [e'V(\gamma'\alpha/J)^{-1}e]^{-1},$$

which is the aforementioned result.   Q.E.D.

Example 7.17.

In order to illustrate the difficulties in studying the variation of the portfolio as a function of the information, we consider a simple example of a return series (ρ_t), with an autoregressive representation of order 1 based on a standard independent white noise:

$$\rho_t - \bar{\rho} = R[\rho_{t-1} - \bar{\rho}] + \varepsilon_t, \quad E\varepsilon_t = 0, \quad V\varepsilon_t = Id,$$

where R satisfies the usual stability conditions. Let us then examine how the efficient portfolios are composed if the information is $I_h = \rho_{t-h}$. These information sets become more and more precise as h diminishes. We have

$$m_h = E(\rho_t/I_h) = \bar{\rho} + R^h(\rho_{t-h} - \bar{\rho}),$$
$$\Sigma_h = V(\rho_t/I_h) = Id + RR' + \ldots + R^{h-1}R'^{h-1}.$$

The expressions of the basic portfolios α_h^* and α_h^{**} cannot be simplified. In the particular case where the matrices R and R' commute, we have $\Sigma_h = [Id - RR']^{-1}[Id - R^h R'^h]$ and, for instance,

$$\alpha_h^{**} = [\text{diag } p]^{-1} \frac{[Id - RR']^{-1}[Id - R^h R'^h]e}{e[Id - R^h R'^h]^{-1}[Id - RR']e}.$$

7.3.3   Aggregation

Up until now, we have essentially considered the case of a unique individual. We may also examine what the global portfolio of a group of individuals would be if each one behaved independently. The individual i has an available budget c_{i0}, an information set I_i and a risk aversion $a_i(I_i)$, $i = 1, \ldots, n$. Then, the set of n individuals globally asks for a portfolio

$$\hat{\alpha} = \sum_{i=1}^{n} \left\{ \frac{1}{2a_i(I_i)} (\text{diag } p)^{-1} \left\{ \Sigma_i^{-1}m_i - \frac{e'\Sigma_i^{-1}m_i}{e'\Sigma_i^{-1}e} \Sigma_i^{-1}e \right\} \right.$$
$$\left. + c_{0i} (\text{diag } p)^{-1} \frac{\Sigma_i^{-1}e}{e'\Sigma_i^{-1}e} \right\}.$$

A priori, as soon as there is individual heterogeneity, the portfolio that is globally in demand is not a function of only two underlying basic portfolios but rather of $2n$ portfolios. It is worth providing additional conditions that would allow us to find again a small number of underlying portfolios.

Let us suppose that the several individuals have common information, for instance, the past prices $\underline{p_t}$, and specific information sets $J_i : I_i = [\underline{p_t}, J_i]$. A number of basic portfolios equal to two would obviously be found again if the distribution of the return R_{t+1} given $[p_t, J_i]$ were the same as the distribution of R_{t+1} given $[p_t]$, that is, if all of the information that is useful to forecast the return were contained in the sequence of the past prices. It is a strong condition of market efficiency that especially implies an autonomous price fixation, that is, without effect of the exogenous shocks of the real economy. However, it is interesting to consider such an assumption. If it is satisfied, we have

$$\hat{\alpha} = \sum_{i=1}^{n} \frac{1}{2a_i(I_i)} (\operatorname{diag} p)^{-1} \left\{ \Sigma^{-1} m - \frac{e' \Sigma^{-1} m}{e' \Sigma^{-1} e} \Sigma^{-1} e \right\}$$
$$+ \sum_{i=1}^{n} c_{0i} (\operatorname{diag} p)^{-1} \frac{\Sigma^{-1} e}{e' \Sigma^{-1} e},$$

with $\Sigma = V(R_{t+1}/p_t)$ and $m = E(R_{t+1}/p_t)$.

The set of the $2n$ individuals may then be reduced to only one individual having a mean variance behavior with an information (p_t) (or I_i), an available budget $\sum_{i=1}^{n} c_{0i}$ and a risk coefficient $a = \left[\sum_{i=1}^{n} \frac{1}{a_i(I_i)} \right]^{-1}$ equal to the harmonic mean of the individual risk coefficients.

7.4 Hedging Portfolios

In the preceding sections, we explained how to select portfolios according to the mean variance criterion s.t. constraint. In practice, other criteria and constraints may be retained.

For instance, one may want to build a portfolio using a small number of given securities with returns close to the evolution of interest. This problem appears in different contexts, three examples of which are provided below.

i) Some developing countries are facing important repayment charges of their foreign debt. This debt is subscribed in several currencies: Dollars, Yen, Deutschmarks, etc., which may vary with respect to one another in quite different ways. It is obvious that the repartition of the debt between the several currencies has to be managed in order to hedge against exchange rate risks. Since this debt is mainly repaid with the commercial surplus, it may appear natural to choose the repartition of the debt among the basic currencies so that the charge of repayment is as close as possible to a given part of the commercial surplus.

ii) Some financial institutions desire to offer managed portfolios that allow them to replicate general price indices [Standard & Poor's, CAC 40 (the French market index), etc.] and even to go a little beyond this index without much additional risk.

iii) On the commodity markets such as metals, coffee, corn, etc., one often considers the possibility of using calls or puts; the idea is to allow the firms to hedge against speculative variations of the price. It may be interesting to examine how the option and the risk-free security permit reconstitution of the return of the support security that bears the option.

In other practical questions, the constraint more than the criterion will be modified. For instance, a producer will try to make sure that he gets the quantities of the commodities that he needs in every period, programming at the best his purchases of goods over time. These transactions may be accomplished on the spot or future market, or by buying options. The budget constraint here is replaced by a constraint of available quantities date by date.

These different questions have a common characteristic: they all have to be solved while avoiding large risk (at least in a first approach).

7.4.1 Determination of a Portfolio Mimicking a Series of Interest

We use the same notation as before for the securities used to build the portfolio and for the portfolio itself. The series of interest is (Z_t), and its evolution is measured by: $\frac{Z_{t+1}}{Z_t} = 1 + \frac{Z_{t+1} - Z_t}{Z_t}$. The portfolio is chosen in order to have a gross return as close as possible to $\frac{Z_{t+1}}{Z_t}$. The problem is defined up to a scale factor so that it is possible to constrain the desired portfolio to have a unit cost without loss of generality. The portfolio is then defined as a solution of

$$
\begin{cases}
\min_{\alpha} E_t \left[\sum_{i=1}^{n} \alpha_i \, p_{i,t} \, R_{i,t+1} - Z_{t+1}/Z_t \right]^2 \\
\text{s.t. } \sum_{i=1}^{n} \alpha_i \, p_{i,t} = 1.
\end{cases}
\tag{7.18}
$$

Let us consider the form of the solution if there is a risk-free security with a known gross return $R_{0,t+1}$. As in the previous section, this risk-free security is added to the list of the n risky securities so that the problem becomes

$$
\begin{cases}
\min_{\alpha} E_t \left[\alpha_0 R_{0,t+1} + \sum_{i=1}^{n} \alpha_i \, p_{i,t} \, R_{i,t+1} - Z_{t+1}/Z_t \right]^2 \\
\text{s.t. } \alpha_0 + \sum_{i=1}^{n} \alpha_i \, p_{i,t} = 1.
\end{cases}
$$

Replacing α_0 by its expression deduced from the budget constraint yields the optimization problem

$$
\min_{\alpha_1,\ldots,\alpha_n} E_t \left[\sum_{i=1}^{n} \alpha_i \, p_{i,t+1}(R_{i,t+1} - R_{0,t+1}) - (Z_{t+1}/Z_t - R_{0,t+1}) \right]^2,
$$

which depends only on the differences between the returns on risky assets and the return on the risk-free security. The solution of this problem is known from the linear regression theory.

Let us write $p_t = (p_{1,t}, \ldots, p_{n,t})'$, $R_{t+1} = (R_{1,t+1}, \ldots, R_{n,t+1})'$; the solution is

$$
\begin{aligned}
\text{diag}[p_t]\hat{\alpha} = {} & [E_t(R_{t+1} - R_{0,t+1}e)(R_{t+1} - R_{0,t+1}e)']^{-1} \\
& \left[E_t(R_{t+1} - R_{0,t+1}e)\left(\frac{Z_{t+1}}{Z_t} - R_{0,t+1}\right)'\right].
\end{aligned}
\tag{7.19}
$$

It may be expressed as a function of the expected returns and the volatility of the returns.

$$
\begin{aligned}
\text{diag}[p_t]\hat{\alpha} = {} & [\Sigma_t + (m_t - R_{0,t+1}e)(m_t - R_{0,t+1}e)']^{-1} \\
& \{\text{Cov}_t(R_{t+1}, Z_{t+1}/Z_t) \\
& + (m_t - R_{0,t+1}e)[E_t(Z_{t+1}/Z_t) - R_{0,t+1}]\}.
\end{aligned}
\tag{7.20}
$$

7.4.2 A Model for the Call Seller Behavior

i) Description of the Behavior

The agents trading on the options market show a variety of behaviors. They want to secure options either to hedge against large risks (case of the firm) or to build efficient portfolios. They are faced with suppliers who may either be individuals having secured options in preceding periods and putting them on the market or specialists whose business is to put such options in the market. The latter ones, called "**market-makers**", are generally considered as traders taking a fixed margin of profit for each operation, without speculative behavior.

In this subsection, we describe the behavior of these agents. For notational convenience, we consider a call brought on the market at date t, with an exercise date $t + 1$.

This market-maker sells options at a price C_t, which he has to choose as the best. We are discussing his choice procedure. Let us suppose that he writes an option with strike K_t and finds a buyer. He then receives a sum C_t, which may be used to build a hedging portfolio. We consider the case where this portfolio is formed using the risk-free security (quantity α_0) and the underlying security (quantity α_1). The risk-free security costs 1 at date t and pays $R_{0,t}$ at the following date. The risky security costs S_t at t and pays S_{t+1} at date $t + 1$. The portfolio is such that

$$
\alpha_0 + \alpha_1 S_t = C_t.
\tag{7.21}
$$

At the following date, the value of the portfolio is

$$
\alpha_0 R_{0,t} + \alpha_1 S_{t+1}.
$$

Two cases may be distinguished:

(*) If the price of the security is lower than the strike $S_{t+1} < K_t$, the owner does not exercise the option and the profit of our agent is

$$G_{t+1} = \alpha_0 R_{0,t} + \alpha_1 S_{t+1} = C_t R_{0,t} + \alpha_1 (S_{t+1} - R_{0,t} S_t).$$

(**) If the price of the underlying security is larger than the strike, the owner exercises the option, and the gain of our agent is

$$\begin{aligned} G_{t+1} &= \alpha_0 R_{0,t} + \alpha_1 S_{t+1} - (S_{t+1} - K_t) \\ &= C_t R_{0,t} + \alpha_1 (S_{t+1} - R_{0,t} S_t) - (S_{t+1} - K_t). \end{aligned}$$

Thus, the gain is

$$G_{t+1} = C_t R_{0,t} + \alpha_1 (S_{t+1} - R_{0,t} S_t) - (S_{t+1} - K_t) \mathbb{I}_{S_{t+1} > K_t}. \tag{7.22}$$

This gain is random, and our risk-averse agent may try to approach as close as possible an a priori given benefit G_0. He may select the hedging portfolio and the selling price in order to minimize

$$\min_{\alpha_1, C_t} E_t (G_{t+1} - G_0)^2. \tag{7.23}$$

ii) Solutions of the Optimization Problem

The problem may be written as

$$\min_{\alpha_1, C_t} E_t (C_t R_{0,t} - G_0 + \alpha_1 (S_{t+1} - R_{0,t} S_t) - (S_{t+1} - K_t) . \mathbb{I}_{S_{t+1} > K_t})^2.$$

Its solutions $\hat{\alpha}_1$ and $\hat{C}_t$ are

$$\begin{cases} \hat{\alpha}_1 = \dfrac{\text{Cov}_t \left(S_{t+1} - R_{0,t} S_t, (S_{t+1} - K_t) \mathbb{I}_{S_{t+1} > K_t} \right)}{V_t \left(S_{t+1} - R_{0,t} S_t \right)}, \\[2ex] C_t R_{0,t} + \hat{\alpha}_1 E_t (S_{t+1} - R_{0,t} S_t) - E_t \left((S_{t+1} - K_t) \mathbb{I}_{S_{t+1} > K_t} \right) = G_0. \end{cases} \tag{7.24}$$

Note that we encounter here a classical least squares regression. Applying the Frisch–Waugh theorem, we see that the agent will proceed in two steps:

(*) First, search for $\hat{\alpha}_1$ to minimize the risk:

$$\min_{\alpha_1} V_t (G_{t+1} - G_0) = V_t (\alpha_1 (S_{t+1} - R_{0,t} S_t) - (S_{t+1} - K_t) \mathbb{I}_{S_{t+1} > K_t}).$$

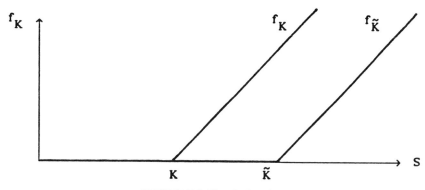

FIGURE 7.3. The f_K function.

(**) Then fix the option price so that the average profit associated with the choice of $\hat{\alpha}_1$ coincides with G_0.

The expression of $\hat{\alpha}_1$ may be rewritten in an alternative way. Indeed, we have

$$\text{Cov}_t(S_{t+1} - R_{0,t} S_t, (S_{t+1} - K_t).\mathbb{I}_{S_{t+1} > K_t})$$
$$= \text{Cov}_t(S_{t+1} - K_t, (S_{t+1} - K_t)\mathbb{I}_{S_{t+1} > K_t})$$
$$= E_t\left((S_{t+1} - K_t)^2 \mathbb{I}_{S_{t+1} > K_t}\right) - E_t(S_{t+1} - K_t) E_t\left((S_{t+1} - K_t)\mathbb{I}_{S_{t+1} > K_t}\right)$$
$$= E_t(\text{Max}(S_{t+1} - K_t, 0)^2) - E_t(S_{t+1} - K_t) E_t(\text{Max}(S_{t+1} - K_t), 0)).$$

Then, the regression coefficient is

$$\hat{\alpha}_1 = \frac{E_t(\text{Max}(S_{t+1} - K_t, 0)^2) - E_t(S_{t+1} - K_t) E_t(\text{Max}(S_{t+1} - K_t, 0))}{V_t(S_{t+1} - R_{0,t} S_t)}.$$

iii) $\hat{\alpha}_1$ and C_t as Functions of the Strike

Let us consider the function $f_K : S \to \text{Max}(S - K, 0)$. This function is piecewise linear and decreases with the value of K (see figure 7.3).

The difference between two such functions $f_K - f_{\tilde{K}}$, with $K < \tilde{K}$, is

$$f_K(S) - f_{\tilde{K}}(S) = \begin{cases} 0, & \text{if } S \leq K, \\ S - K, & \text{if } K \leq S \leq \tilde{K}, \\ \tilde{K} - K, & \text{if } \tilde{K} \leq S, \end{cases}$$

and the plots of figure 7.4 reveal its pattern. It is an increasing function of S. In particular, we deduce that, for $\tilde{K} \geq K$,

$$\text{Cov}_t(S_{t+1}, \text{Max}(S_{t+1} - K, 0) - \text{Max}(S_{t+1} - \tilde{K}, 0)) \geq 0,$$
$$\text{Cov}_t\left(S_{t+1}, \text{Max}(S_{t+1} - K, 0)\right) \geq \text{Cov}_t\left(S_{t+1}, \text{Max}(S_{t+1} - \tilde{K}, 0)\right).$$

This inequality may also be applied directly to the coefficient $\hat{\alpha}_1$.

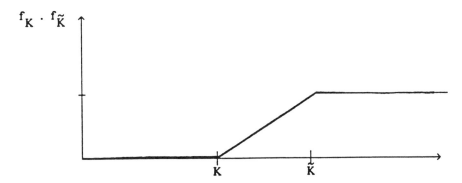

FIGURE 7.4. Difference between f_K and $f_{\tilde{K}}$.

Property 7.25. *The coefficient $\hat{\alpha}_1(K)$ is a decreasing function of K. For the limiting values of the strike, it equals*

$$\hat{\alpha}_1(+\infty) = \frac{\mathrm{Cov}_t(S_{t+1}, 0)}{V_t S_{t+1}} = 0,$$

$$\hat{\alpha}_1(0) = \frac{\mathrm{Cov}_t(S_{t+1}, S_{t+1})}{V_t S_{t+1}} = 1.$$

Thus, the greater the strike, the less frequently the option is exercised, and in consequence the agent is less willing to hedge against the risk by buying the underlying security. The option price also depends on K_t. Namely,

$$C_t(K_t) = \frac{1}{R_{0,t}} \left\{ G_0 - \hat{\alpha}_1(K_t) E_t(S_{t+1} - R_{0,t} S_t) + E_t \left((S_{t+1} - K_t) \mathbb{I}_{S_{t+1} > K_t} \right) \right\}.$$

The option price is determined by the price of the underlying asset and the strike, and it evolves according to the relationship between these two variables. Indeed, $-\hat{\alpha}_1(K_t) E_t(S_{t+1} - R_{0,t} S_t)$ is an increasing function of the strike (because $E_t S_{t+1} > R_{0,t} S_t$, due to the risk premium), and $E_t \left((S_{t+1} - K_t) \mathbb{I}_{S_{t+1} > K_t} \right)$ is a decreasing function of K_t. The first limiting value of the option is

$$C_t(+\infty) = \frac{1}{R_{0,t}} [G_0].$$

(In this limit case, there is no risk because it is known with certainty that the option will not be exercised.) The second case can be summarized as

$$C_t(0) = \frac{1}{R_{0,t}} [G_0 + E_t(R_{0,t} S_t)] = \frac{G_0}{R_{0,t}} + S_t.$$

(In that case, it is certain that the option will be exercised, and one hedges with certainty at a cost S_t augmented by the fix costs.)

iv) A Log-Normal Asset Price Example

Let us consider the particular case where the conditional distribution of $\log[S_{t+1}/(R_{0,t}S_t)]$ is normal with mean a_t and variance σ_t^2. We may wish to evaluate the moments appearing in the formulas yielding $\hat{\alpha}_1$ and C_t. We have (see Appendix 2)

$$E_t S_{t+1} = R_{0,t} S_t \exp(a_t) \exp(\sigma_t^2/2),$$
$$V_t S_{t+1} = R_{0,t}^2 S_t^2 \exp(2a_t) \exp \sigma_t^2 (\exp \sigma_t^2 - 1),$$
$$E_t \operatorname{Max}(S_{t+1} - K, 0) = R_{0,t} S_t \exp(a_t) \exp(\sigma_t^2/2) \Phi(-\tilde{u}_t + \sigma_t) - K_t \Phi(-\tilde{u}_t),$$

where $\tilde{u}_t = \frac{1}{\sigma_t}[\log[K_t/(R_{0,t}S_t)] - a_t]$, and Φ denotes the cumulative distribution function of the standard normal distribution. Finally, the second order moment of the call price at $t+1$ is

$$
\begin{aligned}
&E_t[\operatorname{Max}(S_{t+1} - K, 0)]^2 \\
&= R_{0,t}^2 S_t^2 \exp(2a_t + 2\sigma_t^2) \Phi(-\tilde{u}_t + 2\sigma_t) \\
&\quad - 2K_t R_{0,t} S_t \exp(a_t + \sigma_t^2/2) \Phi(-\tilde{u}_t + \sigma_t) + K_t^2 \Phi(-\tilde{u}_t).
\end{aligned}
$$

We deduce

$$
\begin{aligned}
&\operatorname{Cov}_t(S_{t+1} - R_{0,t} S_t, (S_{t+1} - K_t)\mathbb{I}_{S_{t+1} > K_t}) \\
&= E_t(\operatorname{Max}(S_{t+1} - K_t, 0)^2) - E_t(S_{t+1} - K_t) E_t(\operatorname{Max}(S_{t+1} - K_t, 0)) \\
&= R_{0,t}^2 S_t^2 \exp(2a_t + 2\sigma_t^2) \Phi(-\tilde{u}_t + 2\sigma_t) \\
&\quad - 2K_t R_{0,t} S_t \exp(a_t + \sigma_t^2/2) \Phi(-\tilde{u}_t + \sigma_t) - K_t^2 \Phi(-\tilde{u}_t) \\
&\quad - [R_{0,t} S_t \exp(a_t) \exp(\sigma_t^2/2) - K_t] \\
&\quad\quad [R_{0,t} S_t \exp(a_t) \exp(\sigma_t^2/2) \Phi(-\tilde{u}_t + \sigma_t) - K_t \Phi(-\tilde{u}_t)] \\
&= R_{0,t}^2 S_t^2 \exp(2a_t + 2\sigma_t^2) \Phi(-\tilde{u}_t + 2\sigma_t) \\
&\quad - [K_t R_{0,t} S_t \exp(a_t) \exp(\sigma_t^2/2) \\
&\quad + R_{0,t}^2 S_t^2 \exp(2a_t + \sigma_t^2)] \Phi(-\tilde{u}_t + \sigma_t) + K_t R_{0,t} S_t \exp(a_t + \sigma_t^2/2) \Phi(-\tilde{u}_t)].
\end{aligned}
$$

The regression coefficient is then

$$
\hat{\alpha}_1 = \frac{1}{\exp \sigma_t^2 - 1} \{\exp \sigma_t^2 \Phi(-\tilde{u}_t + 2\sigma_t) - [L_t + 1]\Phi(-\tilde{u}_t + \sigma_t) + L_t \Phi(-\tilde{u}_t)\},
$$

with

$$
\begin{aligned}
L_t &= K_t[R_{0,t} S_t \exp(a_t + \sigma_t^2/2)]^{-1} \\
&= K_t/E_t(S_{t+1}), \\
\tilde{u}_t &= \frac{1}{\sigma_t} \log L_t + \frac{\sigma_t}{2}.
\end{aligned}
$$

7.4.3 The Firm Behavior

i) The Model

Let us now consider the same type of market as in the preceding section with one asset traded (a commodity like corn, for example), one option with a unitary maturity written on this asset, and a risk-free asset. We suppose that the firm has to possess a given quantity of the commodity at date $t + 1$. By convention, this quantity is fixed to one. In order to obtain this quantity, it may buy some good at date t at price S_t and keep it until the following date; otherwise, buy options or simply keep the money and buy the commodity at date $t + 1$ on the market.

Let a denote the immediate quantity of the commodity purchased at a total cost of $a S_t$ and b the quantity of options acquired at a total cost $b C_t$. The total cost of these operations evaluated at date $t + 1$ is

$$a R_{0,t} S_t + b R_{0,t} C_t.$$

At date $t + 1$, the value of the portfolio built is

$$a S_{t+1} + b \operatorname{Max}(S_{t+1} - K_t, 0)$$

and is exchanged against one unit of the commodity for the sum S_{t+1}. In summary, the purchase cost of a unit of corn discounted at date $t + 1$ is

$$Q_{t+1} = S_{t+1} + b R_{0,t} C_t + a R_{0,t} S_t - a S_{t+1} - b \operatorname{Max}(S_{t+1} - K_t, 0).$$

$$(7.26)$$

ii) Portfolio Determination

According to the mean variance approach, the firm will hold a portfolio that minimizes

$$\min_{a,b} E_t Q_{t+1} + \alpha V_t Q_{t+1}, \qquad (7.27)$$

where the positive parameter α is a risk-aversion measure. We have

$$E_t Q_{t+1} = b R_{0,t} C_t - b E_t \operatorname{Max}(S_{t+1} - K_t, 0) + a R_{0,t} S_t + (1 - a) E_t S_{t+1},$$
$$V_t Q_{t+1} = (1 - a)^2 V_t S_{t+1} + b^2 V_t \operatorname{Max}(S_{t+1} - K_t, 0)$$
$$- 2b(1 - a) \operatorname{Cov}_t[S_{t+1}, \operatorname{Max}(S_{t+1} - K_t, 0)].$$

The solution of this optimization problem yields the coefficients a and b such that

$$\begin{bmatrix} b \\ a - 1 \end{bmatrix} = \frac{1}{2\alpha} \frac{1}{V_t(S_{t+1})V_t \operatorname{Max} - \operatorname{Cov}_t(S_{t+1}, \operatorname{Max})} \times \begin{bmatrix} V_t(S_{t+1}) & \operatorname{Cov}_t(S_{t+1}, \operatorname{Max}) \\ \operatorname{Cov}_t(S_{t+1}, \operatorname{Max}) & V_t \operatorname{Max} \end{bmatrix} \begin{bmatrix} E_t \operatorname{Max} - R_{0,t} C_t \\ E_t S_{t+1} - R_{0,t} S_t \end{bmatrix}$$

$$(7.28)$$

where Max denotes $\text{Max}(S_{t-1} - K_t, 0)$. A totally risk-averse firm will buy the whole quantity of the commodity at date t. In formula (7.28), this occurs when $\alpha = \infty$, and we find $b = 0, a = 1$.

7.5   Empirical Study of Performance Measures

7.5.1   Performances of a Set of Assets

Let us consider the case where, in addition to the n basic risky assets, a risk-free asset exists. The optimal portfolio allocations are [see (7.10), (7.11)]

$$\hat{\alpha}_{0t} = c_0 - p_t'\hat{\alpha}_t, \quad \hat{\alpha}_t = \frac{1}{2a}(\text{diag } p_t)^{-1}\Sigma_t^{-1}(m_t - R_{0,t}e),$$

depending explicitly on time. The optimal value of the mean variance criterion function is

$$u_t = R_{0,t}c_0 + \frac{1}{2a}(m_t - R_{0,t}e)'\Sigma_t^{-1}(m_t - R_{0,t}e).$$

It is an increasing function of the quantity

$$S_t = (m_t - R_{0,t}e)'\Sigma_t^{-1}(m_t - R_{0,t}e). \tag{7.29}$$

This arises as a natural generalization of Sharpe's performance measure to the n assets case.

Definition 7.30. *The quantity*

$$S_t = (m_t - R_{0,t}e)'\Sigma_t^{-1}(m_t - R_{0,t}e)$$

is called Sharpe's performance measure.

In practice, it is important to estimate this measure for each successive date. This estimation is easily performed if a dynamic ARCH model is fitted to the returns (or to the logarithms of the price) and estimated. If the model is defined by

$$\begin{cases} E(R_{t+1}/I_t) = m_t(\theta), \\ V(R_{t+1}/I_t) = H_t(\theta), \end{cases}$$

and if $\hat{\theta}$ denotes a consistent estimator of θ, the estimated performance measure is

$$\hat{S}_t = (m_t(\hat{\theta}) - R_{0,t}e)'H_t(\hat{\theta})^{-1}(m_t(\hat{\theta}) - R_{0,t}e). \tag{7.31}$$

These estimations are useful for comparing the respective performances of two groups of assets. One will then be willing to evaluate the performances of each of the groups with respect to the *same information set* I_t, for instance, the one consisting of the observations on the prices of assets that appear in the two groups.

7.5.2 Improving the Efficiency

In order to find profit making portfolios, it is often useful to apply a sequential approach. For instance, we begin by comparing the individual returns on some assets and retaining the best one within the portfolio. In the second step, we add the one that results in the greatest profit increase, etc. Such a procedure does not necessarily lead to an optimal portfolio, but it often yields satisfactory results.

In order to understand the sequential approach, we have to study how the performance varies if the set of considered assets is enlarged. Therefore, let us consider two disjoint groups of assets. The expected returns are denoted $\begin{pmatrix} m_{1t} \\ m_{2t} \end{pmatrix}$ and the volatilities and covolatilities by

$$\begin{pmatrix} \Sigma_{11t} & \Sigma_{12t} \\ \Sigma_{21t} & \Sigma_{22t} \end{pmatrix}.$$

The performance of the first group of assets is

$$S_{1t} = (m_{1t} - R_{0,t}e_1)'\Sigma_{11t}^{-1}(m_{1t} - R_{0,t}e_1),$$

where e_1 denotes the vector of ones of length equal to the number of assets in the first group. The performance of the entire set consisting of the two groups is

$$S_{1,2t} = \begin{pmatrix} m_{1t} - R_{0,t}e_1 \\ m_{2t} - R_{0,t}e_2 \end{pmatrix}' \begin{pmatrix} \Sigma_{11t} & \Sigma_{12t} \\ \Sigma_{21t} & \Sigma_{22t} \end{pmatrix}^{-1} \begin{pmatrix} m_{1t} - R_{0,t}e_1 \\ m_{2t} - R_{0,t}e_2 \end{pmatrix}.$$

Property 7.32. *The performance gain due to the addition to the first group of the assets of the second group is*

$$S_{1,2t} - S_{1t} = \left\{ m_{2t} - R_{0,t}e_2 - \Sigma_{21t}\Sigma_{11t}^{-1}(m_{1t} - R_{0,t}e_1) \right\}'$$

$$[\Sigma_{22t} - \Sigma_{21t}\Sigma_{11t}^{-1}\Sigma_{12t}]^{-1} \left\{ m_{2t} - R_{0,t}e_2 - \Sigma_{21t}\Sigma_{11t}^{-1}(m_{1t} - R_{0,t}e_1) \right\}.$$

Proof. See exercise 7.9.

In particular, it is useless to add the second subgroup to the first one to build an optimal portfolio iff

$$\{m_{2t} - R_{0,t}e_2 - \Sigma_{21t}\Sigma_{11t}^{-1}(m_{1t} - R_{0,t}e_1)\} = 0. \tag{7.33}$$

This constraint may obviously be tested empirically. We do not discuss these tests here since they are described in detail in section 8.2.

7.5.3 Estimation of the Efficient Portfolio and its Performance in the Static Case

In order to illustrate the practical use of the notions of efficient portfolio and performance, we present estimation and tests in a static framework, that is, of independent identically distributed (i.i.d.) returns. The more general case taking into account the dynamic aspects of a return series is discussed in section 8.

i) Allocation of the Efficient Portfolio

We know [see (7.10)] that the allocation of the efficient portfolio is

$$\alpha = \Sigma^{-1}(m - R_0 e),$$

where m and Σ are the mean and variance of the returns. If we have observations on the returns $R_1, \ldots, R_T$ for several dates, we may compute the empirical mean of the returns:

$$\hat{m}_T = \frac{1}{T} \sum_{t=1}^{T} R_t,$$

and their empirical variance

$$\hat{\Sigma}_T = \frac{1}{T} \sum_{t=1}^{T} (R_t - \hat{m}_T)(R_t - \hat{m}_T)'.$$

The allocation of the efficient portfolio is then naturally estimated by

$$\hat{\alpha}_T = \hat{\Sigma}_T^{-1}[\hat{m}_T - R_0 e]. \qquad (7.34)$$

The asymptotic properties of this estimator are stated below and derived in Appendix 3.

Property 7.35. *Under the assumption of i.i.d. returns, the estimated allocation is consistent, asymptotically normal:*

$$\sqrt{T}(\hat{\alpha}_T - \alpha) \xrightarrow{d} N(0, \Omega),$$
$$\text{with } \Omega = \Sigma^{-1}(1 + S)\Sigma^{-1}(m - R_0 e)(m - R_0 e)'\Sigma^{-1}$$
$$= \Sigma^{-1}(1 + S) + \alpha\alpha',$$

where $S = (m - R_0 e)'\Sigma^{-1}(m - R_0 e)$ is the Sharpe performance measure of the set of assets.

ii) Estimation of the Performance

Similarly, we may consider the estimation of the performance S by

$$\hat{S}_T = (\hat{m}_T - R_0 e)' \hat{\Sigma}_T^{-1}(\hat{m}_T - R_0 e) \qquad (7.36)$$
$$= \hat{\alpha}_T' \hat{\Sigma}_T^{-1} \hat{\alpha}_T.$$

The asymptotic properties of this estimator are described below and proven in Appendix 3.

Property 7.37. *Under the assumption of i.i.d. returns:*

$$\sqrt{T}(\hat{S}_T - S) \xrightarrow{d} N[0, 2S(2 + S)].$$

Thus, the asymptotic properties of the estimated performance depend only on the performance itself. The relative error committed in this evaluation, which is twice the standard error divided by the quantity to be estimated, equals

$$e_R = \frac{2\sqrt{2S(2+S)}}{S\sqrt{T}}$$

$$= \frac{4}{\sqrt{T}}\sqrt{1 + \frac{1}{2S}}.$$

It is always greater than $\frac{4}{\sqrt{T}}$.

iii) Comparison of Performances

The preceding result may be easily generalized to two subsets of assets derived from the set of initial assets. We will use a group $j = 1, 2$, and, following the same notations as above, we write the estimated performances of these two groups

$$\hat{S}_{jT} = (\hat{m}_{jT} - R_0 e_j)' \hat{\Sigma}_{jT}^{-1} (\hat{m}_{jT} - R_0 e_j),$$

where $\hat{m}_{jT}$ denotes the returns on the assets of group j. The analog of property 7.37, whose proof is left as an exercise, is

Property 7.38. *Under the assumption of i.i.d. returns:*

$$\sqrt{T}\left(\begin{array}{c} \hat{S}_{1T} - S_1 \\ \hat{S}_{2T} - S_2 \end{array} \right) \xrightarrow{d} N[0, \left[\begin{array}{cc} 2S_1(2+S_1) & 2S_{12}(2+S_{12}) \\ 2S_{12}(2+S_{12}) & 2S_2(2+S_2) \end{array} \right]],$$

with

$$S_{12} = (m_1 - R_0 e_1)' \Sigma_{11}^{-1} \Sigma_{12} \Sigma_{22}^{-1} (m_2 - R_0 e_2)$$
$$= \alpha_1' \Sigma_{12} \alpha_2,$$

where Σ_{12} denotes the covariances between the unitary returns of the assets of the first and second groups.

This property may be used for testing if two subsets of assets have the same performance (and alternatively, to classify the set of assets by their decreasing performance). Let us consider the hypothesis of equal performances:

$$H_0 = \{S_1 = S_2\}.$$

A statistic to test the hypothesis H_0 may be based on the difference between the two estimated performances:

$$\hat{S}_{1T} - \hat{S}_{2T} \approx N\left[S_1 - S_2; \frac{1}{T}[2S_1(2+S_1) + 2S_2(2+S_2) - 4S_{12}(2+S_{12})] \right].$$

Dividing this difference by the estimated standard error, we obtain the following test statistic:

$$\xi = \frac{T(\hat{S}_{1T} - \hat{S}_{2T})^2}{2\hat{S}_{1T}(2 + \hat{S}_{1T}) + 2\hat{S}_{2T}(2 + \hat{S}_{2T}) - 4\hat{S}_{12T}(2 + \hat{S}_{12T})}. \tag{7.39}$$

Property 7.40. *If the asymptotic variance $V_{as}[\sqrt{T}(\hat{S}_{1T} - \hat{S}_{2T})]$ is different from zero, the statistic ξ asymptotically follows a chi-square distribution with one degree of freedom under the null hypothesis. Let us denote by $\chi^2_{95\%}$ the 95% quantile of this distribution. The test consists in*

- *rejecting the equality if $\xi > \chi^2_{95\%}$,*

- *accepting the equality otherwise.*

It is useful to note that there exist interesting cases where the asymptotic variance $V_{as}[\sqrt{T}(\hat{S}_{1T} - \hat{S}_{2T})]$ equals zero under the null hypothesis H_0. In such a case, the preceding test cannot be applied. Let us assume that the efficient portfolio built using the two subgroups of assets includes only assets of the first group. We then know that the constraint (7.33) is satisfied:

$$m_2 - R_0 e_2 - \Sigma_{21} \Sigma_{11}^{-1}(m_1 - R_0 e_1) = 0.$$

Multiplying the left side by $(m_2 - R_0 e_2)' \Sigma_{22}^{-1}$, we deduce that

$$S_{21} = S_2.$$

Under the null hypothesis $S_{12} = S_2 = S_1$, the asymptotic variance $V_{as}[\sqrt{T}(\hat{S}_{1T} - \hat{S}_{2T})]$ is zero. Therefore, the last test is relevant only if none of the two subgroups is efficient. The case of efficiency of one of the subgroups is studied in detail in chapter 8.

Appendix 1: Presentation in Terms of Utility

1. Selection of an Efficient Portfolio

The choice of the investor may be studied in the usual framework of consumer theory where the individual chooses the consumption pattern by optimizing his or her utility s.t. the budget constraint. In this appendix, we suppose that the utility is only a function of the profit associated with the portfolio chosen and that, in an uncertain environment, the consumer maximizes the expectation of the utility at the next date. In this approach, the utility has a cardinal aspect, the problem being invariant in the case of an increasing *linear* transformation of the utility. In addition, the dynamic is limited since the expectation is not extended over the entire life of the investor; rather, the approximations are performed separately for each period (myopic behavior). The optimization problem is

$$\begin{cases} \max_{\alpha} Eu(\gamma'\alpha) = Eu(\alpha' \operatorname{diag} p \, R - \alpha' p) \\ \text{s.t. } \alpha' p = c_0. \end{cases} \tag{A.1}$$

The utility will generally be represented by an increasing (preference for high profit) and concave (risk-aversion) function.

The first order conditions are deduced from the optimization of the Lagrangian:

$$\mathcal{L} = Eu(\alpha' \operatorname{diag} p \ R - c_0) - \lambda(\alpha' p - c_0).$$

By assuming u differentiable and the possibility of commuting expectation and derivation, we obtain the equations

$$\begin{cases} E\left\{\operatorname{diag} p \ R \ \dfrac{du}{dy}(\alpha' \operatorname{diag} p \ R - c_0)\right\} - \lambda p = 0, \\ \alpha' p = c_0. \end{cases} \tag{A.2}$$

Then the value of the Lagrange multiplier is

$$\lambda = \frac{1}{c_0} E\left\{\alpha' \operatorname{diag} p \ R \frac{du}{dy}(\alpha' \operatorname{diag} p \ R - c_0)\right\},$$

and the implicit equation satisfied by the optimal allocation is

$$\begin{aligned} c_0 E &\left\{\operatorname{diag} p \ R \frac{du}{dy}(\alpha' \operatorname{diag} p \ R - c_0)\right\} \\ &- E\left\{\alpha' \operatorname{diag} p \ R \frac{du}{dy}(\alpha' \operatorname{diag} p \ R - c_0)\right\} p = 0. \end{aligned} \tag{A.3}$$

In general, there is no closed form solution, as it depends on several characteristics of the conditional distribution of the returns.

2. Constant Absolute Risk Aversion

Among the various utility functions, one often considers those for which the absolute risk aversion defined by $-\frac{d^2u(y)}{dy^2}/\frac{du(y)}{dy}$ is constant. If a denotes this positive constant, we see that the utility function is

$$u(y) = -\exp(-ay). \tag{A.4}$$

The first order condition becomes

$$\begin{cases} aE\{\operatorname{diag} p \ R \exp a(c_0 - \alpha' \operatorname{diag} p \ R)\} - \lambda p = 0, \\ \alpha' p = c_0. \end{cases}$$

The solution depends on the entire conditional distribution of the returns because it depends on the whole Laplace transform of this distribution. If the set of assets includes a risk-free asset, the initial optimization problem becomes

$$\begin{cases} \max_{\alpha_0, \alpha} E\{u(\alpha_0 R_0 + \alpha' \operatorname{diag} p \ R - c_0)\} \\ \text{s.t. } \alpha_0 + \alpha' p = c_0. \end{cases}$$

Eliminating the quantity α_0 of risk-free assets yields a problem where only the quantities of risky assets matter:

$$\max_{\alpha} Eu(\alpha' \operatorname{diag} p(R - R_0 e) + c_0 R_0 - c_0).$$

If the utility function has an exponential form, the problem is

$$\max_{\alpha} Eu[\alpha' \operatorname{diag} p(R - R_0 e)].$$

Property A.5. *If the utility function exhibits constant absolute risk aversion, the optimal quantities of risky assets do not depend on the initial endowment c_0.*

Thus, the demand for a risk-free asset appears as a kind of residual demand.

3. Conditional Normality

i) Form of the Objective Function

Optimization problems such as (A.1) are often examined under the simplifying assumption of conditional normality of the returns. Let us recall that this is a *very strong assumption* since in the case of path-dependent variability it cannot be simultaneously satisfied for two different horizons.

We are nevertheless discussing this approach to present the corresponding criterion functions. Under the normality assumption, the conditional distribution of the returns is characterized by its conditional mean and conditional variances; this remains valid for the conditional distribution of the gain. We see that the expected utility is a known function of these two statistics.

$$Eu(\gamma'\alpha) = v[E(\gamma'\alpha), V(\gamma'\alpha)]. \tag{A.6}$$

In addition, since u is increasing and concave, it is easy to show that the function v is increasing in the mean and decreasing in the variance. It is then obvious that the search for an efficient portfolio may be carried out directly by means of an objective function like (A.6) and that this form generalizes the linear framework exploited in section 7.1.

Note A.7. If the utility function exhibits constant absolute risk aversion, we have

$$Eu(\gamma'\alpha) = -E(\exp{-a\gamma'\alpha}) = -\exp\left[-aE(\gamma'\alpha) + \frac{a^2}{2}V(\gamma'\alpha)\right],$$

and the maximization problem is equivalent to maximizing a linear function of the mean and variance:

$$\max_{\alpha} Eu(\gamma'\alpha) - \frac{a}{2}V(\gamma'\alpha).$$

Thus, the criterion introduced in section 7.1 may be associated with an exponential utility function under the assumption of conditional normality of the returns.

ii) First Order Conditions (Case of a Risk-Free Asset)

Let us consider the case of a risk-free asset. The optimization problem is

$$\begin{cases} \max_{\alpha_0,\alpha} v[\alpha_0 R_0 + m' \operatorname{diag} p\, \alpha - c_0, \alpha' \operatorname{diag} p\, \Sigma \operatorname{diag} p\, \alpha]. \\ \text{s.t. } \alpha_0 + p'\alpha = c_0, \end{cases}$$

or, after eliminating α_0,

$$\max v[(m - R_0 e)' \operatorname{diag} p\, \alpha + c_0 R_0 - c_0, \alpha' \operatorname{diag} p\, \Sigma \operatorname{diag} p\, \alpha].$$

The first order condition is

$$\text{diag } p(m - R_0 e)\frac{\partial v}{\partial \mu} + 2 \text{ diag } p \, \Sigma \text{ diag } p \, \alpha \frac{\partial v}{\partial \eta^2} = 0,$$

denoting by $\frac{\partial v}{\partial \mu}$ and $\frac{\partial v}{\partial \eta^2}$ the derivatives of the criterion function with respect to the mean and the variance.

We then obtain a formula similar to (7.10):

$$\hat{\alpha} = -\frac{\partial v/\partial \mu}{2(\partial v/\partial \eta^2)}[\text{diag } p]^{-1}\Sigma^{-1}(m - R_0 e), \tag{A.8}$$

in which the risk-aversion coefficient generally depends on time, through $E(\gamma'\alpha)$ and $V(\gamma'\alpha)$.

Appendix 2: Moments of the Truncated Log-Normal Distribution

In the following, u denotes a standard normal variable and m, σ, K real constants.

1) We have

$$E[\exp(m + \sigma u)] = \exp\left(m + \frac{\sigma^2}{2}\right)$$

using the generating function of the standard normal distribution.

2) Likewise,

$$\begin{aligned} V&[\exp(m + \sigma u)] \\ &= E[\exp(2m + 2\sigma u)] - (E \exp(m + \sigma u))^2 \\ &= \exp(2m + 2\sigma^2) - \exp(2m + \sigma^2) \\ &= \exp(2m + \sigma^2)(\exp \sigma^2 - 1) \end{aligned}$$

3) and

$$E \text{ Max}(\exp(m + \sigma u) - K, 0)$$

$$= \int_{u > \frac{\log K - m}{\sigma} = \tilde{u}} (\exp(m + \sigma u) - K)\varphi(u)\, du,$$

where φ denotes the density function of the standard normal distribution.

$$E \text{ Max}(\exp(m + \sigma u) - K, 0)$$

$$= \int_{\tilde{u}}^{\infty} \exp(m + \sigma u)\frac{1}{\sqrt{2\pi}}\exp\left(-\frac{u^2}{2}\right)du - K[1 - \Phi(\tilde{u})]$$

$$= \exp\left(m + \frac{\sigma^2}{2}\right)\int_{\tilde{u}}^{\infty} \varphi(u - \sigma)\, du - K\Phi(-\tilde{u})$$

$$= \exp\left(m + \frac{\sigma^2}{2}\right)\Phi(\sigma - \tilde{u}) - K\Phi(-\tilde{u}).$$

4) Finally,

$$E\,[\text{Max}(\exp(m+\sigma u)-K,0)]^2$$

$$= \int_{\tilde{u}}^{\infty} [\exp(m+\sigma u)-K]^2 \varphi(u)\,du$$

$$= \int_{\tilde{u}}^{\infty} \exp(2m+2\sigma u)\varphi(u)\,du$$

$$- 2K \int_{\tilde{u}}^{\infty} \exp(m+\sigma u)\varphi(u)\,du + K^2 \int_{\tilde{u}}^{\infty} \varphi(u)\,du$$

$$= \exp(2m+2\sigma^2)\,\Phi(2\sigma-\tilde{u}) - 2K\exp\left(m+\frac{\sigma^2}{2}\right)\Phi(\sigma-u) + K^2\Phi(-\tilde{u}).$$

Appendix 3: Asymptotic Properties of the Estimators

1. Asymptotic Distribution of the Estimated Efficient Allocation

This distribution will be determined from a Taylor expansion of the estimators in the neighborhood of their limiting values. For that, it is useful to introduce the centered returns $u_t = R_t - m$ and their empirical variance

$$\tilde{\Sigma}_T = \frac{1}{T}\sum_{t=1}^{T}(R_t-m)(R_t-m)'.$$

The matrix differs from $\hat{\Sigma}_T$ since the mean m is not replaced by its estimator. We have

$$\sqrt{T}(\hat{\alpha}_T-\alpha)$$
$$= \sqrt{T}[\hat{\Sigma}_T^{-1}(\hat{m}_T-R_0e) - \Sigma^{-1}(m-R_0e)]$$
$$= \sqrt{T}[\hat{\Sigma}_T^{-1}(\hat{m}_T-m) - (\hat{\Sigma}_T^{-1}-\Sigma^{-1})(m-R_0e)]$$
$$\approx \Sigma^{-1}\sqrt{T}(\hat{m}_T-m) - \Sigma^{-1}\sqrt{T}(\hat{\Sigma}_T-\Sigma)\Sigma^{-1}(m-R_0e)$$
$$\approx \Sigma^{-1}\sqrt{T}(\hat{m}_T-m) - \Sigma^{-1}\sqrt{T}(\tilde{\Sigma}_T-\Sigma)\Sigma^{-1}(m-R_0e)$$
$$\approx \Sigma^{-1}\sqrt{T}\frac{1}{T}\sum_{t=1}^{T}u_t - \Sigma^{-1}\sqrt{T}\left(\frac{1}{T}\sum_{t=1}^{T}u_t u_t' - \Sigma\right)\Sigma^{-1}(m-R_0e).$$

We deduce that the estimator is asymptotically a linear transformation of

$$\sqrt{T}(\hat{m}_T-m),\ \sqrt{T}\left(\frac{1}{T}\sum_{t=1}^{T}u_t u_t' - \Sigma\right),$$

i.e., variables that are asymptotically normal according to the central limit theorem.

Therefore, $\sqrt{T}(\hat{\alpha}_T-\alpha)$ is also asymptotically normal. The asymptotic precision remains to be stated. It is given by

$$V_{as}[\sqrt{T}(\hat{\alpha}_T-\alpha)] = V[\Sigma^{-1}u - \Sigma^{-1}uu'\Sigma^{-1}(m-R_0e)].$$

Let us consider the associated bilinear form. Let a and b be two vectors. We have

$$a' V_{as}[\sqrt{T}(\hat{\alpha}_T - \alpha)]b =$$
$$\text{Cov}[a'\Sigma^{-1}u - a'\Sigma^{-1}uu'\Sigma^{-1}(m - R_0 e), \, b'\Sigma^{-1}u - b'\Sigma^{-1}uu'\Sigma^{-1}(m - R_0 e)].$$

The vector $[a'\Sigma^{-1}u, b'\Sigma^{-1}u, (m - R_0 e)\Sigma^{-1}u]$ is Gaussian, and its cross moments may be derived easily by using the results of exercise 7.10. We have

$$a' V_{as}[\sqrt{T}(\hat{\alpha}_T - \alpha)]b$$
$$= \text{Cov}[a'\Sigma^{-1}u, b'\Sigma^{-1}u] + 2\,\text{Cov}(a'\Sigma^{-1}u, (m - R_0 e)'\Sigma^{-1}u)$$
$$\text{Cov}(b'\Sigma^{-1}u, (m - R_0 e)'\Sigma^{-1}u)$$
$$+ \text{Cov}(a'\Sigma^{-1}u, (m - R_0 e)'\Sigma^{-1}u)\,\text{Cov}(b'\Sigma^{-1}u, (m - R_0 e)'\Sigma^{-1}u)$$
$$= a'\Sigma^{-1}b[1 + (m - R_0 e)'\Sigma^{-1}(m - R_0 e)] + a'\Sigma^{-1}(m - R_0 e)(m - R_0 e)'\Sigma^{-1}b.$$

This provides the desired form of the asymptotic variance of the estimated allocation.

2. Asymptotic Distribution of the Performance

The Taylor expansion of the difference between the estimated and the true performances gives

$$\sqrt{T}(\hat{S}_T - S)$$
$$= \sqrt{T}[(\hat{m}_T - R_0 e)'\hat{\Sigma}_T(\hat{m}_T - R_0 e) - (m - R_0 e)'\Sigma^{-1}(m - R_0 e)]$$
$$\approx 2(m - R_0 e)'\Sigma^{-1}\sqrt{T}(\hat{m}_T - m)$$
$$+ (m - R_0 e)'\Sigma^{-1}\sqrt{T}(\hat{\Sigma}_T - \Sigma^{-1})\Sigma(m - R_0 e)$$

Here, the asymptotic normality once more is implied by the central limit theorem. The expression of the asymptotic precision is derived noting that

$$V_{as}[\sqrt{T}(\hat{S}_T - S)]$$
$$= V[2(m - R_0 e)'\Sigma^{-1}u + (m - R_0 e)\Sigma^{-1}uu'\Sigma^{-1}(m - R_0 e)]$$
$$= 4V[(m - R_0 e)'\Sigma^{-1}u] + 2[V((m - R_0 e)'\Sigma^{-1}u)]^2$$
$$= 4S + 2S^2 = 2S[2 + S]$$

(the second equality results from exercise 7.10).

7.6   Exercises

Exercise 7.1. Determine the real functions U such that, for every possible distribution of X, $EU(X)$ depends only on EX and EX^2. What do you conclude?

Exercise 7.2. Let us consider a market on which two riskless assets would exist. Their respective returns are R_0 and R_1, $R_0 > R_1$. Verify that it is possible to make a riskless profit. What does such a possibility imply as far as demand and supply of the two assets are concerned?

Exercise 7.3. Let us consider the two basic portfolios α^* and α^{**} given in Property 7.12. Verify that the portfolios, with returns uncorrelated with those two basic portfolios' returns, have zero cost and a zero expected return. How can they be used for arbitrage?

Exercise 7.4. Verify that the expected return $\mu(\alpha^*)$ of the arbitrage portfolio is always positive. What do you conclude?

Exercise 7.5.

1) Find the solution of the problem

$$
\begin{cases}
\max_{\alpha} E(\gamma'\alpha/I) - aV(\gamma'\alpha/I), \\
\text{s.t. } p(\alpha) = c_0.
\end{cases}
$$

2) Write the variance of the optimal allocation.

3) Give an example showing that it can actually depend on the information set I.

Exercise 7.6. Verify that the Sharpe performance measure introduced in section 7.1.3.iii takes the same value no matter whether it is computed using the gross or net returns.

Exercise 7.7 (important). Let us consider a market where risky assets and a risk-free asset can be exchanged. It is assumed that the risk-free return R_0 is time independent and that the returns of the risky assets associated with the different periods may be regarded as i.i.d. They are linked to the prices by $R_t = p_{t+1}/p_t$.

1) Show that

$$
\text{diag } p_t = \text{diag } p_0 \text{ diag exp} \left(\sum_{\tau=1}^{t} \log R_\tau \right)
$$

$$
= \text{diag } p_0 \text{ diag exp}(t E \log R_1).
$$

2) Deduce that, at date t, the desired quantities of the assets would be given by (see section 7.10)

$$
\hat{\alpha}_t \approx \frac{1}{2a} (\text{diag } p_0)^{-1} [\text{diag exp}(t E \log R_1)]^{-1} \Sigma^{-1} (m - R_0 e),
$$

with $\Sigma = V R_1$ and $m = E R_1$.

3) What can be said about the quantities $\hat{\alpha}_t$ if t tends to infinity? What do you conclude?

Exercise 7.8 (important). The conditions of section 7.1.3.iii are satisfied, and it is assumed that the expectations are evaluated at horizon h with a risk-aversion coefficient a independent of h.

1) Explain why it is preferable that Σ and $m - R_0$ depend on h so that

$$
\Sigma_h^{-1}(m_h - R_{0,h} e)
$$

converges towards a limit without zero component.

2) Compare this condition with the one linking the orders of the drift and volatility in a diffusion equation (see chapter 5).

Exercise 7.9. Let $\begin{pmatrix} X \\ Y \end{pmatrix}$ be a pair of random Gaussian vectors

$$N\left[\begin{pmatrix} 0 \\ 0 \end{pmatrix} ; \begin{pmatrix} \Sigma_{XX} & \Sigma_{XY} \\ \Sigma_{YX} & \Sigma_{YY} \end{pmatrix} \right].$$

1) Find the conditional distribution of Y given X.

2) Write that the density function of the pair $\begin{pmatrix} X \\ Y \end{pmatrix}$ is the product of the marginal density function of X and of the conditional density of Y given X. Deduce that

$$\begin{pmatrix} X \\ Y \end{pmatrix}' \begin{pmatrix} \Sigma_{XX} & \Sigma_{XY} \\ \Sigma_{YX} & \Sigma_{YY} \end{pmatrix}^{-1} \begin{pmatrix} X \\ Y \end{pmatrix} = X' \Sigma_{XX}^{-1} X$$

$$+ (Y' - \Sigma_{YX} \Sigma_{XX}^{-1} X)' \left(\Sigma_{YY} - \Sigma_{YX} \Sigma_{XX}^{-1} \Sigma_{XY} \right)^{-1} \left(Y - \Sigma_{YX} \Sigma_{XX}^{-1} X \right).$$

Exercise 7.10. Let $(X, Y, Z, T)'$ be a centered Gaussian vector. Using the form of the characteristic function, verify that

$$E\left(X\, Y\, Z\, T \right) = \mathrm{Cov}(X, Z)\, \mathrm{Cov}(Y, T) + \mathrm{Cov}(X, T)\, \mathrm{Cov}(Y, Z)$$

$$+ \mathrm{Cov}(X, Y)\, \mathrm{Cov}(Z, T).$$

$$+ \mathrm{Cov}(X, Y)\, \mathrm{Cov}(Z, T).$$

Show that

$$E\left(X\, Y\, Z^2 \right) = 2\, \mathrm{Cov}(X, Z)\, \mathrm{Cov}(Y, Z) + \mathrm{Cov}(X, Y)\, V(Z),$$

$$E\left(X^2\, Z^2 \right) = 2\, \mathrm{Cov}(X, Z)^2 + V(X)\, V(Z),$$

$$E\left(X^4 \right) = 3\, (V X)^2.$$

8

Factor Models, Diversification and Efficiency

The simultaneous study of several financial or currency series often shows similar evolutions. These can be modelled in two different ways, either introducing underlying series, observable or not, that explain this common evolution or identifying approximated relations satisfied by the series. The first approach leads to factor models similar to the ones introduced in chapter 6, and the second approach leads to techniques like cointegration and codependence.

In the first section, we give a general definition of factors and discuss the possibility of choosing them endogenously, i.e., as linear functions of the asset gains. We show that the existence of factors is equivalent to the existence of static relations between gains, and then we give a characterization of factor models using dynamic expressions of the conditional means and variances. Finally, we establish the link with the dynamic properties of the set of efficient portfolios.

The second section is devoted to the diversification problem. We consider a factor model with uncorrelated errors between the asset returns and suppose that the number of assets is very large (even infinite). It is then possible to build portfolios whose initial value is zero (**arbitrage portfolios**), which are not linked to the factors (**zero beta portfolio**) and are not risky because of their balanced composition in the several assets (**diversified portfolios**). Applying an arbitrage argument, we deduce that the expected return of this portfolio is zero. That condition implies a relation between the expected returns and the factors on which the APT (Arbitrage Pricing Theory) is based.

The following section is then devoted to testing procedures. May a set of series a priori given be considered as a set of factors associated with the gains? If so, does every factor have an impact on the gains? In the case where the factors are endogenous, we establish the link to efficiency tests and Sharpe performance measures. Finally, we present some procedures for the analysis of diversification.

8.1 Factor Models

Throughout this section, we define the models for the series of net gains of the several assets $Y_t = \gamma_t - R_{0,t-1} p_t$. The net gain of a portfolio whose composition α is fixed is simply the linear combination $\alpha' Y_t$ of the net gains of the basic assets. Thus, we may identify any linear combination of the variables with a portfolio.

8.1.1 Linear Factor Representation

The model is defined from the underlying series that explain the joint evolution of the net gains. These series are called **factors** and are denoted by $F = (F_t)$, where F is a process of dimension K. The joint information set associated with the basic series Y and the factors F is $J_{t-1} = (Y_{t-1}, F_{t-1})$.

Definition 8.1. *The net gains satisfy a linear representation with factors F if*

$$Y_t = B F_t + u_t, \tag{8.2}$$

with $E(u_t / J_{t-1}) = 0$,
           $V(u_t / J_{t-1}) = \Omega$, *time independent*,
           $\text{Cov}(u_t, F_t / J_{t-1}) = 0$.
The columns of B are called factor directions or betas (of the basic assets on the factors).

A residual term $u = (u_t)$ occurs in the equation linking the factors and the basic series; it is such that

$$E(u_t / u_{t-1}) = 0, \; V(u_t / u_{t-1}) = \Omega.$$

Its evolution is not linked to the past, so that the whole dynamic of the model comes from the function of the factors $B F_t$. A linear factor representation being given, factors and factor directions are not unique.

(*) If the rank of the matrix B is strictly lower than K, it is possible to keep the same kind of representation diminishing the number of factors by aggregation. We assume in the following that such an aggregation has already been carried out, i.e., $rk\, B = K$. This implies that the number of factors is lower than the number of basic series n.

(**) Even under this condition, there exists a multiplicity of definitions of the factors and factor directions up to an invertible linear transformation. Indeed, if P is an invertible square matrix of size K, we may write

$$Y_t = B P^{-1} P F_t + u_t = \tilde{B} \tilde{F}_t + u_t,$$

with $\tilde{B} = BP^{-1}$, $\tilde{F}_t = PF_t$. As $\tilde{J}_{t-1} = (Y_{t-1}, \tilde{F}_{t-1}) = J_{t-1}$, we immediately verify the conditions for the conditional moments of the residual term with respect to the information set $\tilde{J}_{t-1}$. It corresponds to a linear factor representation that is equivalent to the initial one.

Note 8.3. The existence of the representation (8.2) does not presuppose the observability of the factors. Some of them may be observable: it will occur if we explain the gains as functions of the interest rates, of the consumption level, etc. Some may not be observable, and we have to find out the evolution and influence of these latent factors.

8.1.2 Representation with Endogenous Factors

We have seen that for a given information set $J_{t-1} = \tilde{J}_{t-1}$, there exist several possible definitions of the factors. We now establish that there exist other factor representations if the information set J_{t-1} is allowed to vary. Among them, we present one with factors

$$F_t^* = A'Y_t \tag{8.4}$$

that are linear functions of the net gains. Such **factors** are said to be **endogenous**. This result is important for understanding the notion of a factor model. It means that it is impossible to answer a question like: Are the unobservable latent factors exogenous or endogenous? Indeed, a series admitting a representation with exogenous factors also admits a representation with endogenous factors. The latter may then be considered as portfolios whose net gains would summarize the dynamic of the exogenous factors.

In order to point out these endogenous factors $F^* = A'Y_t$, we look for portfolio composition A such that the linear regression of Y_t on F_t^*, F_t given the information set J_{t-1} does not depend on F_t.

This linear regression is (see exercise 8.1)

$$Y_t = \Omega A[A'\Omega A]^{-1}A'Y_t \tag{8.5}$$
$$+ [Id - \Omega A[A'\Omega A]^{-1}A']BF_t + v_t.$$

In order to eliminate the initial factors, we have to choose A such that

$$\{Id - \Omega A[A'\Omega A]^{-1}A'\}B = 0$$
$$\Leftrightarrow [Id - \Omega^{1/2}A[(\Omega^{1/2}A)'(\Omega^{1/2}A)]^{-1}(\Omega^{1/2}A)']\Omega^{-1/2}B = 0.$$

The matrix in brackets corresponds to an orthogonal projector on the orthogonal subspace of the space generated by the columns of $\Omega^{1/2}A$. The condition is then equivalent to

$$Rg\,(\Omega^{-1/2}B) \subset Rg\,(\Omega^{+1/2}A)$$
$$\Leftrightarrow Rg\,(\Omega^{-1}B) \subset Rg\,A.$$

Therefore, there are several possible choices for the endogenous factors whose evolution summarizes one of the initial factors. Among these choices, some lead to the minimal number of independent factors; for instance, we may take $\tilde{A} = \Omega^{-1}B$. With this choice, formulation (8.5) becomes

$$Y_t = B[B'\Omega^{-1}B]^{-1}B'\Omega^{-1}Y_t + v_t,$$
$$Y_t = Q_B Y_t + (Id - Q_B)u_t,$$

where Q_B denotes the projector on the columns of B for the scalar product associated with Ω^{-1}. By defining the factors and factor directions up to an invertible matrix of dimension K, we may also select $A = \Omega^{-1}B'[B'\Omega^{-1}B]^{-1}$ and then arrive at a model

$$Y_t = BA'Y_t + (Id - Q_B)u_t, \tag{8.6}$$

in which the factor directions (columns of B) are identical to those of the initial factor model. Finally, to interpret (8.6) as another factor representation, it remains to verify the conditions on the moments of the residual term. We have

$$E(u_t/J_{t-1}) = 0, \quad V(u_t/J_{t-1}) = \Omega,$$

and by iterated expectations and variance analysis

$$E(u_t/\underline{Y_{t-1}}) = 0, \quad V(u_t/\underline{Y_{t-1}}) = \Omega.$$

Then, we have

$$\left\{ \begin{array}{l} E(v_t/\underline{Y_{t-1}}) = (Id - Q_B)\,E(u_t/\underline{Y_{t-1}}) = 0, \\ V(v_t/\underline{Y_{t-1}}) = (Id - Q_B)\,\Omega\,(Id - Q_B)', \text{ independent of time,} \\ \text{Cov}(v_t, Q_B Y_t/\underline{Y_{t-1}}) = (Id - Q_B)\Omega Q_B' = 0, \\ \text{and then also } \text{Cov}(v_t, F_t^*/\underline{Y_{t-1}}) = 0. \end{array} \right.$$

We find that the conditions on the conditional moments given $(\underline{Y_{t-1}}) = (\underline{Y_{t-1}}, \underline{F_{t-1}^*})$ are satisfied.

Property 8.7. *Any series of net gains with a linear factor representation also admits a linear endogenous factor representation*

$$Y_t = BF_t^* + v_t, \tag{8.8}$$

with $F_t^* = A'Y_t,$
$\quad E(v_t/\underline{Y_{t-1}}) = 0, \quad V(v_t/\underline{Y_{t-1}}) = 0,$
$\quad \text{Cov}(v_t, F_t^*/\underline{Y_{t-1}}) = 0.$
The number of endogenous factors may be taken equal to the number of initial factors, and the matrix A may be chosen such that $BA' = Q_B$ is the orthogonal projector on B for the scalar product associated with Ω^{-1}.

If our observations refer only to the values of net gain series and not to the initial factors, the endogenous representation (8.8) is the only factor representation that may be identified.

The initial model admits a recursive form

$$\begin{cases} Y_t = B(A'Y_t) + v_t, & E(v_t/J_{t-1}) = 0, \ V(v_t/J_{t-1}) = \Omega^*, \\ A'Y_t = A'BF_t + A'u_t, & E(u_t/J_{t-1}) = 0, \ V(u_t/J_{t-1}) = \Omega^*, \\ & \text{Cov}(v_t, A'u_t/J_{t-1}) = 0, \end{cases} \tag{8.9}$$

in which the first subsystem corresponds to the representation with endogenous factors, and the second subsystem gives the connection between initial and endogenous factors. If F is not observed, the second subsystem cannot be studied, contrary to the first one. This recursive representation shows that the system with endogenous factors generally includes less information than the model with initial factors, and these two systems are not equivalent.

8.1.3 Structure of the Conditional Moments

A linear factor representation of the type (8.2) implies some constraints on the conditional moments m_t and Σ_t. From (8.2), we get

$$\begin{cases} m_t = BE(F_{t+1}/\underline{Y_t}), \\ \Sigma_t = BV(F_{t+1}/\underline{Y_t})B' + \Omega. \end{cases} \tag{8.10}$$

Therefore, the expected net gain is a linear combination of fixed vectors (the factor directions) with time dependent coefficients

$$m_t = B\mu_t = \sum_{k=1}^{K} B_k \mu_{kt}, \tag{8.11}$$

where B_k is the k-th column of B and $\mu_{kt} = E(F_{k,t+1}/\underline{Y_t})$.

Similarly, we have

$$\Sigma_t = B\Lambda_t B' + \Omega = \sum_{k=1}^{K} \sum_{l=1}^{K} \lambda_{klt} B_k B'_l + \Omega, \tag{8.12}$$

where $\Lambda_t = V(F_t/\underline{Y_t})$ is a positive definite symmetric matrix. The last decomposition looks like a singular value decomposition of the volatility matrix, and the search for factor directions may likely be performed by canonical analysis (see section 8.3).

Property 8.13. *The conditional means and variances may be decomposed as*

$$m_t = B\mu_t, \ \Sigma_t = B\Lambda_t B' + \Omega,$$

$\Omega \gg 0, \ \Lambda_t \gg 0, \ \forall t$, *if and only if the series Y has a linear representation with endogenous factors and factor directions B.*

Proof. The sufficient part has already been established, and it remains to check the necessary part. Let us suppose (8.11) and (8.12). We can always write

$$Y_t = Q_B Y_t + (Id - Q_B) Y_t. \tag{8.14}$$

We then verify

$$E((Id - Q_B)Y_t / \underline{Y_{t-1}}) = (Id - Q_B)m_{t-1} = 0,$$

$$V((Id - Q_B)Y_t / \underline{Y_{t-1}}) = (Id - Q_B)\Sigma_{t-1}(Id - Q_B)'$$

$$= (Id - Q_B)\Omega(Id - Q_B)', \text{ independent of time,}$$

$$\text{Cov}(Q_B Y_t, (Id - Q_B)Y_t / \underline{Y_{t-1}}) = Q_B \Sigma_{t-1}(Id - Q_B)'$$

$$= Q_B \Omega(Id - Q_B)' = 0.$$

It follows that the decomposition (8.14) is with endogenous factors.   Q.E.D.

Note 8.15. This characterization of the factor representation allows us to discuss the choice of the time unit. Indeed, suppose that we are interested in a larger time unit, for instance, weekly data instead of daily data. We may introduce the initial information set $I_t = (\underline{Y_t})$ (daily) and the less precise information set

$$\tilde{I}_t = (\underline{\tilde{Y}_{ht}}) = (\tilde{Y}_{ht}, \tilde{Y}_{h(t-1)}, \tilde{Y}_{h(t-2)}, \ldots),$$

with $\tilde{Y}_t = Y_{ht} + Y_{ht-1} + \ldots + Y_{ht-h+1}$. Likewise, we may introduce the conditional moments with respect to the initial series

$$m_t = E(Y_{t+1}/I_t), \quad \Sigma_t = V(Y_{t+1}/I_t),$$

and the moments with respect to the time aggregated series

$$\tilde{m}_t = E(\tilde{Y}_{t+1}/\tilde{I}_t), \quad \tilde{\Sigma}_t = V(\tilde{Y}_{t+1}/\tilde{I}_t).$$

We have

$$\tilde{m}_t = E(\tilde{Y}_{t+1}/\tilde{I}_t) = E(Y_{h(t+1)} + \ldots + Y_{ht+1}/\tilde{I}_t)$$

$$= E(m_{h(t+1)} + \ldots + m_{ht+1}/\tilde{I}_t) \text{ by iterated expectations}$$

$$= B[E(\mu_{h(t+1)}/\tilde{I}_t) + \ldots + E(\mu_{ht+1}/\tilde{I}_t)].$$

The factor directions for the expected aggregated gains belong to the space generated by the initial factor directions. They are not necessarily the same, because some of them could be noneffective, when $E(\mu_{h(t+1)}/\tilde{I}_t) + \ldots + E(\mu_{ht+1}/\tilde{I}_t)$ has zero components.

By analogy, one may compute $\tilde{\Sigma}_t$. By variance analysis (see exercise 8.2), we obtain an expression of the kind

$$\tilde{\Sigma}_t = B\tilde{\Lambda}_t B' + \Omega,$$

with $\tilde{\Lambda}_t \gg E(\Lambda_{h(t+1)}/\tilde{I}_t) + \ldots + E(\Lambda_{ht+1}/\tilde{I}_t)$. Therefore, the notion of linear factor representation is maintained by increasing the time unit. The number of factors with a real impact on the mean may eventually decrease, and the part due to the factors in the decomposition of the variance may increase.

8.1.4   Cofactors

We have seen that the residual term $v_t = (Id - Q_B)u_t$ is such that

$$E(v_t/\underline{Y_{t-1}}) = 0, \quad V(v_t/\underline{Y_{t-1}}) = (Id - Q_B)\Omega(Id - Q_B)'.$$

The matrix $Id - Q_B$ has rank $n - K$ and admits $n - K$ independent rows, which may be gathered into an $(n - K, n)$ matrix C' with rank $n - K$. The vector $C'Y_t$ is a conditionally homoscedastic martingale difference sequence since

$$E(C'Y_t/\underline{Y_{t-1}}) = 0, \quad V(C'Y_t/\underline{Y_{t-1}}) = C'\Omega C.$$

Property 8.16. *The process of the net gains admits a linear representation with endogenous factors if and only if there exist linear transformations of the initial series $C'Y_t$ satisfying*

$$E(C'Y_t/\underline{Y_{t-1}}) = 0, \quad V(C'Y_t/\underline{Y_{t-1}}) = C'\Omega C,$$

with $\Sigma_t \gg \Omega \gg 0, \forall t$. The columns of C are called cofactors.

Proof. See exercise 8.3.

There exist close links between cofactors and factor directions. A cofactor is associated with every direction orthogonal to every factor direction and vice versa. Thus, we may always choose for C a matrix whose columns constitute an orthogonal basis of the range of B. If the minimal number of factors is K, the possible maximal number of cofactors is $n - K$. The cofactors are associated with portfolios whose net gains satisfy $C'Y_t = w_t$, where w_t is a white noise.

8.1.5   Characterization with the Matrix Defining the Endogenous Factors

A last characterization may be obtained from the matrix A defining the endogenous factors

$$F_t^* = A'Y_t.$$

The existence of a representation with endogenous factors F_t^* requires three conditions on the regression of Y_{t+1} on F_{t+1}^* given the information set $\underline{Y_t}$:

(i) The regression coefficient is time independent.

(ii) The specific effect of $\underline{Y_t}$, once F_{t+1}^* is taken into account, is zero.

(iii) The residual variance is time independent.

The conditions are

$$\left|\begin{array}{ll} (i) & \Sigma_t A(A'\Sigma_t A)^{-1} \text{ time independent} \\ (ii) & m_t - \Sigma_t A(A'\Sigma_t A)^{-1} A'm_t = 0; \\ (iii) & \Sigma_t - \Sigma_t A(A'\Sigma_t A)^{-1} A'\Sigma_t \text{ time independent.} \end{array}\right.$$

The second equality is equivalent to

$$m_t - \Sigma_t^{1/2}(\Sigma_t^{1/2}A)\left[(\Sigma_t^{1/2}A)'(\Sigma_t^{1/2}A)\right]^{-1}(\Sigma_t^{1/2}A)'\Sigma_t^{-1/2}m_t = 0$$

$$\Leftrightarrow \Sigma_t^{-1/2}m_t \in Rg(\Sigma_t^{1/2}A)$$

$$\Leftrightarrow \Sigma_t^{-1}m_t \in Rg(A).$$

This means that the efficient portfolios, whose true compositions vary over time, may be built using K portfolios with time-invariant compositions.

Property 8.17. *The net gains series has a representation with endogenous factors* $F_t^* = A'Y_t$ *if and only if*

(i) *The betas of the basic assets on the basic portfolios associated with the columns of A are time independent.*

(ii) *The basic portfolios generate the set of efficient portfolios.*

(iii) *The residual risk is time independent.*

8.2   Arbitrage Theory

8.2.1   *Absence of Arbitrage Opportunities*

The **Arbitrage Pricing Theory** (APT) was introduced by Ross (1976). It is based on the **absence of arbitrage opportunities** (AAO), which requires that a zero cost portfolio cannot have a strictly positive return. This condition was underlying the entire analysis of chapter 7: we have indeed assumed that the conditional variability matrix of the returns is invertible. The only portfolio with a deterministic return is then composed only of the risk-free asset. The cost of such a portfolio is α_0, where α_0 denotes the quantity of a risk-free asset, and it is zero only if $\alpha_0 = 0$. This portfolio, which consists of no intervention in the market, has a zero return, and the condition of absence of arbitrage opportunities is satisfied. Imposing such a condition in the framework of chapter 7 implies no new restriction. The Ross contribution consists in extending the idea to the case of a market composed of a large number of assets, growing to infinity. In that case, it is possible to keep the same notation as before, as soon as we introduce a gain vector and a price vector with infinite dimension. The conditional moments are symbolized by matrices with dimension $(\infty, 1)$ for the means and (∞, ∞) for the variance. These matrices are defined element by element, which always makes sense. Some difficulty occurs with respect to the definition of the portfolios. In the easiest case, they are defined by their composition $(\alpha_{0t}, \alpha_{it}, i = 1, 2, \ldots)$ and their gain

$$\alpha_{0t}R_{0t} + \sum_{i=1}^{\infty}\alpha_{it}\gamma_{it+1}$$

in such a way that it is possible to compute the conditional mean and variance

$$E\left[\left(\alpha_{0t} R_{0t} + \sum_{i=1}^{\infty} \alpha_{it} \gamma_{it+1}\right)^2 / \underline{\gamma_t}\right] < +\infty. \tag{8.18}$$

This condition on the second order moments implies joint restrictions on the composition of the portfolio and the risk of the basic assets. In this context, we may define the absence of arbitrage opportunities as follows.

Definition 8.19. *The market with an infinite number of assets satisfies the absence of arbitrage opportunities if we cannot find a sequence of portfolios* $(\alpha_{0t}^n, \alpha_t^n)$ *with zero cost and square integrable gains, such that*

$$\begin{cases} \lim_{n \to \infty} E\left(\alpha_{0t}^n R_{0t} + \sum_{i=1}^{\infty} \alpha_{it}^n \gamma_{i\,t+1} / \underline{\gamma_t}\right) = +\infty, \\ \lim_{n \to \infty} V\left(\alpha_{0t}^n R_{0t} + \sum_{i=1}^{\infty} \alpha_{it}^n \gamma_{it+1} / \underline{\gamma_t}\right) = 0. \end{cases}$$

If the condition were not satisfied, we could build portfolios for which the risk would become negligible and the expected gain simultaneously infinitely large. The fact that the portfolio has zero cost implies the following constraint:

$$\alpha_{0t}^n + \sum_{i=1}^{\infty} \alpha_{it}^n p_{it} = 0.$$

The net gain of this portfolio may then be written as

$$-\left(\sum_{i=1}^{\infty} \alpha_{it}^n p_{it}\right) R_{0t} + \sum_{i=1}^{\infty} \alpha_{it}^n \gamma_{i\,t+1} = \sum_{i=1}^{\infty} \alpha_{it}^n (\gamma_{i\,t+1} - p_{it} R_{0t}) = \sum_{i=1}^{\infty} \alpha_{it}^n Y_{i\,t+1}.$$

The absence of the arbitrage opportunities condition may then be written in terms of net gains.

8.2.2 Diversification and Pricing Model

In the following, we assume that the evolution of the unit net gains satisfies the factor representation

$$Y_{t+1} = m_t + B f_{t+1} + u_{t+1}, \tag{8.20}$$

where m_t is the vector with infinite dimension giving the expected net gains, B is a (∞, K) matrix, f_{t+1} is a set of K centered factors and u_t is a residual term. The conditional variance–covariance matrix of u_t is assumed time independent, diagonal,

$$\omega_{ij} = \text{Cov}(u_{it}, u_{jt}) = 0, \text{ if } i \neq j, \tag{8.21}$$

and such that there is not much heteroscedasticity between the assets:

$$\max_i \omega_{ii} = \max_i V u_{it} < \infty. \tag{8.22}$$

The model (8.20), (8.21), (8.22) differs from the factor models considered in section 8.1 in two features:

(*) The factor aspect of the dynamic appears in the variance of the gains and not in their mean, because m_t may a priori have any evolution.

(**) The factors (f_t) are factors not only from a dynamic point of view but also since they eliminate the possible correlations between asset returns [condition (8.21)].

We have then introduced two interpretations of factor models, depending on whether the time index (case of section 8.1) or the asset aspect is privileged. We now deal with the latter one.

Let us then consider an arbitrage portfolio whose composition in the risky assets is α^n. The gain of the portfolio is

$$\alpha^{n'} Y_{t+1} = \alpha^{n'} m_t + \alpha^{n'} B f_{t+1} + \alpha^n u_{t+1}.$$

It includes three components: the expected gain $\alpha^{n'} m_t$, a variable part linked to the factors $\alpha^{n'} B f_{t+1}$ and a variable residual part $\alpha^{n'} u_{t+1}$.

Property 8.23. *In the absence of arbitrage opportunities, there exists a vector μ_t with dimension K such that*

$$\|m_t - B\mu_t\|^2 = \sum_{i=1}^{\infty}(m_{it} - \sum_{k=1}^{K} b_{ik}\mu_{kt})^2 < +\infty.$$

Proof. Huberman (1982).

In order to establish such a result, we may choose μ_t such that

$$\|m_t - B\mu_t\|^2 = \min_{\mu} \|m_t - B\mu\|^2;$$

$B\mu_t$ is then the orthogonal projection of m_t on $\{B\mu\}$. We denote by $d_t = m_t - B\mu_t$ the residual term.

Let us suppose that the necessary condition of property (8.23) is not satisfied, that is, $\|d_t\|^2 = \infty$. Then we exhibit a sequence of arbitrage portfolios whose risks become negligible, whereas the expected returns tend to infinity.

For that purpose, we introduce the vectors and matrices m_t^n, B^n obtained by selecting the n first lines of m_t, B. We consider the orthogonal projections of m_t^n on the columns of B^n, which provides a decomposition $m_t^n = B^n \mu_t^n + d_t^n$. Then, if n tends to infinity,

$$\lim_{n\to\infty} \mu_t^n = \mu_t \text{ and } \lim_{n\to\infty} \|d_t^n\|^2 = +\infty.$$

Let us study the sequence of portfolios

$$\alpha_t^n = \|d_t^n\|^{-3/2}\tilde{d}_t^n, \tag{8.24}$$

where $\tilde{d}_t^n$ has its n first components equal to the ones of d_t^n, the other components being zero.

According to the definition of d_t^n, we have $d_t^{n'} B = 0$, and consequently $\alpha_t^{n'} B f_t = 0$. The portfolio has a gain which is not influenced by the factors. Such a **portfolio** is called **zero beta**, because its composition is orthogonal to the vectors of betas. Furthermore,

$$\alpha_t^{n'} m_t = \alpha_t^{n'} m_t^n = \alpha_t^{n'} B^n \mu_t^n + \alpha_t^{n'} d_t^n$$
$$= \alpha_t^{n'} d_t^n = \|d_t^n\|^{1/2},$$
$$V(\alpha_t^{n'} u_{t+1}) \le (\max_i \omega_{ii})\|\alpha_t^n\|^2 = (\max_i \omega_{ii})\|d_t^n\|^{-1}.$$

When n tends to infinity, we get

$$\begin{cases} \lim_{n \to \infty} \alpha_t^{n'} m_t = +\infty, \\ \lim_{n \to \infty} V(\alpha_t^{n'} u_{t+1}) = 0, \end{cases}$$

so that there would be an arbitrage opportunity.   Q.E.D.

Property 8.23 shows that, except for a finite number of assets, where the residual component d_{it} might be important, we can write an approximated relation

$$m_{it} = E(Y_{i\,t+1}/\underline{Y_t}) \approx \sum_{k=1}^{K} b_{ik} \mu_{kt}. \tag{8.25}$$

This relation may be seen as a **pricing model** where the expected gain of asset i depends on the specific risks of each factor. The coefficients μ_{kt} measure the **price of the risk** of each of these factors. Moreover, the portfolios α_t^n have the following structure:

$$\left(\frac{d_{1t}}{\|d_t^n\|^{3/2}}, \frac{d_{2t}}{\|d_t^n\|^{3/2}}, \ldots, \frac{d_{nt}}{\|d_t^n\|^{3/2}}, 0, \ldots, 0, \ldots \right).$$

If n increases, they are modified by adding assets to the preceding portfolio while decreasing the part of the n first ones. At the limit, the part of each of the basic assets in the composition tends to zero.

These portfolios are **well diversified** in the different assets. This possibility of diversification is based mainly on the property of weak correlation (here taken equal to zero) and of approximated homoscedasticity of the residual terms u_{t+1}. If such conditions are satisfied, u_{t+1} is often called an **idiosyncratic term**, i.e., specific to the asset.

Note 8.26. In the absence of arbitrage opportunities, the factor model is written as

$$Y_{t+1} = m_t + B f_{t+1} + u_{t+1}$$
$$\approx B \mu_t + B f_{t+1} + u_{t+1}$$
$$\approx B F_{t+1} + u_{t+1}, \text{ with: } F_{t+1} = \mu_t + f_{t+1}.$$

Therefore, the factor models introduced in section 8.1, whose factor directions with respect to the first order moment are linked to factor directions with respect to the second order moments, are compatible with arbitrage pricing theory.

8.2.3 Diversification and Risk Aversion

The pricing model has been derived from the factor model and the absence of arbitrage opportunities. It does not require conditions with respect to utility functions on which the agents base their choices. Nevertheless, we have seen in section 8.2.2 that, for factors models derived from the spectral decomposition of the variance matrix, a mean variance optimal portfolio has a particular composition. It is a function of the portfolios associated with the most important factorial directions. The diversification idea and the pricing model may then be introduced either by using the absence of arbitrage opportunities condition or by making assumptions on the agents' behaviors. The second approach is considered in the CAPM (chapter 9). For a more detailed discussion of these questions, refer to Connor (1984) and Huang and Litzenberger (1988).

8.3   Efficiency Tests and Diversification

8.3.1   Ex-Ante Efficiency

Let us consider the factor model

$$Y_t = BF_t + u_t, \tag{8.27}$$

where the factors are observable and may eventually be interpreted as endogenous factors $F_t = A'Y_t$. In the last case, the variance–covariance matrix of the residual term u_t is singular and of rank $n - K$. We may always restrict to the case of a regular matrix by deleting K equations from the preceding system.

In practice, the number of assets N is large, and we usually work with a small number of equations (between 10 and 20) obtained by combining the initial equations. Equivalently, we consider the gains of well chosen portfolios defined as functions of the gains of the factor portfolios. The subsystem studied is

$$D'Y_t = D'BF_t + D'u_t.$$

In this subsystem, the variance–covariance matrix of the error $V(D'u_t) = D'\Omega D$ is generally invertible.

Equation (8.27) is a linear regression equation of Y_t on F_t given the past J_{t-1}. In particular, no specific effect of the past exists, and the linear regression of A_t on F_t, X_t, where X_t is any variable function of J_{t-1}, has a zero coefficient for X_t. In the case of endogenous factors $F_t = A'Y_t$, it means that the portfolios associated with the columns of A generate the set of efficient portfolios for all of the dates. Therefore, this test may be viewed as an **efficiency test**.

We may nest the initial model (8.27) into the larger model

$$Y_t = BF_t + DX_t + u_t, \quad t = 1, \ldots, T, \tag{8.28}$$

where X_t is a vector of dimension m and function of the past J_{t-1}. We consider the null hypothesis

$$H_0 = \{D = 0\}. \tag{8.29}$$

Since the errors (u_t) are instantaneously correlated with a fixed and unconstrained variance–covariance matrix Ω, and the explanatory variables F_t, X_t are the same in the n equations, the generalized least squares estimator of B and D is identical to the ordinary least squares estimator determined equation by equation. The OLS estimator of $d = (d'_1, \ldots, d'_n) = \text{vec } D$ is written $\hat{d}_T = (\hat{d}'_{1T}, \ldots, \hat{d}'_{nT})$, where

$$\hat{d}_{iT} = [X'(Id - Q_F)X]^{-1}X'(Id - Q_F)\tilde{Y}_i, \quad i = 1, \ldots, n, \tag{8.30}$$

where X is the (T, m) matrix with rows X'_t, Q_F is the projector $F(F'F)^{-1}F'$, F' is the (T, K) matrix with rows F_t, and $\tilde{Y}_i$ is the vector of dimension T whose components are the i-th components of Y_t.

Equations (8.30) may also be written as

$$\hat{d}_T = \{Id_n \otimes [X'(Id - Q_F)X]^{-1}X'(Id - Q_F)\}y, \tag{8.31}$$

with $y = \text{vec } Y$, Y being the (T, n) matrix with rows Y'_t (and columns $\tilde{Y}_i$).

By writing the initial equation as

$$y = (Id_n \otimes X)d + (Id_n \otimes F)b + u, \tag{8.32}$$

with $Vu = \Omega \otimes Id_T$, we get

$$\hat{d}_T = d + \{Id_n \otimes [X'(Id - Q_F)X]^{-1}X'(Id - Q_F)\}u. \tag{8.33}$$

This estimator is consistent, asymptotically normal under the stationarity assumption. A consistent estimator of the asymptotic variance–covariance matrix of $\sqrt{T}(\hat{d}_T - d)$ is

$$\hat{V}_{as}[\sqrt{T}(\hat{d} - d)] = T\{\hat{\Omega} \otimes [X'(Id - Q_F)X]^{-1}\},$$

with $\hat{\Omega} = \frac{1}{T}\sum_{t=1}^{T} \hat{u}_t\hat{u}'_t$, $\hat{u}_t = Y_t - \hat{B}F_t - \hat{D}X_t$.

From these forms of the estimator and its estimated asymptotic precision, we derive the expression of the Wald statistic to test for $H_0 = \{D = 0\} = \{d = 0\}$:

$$\xi_T^d = y'\{\hat{\Omega}^{-1} \otimes (Id - Q_F)X[X'(Id - Q_F)X]^{-1}X'(Id - Q_F)\}y.$$

The statistic has the following equivalent expression:

$$\xi_T^d = \text{Tr}\left\{\hat{\Omega}^{-1}Y'(Id - Q_F)X[X'(Id - Q_F)X]^{-1}X'(Id - Q_F)Y\right\}$$

$$= T \ \text{Tr}\left\{[Y'(Id - Q_{X,F})Y]^{-1}Y'(Id - Q_F)\right.$$

$$\left. X[X'(Id - Q_F)^{-1}X]^{-1}X'(Id - Q_F)Y\right\}.$$

Let us introduce the matrix of conditional second order canonical moments

$$R^2[Y, X/F] = [Y'(Id - Q_{X,F})Y]^{-1}Y'(Id - Q_F)XX'(Id - Q_F)Y \quad (8.34)$$
$$[X'(Id - Q_F)X]^{-1}$$

and note that the matrix in the brackets in the expression of ξ_T^d equals

$$[Id - R^2(Y, X/F)]^{-1}R^2(Y, X/F); \quad (8.35)$$

we derive the following result.

Property 8.36. *The Wald test for the null hypothesis* $\{D = 0\}$ *admits an asymptotic critical region with level α given by*

$$\xi_T^d \geq \chi_{1-\alpha}^2(nm),$$

where $\xi_T^d = T \sum_{i=1}^n \frac{\hat{\eta}_{iT}}{1-\hat{\eta}_{iT}}$ *and* $\hat{\eta}_{1T}, \ldots, \hat{\eta}_{nT}$ *are the eigenvalues of the matrix* $R^2(Y, X/F)$ *given in (8.35).*

Note 8.37. Other testing procedures like the likelihood ratio or Lagrange multiplier test may be developed. They lead to critical regions similar to the one that we have just described [see Jobson and Korkie (1982, 1989), Gibbons et al. (1989), Gouriéroux et al. (1991) and the exercises].

The test that has been proposed is asymptotic and may not be precise in a finite sample even if the number of equations is large. Two kinds of approaches have been proposed for finite samples:

(*) In analytic approaches, the exact distribution of the statistic ξ_T^d is derived. For this, assumptions have to be introduced on the joint distribution of the factors and residual terms (Jobson and Korkie 1982, 1989; Gibbons et al. 1989). Very strong assumptions are needed that allow for neither time correlation nor conditional heteroscedasticity. The results obtained are then to be handled with caution.

(**) Numerical evaluation by simulations of the finite distance distribution of the statistic ξ_T^d may also be used. Thus, we may apply a Bootstrap procedure (Ferson et al. 1982) with the following steps:

1) First, we estimate by OLS the system (8.28) and compute the residuals $(\hat{u}_t)$.

2) T values are then drawn independently in the residual set $[\hat{u}_1, \ldots, \hat{u}_T]$; these values are denoted by: $\tilde{u}_1, \ldots, \tilde{u}_T$. Simulated values of the gains are then derived by

$$\tilde{Y}_t = \hat{B}F_t + \hat{D}X_t + \tilde{u}_t.$$

3) We deduce from the values $(\tilde{Y}_t, F_t, X_t)$ a simulated value of the statistic ξ_T^d denoted $\tilde{\xi}$.

4) Steps 2 and 3 are repeated S times, which provides S simulated values of the statistic $\tilde{\xi}^1, \ldots, \tilde{\xi}^S$. The finite distance distribution of ξ_T^d may be well approximated by the empirical distribution of $\tilde{\xi}^1, \ldots, \tilde{\xi}^S$.

8.3.2   Ex-Post Efficiency

Once a system of factors summarizing the dynamic is found, we have to examine whether this system is minimal, that is, whether there is no redundant factor. This question concerns the rank of the beta matrix. If the matrix has full rank, all of the factors are useful for summarizing the dynamic; otherwise, we may reduce the number of factors. Therefore, we have to study two problems: the determination of the rank of the beta matrix and the determination of the actual factors. These problems will be solved simultaneously.

We are interested in the sequence of hypotheses

$$H_0^k = \{\text{Rank } B = k\} \tag{8.38}$$
$$= \{\exists\, \beta, \alpha, \text{ matrices of size } (n, k) \text{ and } (k, K) \tag{8.39}$$
$$\text{with rank } k, \text{ such that } B = \beta\alpha'\}$$
$$\text{for } k = 1, \ldots, K.$$

These hypotheses are analyzed in the framework of model (8.27), $Y_t = BF_t + u_t$, and the tests based on the OLS estimator of B. The OLS estimator of $b = (b_1', \ldots, b_n') = \text{vec } B$ is

$$\hat{b} = [Id_n \otimes F(F'F)^{-1}F']y. \tag{8.40}$$

This estimator is asymptotically normal, with mean b, and a consistent estimator of its asymptotic variance matrix is

$$\hat{W} = \hat{V}_{as}[\sqrt{T}(\hat{b} - b)] = T\{\hat{\Omega} \otimes (F'F)^{-1}\}, \tag{8.41}$$

with $\hat{\Omega} = \frac{1}{T}\sum_{t=1}^{T}\hat{u}_t\hat{u}_t'$ and $\hat{u}_t = Y_t - \hat{B}F_t$.

The constraint defining H_0^k may be written by means of the vectorized parameter b:

$$H_0^k = \{b = (Id \otimes \alpha)\text{vec } \beta'\}.$$

Applying asymptotic least squares (Gouriéroux and Monfort 1990), we may introduce the test statistic

$$\xi_T^b = \min_{\alpha,\beta}[\hat{b} - (Id_n \otimes \alpha)\text{vec } \beta']'\hat{W}^{-1}[\hat{b} - (Id_n \otimes \alpha)\text{vec } \beta'], \tag{8.42}$$

which asymptotically follows under the null hypothesis a chi-square distribution with

$$Kn - k(n + K - {}^`k) = (K - k)(n - k)$$

degrees of freedom.

Property 8.43. *The critical region with asymptotic level 5% to test for the rank condition H_0^k is*

$$\xi_T^k \geq \chi_{95\%}^2((K - k)(n - k)),$$

where ξ_T^k is given by (8.41).

Now, it remains to derive the explicit form of the statistic ξ_T^k by a canonical analysis of a well chosen matrix.

The minimization problem (8.41) may be solved in two steps: first by minimizing with respect to β, α being fixed, and then by minimizing with respect to α. The minimization, α being fixed, provides

$$(\text{vec }\hat{\beta}')(\alpha) = [(Id_n \otimes \alpha)'\hat{W}^{-1}(Id_n \otimes \alpha)]^{-1}(Id_n \otimes \alpha)'\hat{W}^{-1}\hat{b},$$

and the value of the concentrated objective function is

$$\begin{aligned}
\xi_T(\alpha) = &\ \hat{b}'\hat{W}^{-1}\hat{b} \\
&- \hat{b}'\hat{W}^{-1}(Id_n \otimes \alpha)[(Id_n \otimes \alpha)'\hat{W}^{-1}(Id_n \otimes \alpha)]^{-1} \\
&(Id_n \otimes \alpha)'\hat{W}^{-1}\hat{b}.
\end{aligned}$$

We are finally led to maximize

$$\begin{aligned}
M(\alpha) = &\ \hat{b}'\hat{W}^{-1}(Id_n \otimes \alpha)[(Id_n \otimes \alpha)'\hat{W}^{-1}(Id_n \otimes \alpha)]^{-1} \\
&(Id_n \otimes \alpha)'\hat{W}^{-1}\hat{b} \\
= &\ \text{Tr}\{[(Id_n \otimes \alpha)'\hat{W}^{-1}(Id_n \otimes \alpha)]^{-1}(Id_n \otimes \alpha)\hat{W}^{-1}\hat{b}\hat{b}'\hat{W}^{-1} \\
&(Id_n \otimes \alpha)\} \\
= &\ \frac{1}{T}\text{Tr}\{[\hat{\Omega}^{-1} \otimes \alpha'F'F\alpha]^{-1}[\hat{\Omega}^{-1} \otimes \alpha F'F]\hat{b}\hat{b}'[\hat{\Omega}^{-1} \otimes F'F\alpha]\}.
\end{aligned}$$

Since α is a regular matrix, we may impose the normalizing convention

$$\alpha'F'F\alpha = Id_k. \tag{8.44}$$

Then the objective function becomes

$$\begin{aligned}
M(\alpha) &= \frac{1}{T}\text{Tr}\{[Id_n \otimes \alpha'F'F]\hat{b}\hat{b}'[\hat{\Omega}^{-1} \otimes F'F\alpha]\} \\
&= \frac{1}{T}\text{Tr}\{\alpha'F'F\hat{B}'\hat{\Omega}^{-1}\hat{B}F'F\alpha\}.
\end{aligned}$$

In order to maximize $M(\alpha)$ under the constraint (8.42), we may diagonalize the matrix $\hat{B}'\hat{\Omega}^{-1}\hat{B}F'F$. Let us denote by $\hat{\mu}_{1T} \geq \hat{\mu}_{2T}, \ldots \geq \hat{\mu}_{KT}$ its eigenvalues ranked in decreasing order and by $\hat{\alpha}_{1T}, \ldots, \hat{\alpha}_{KT}$ a basis of associated eigenvectors satisfying the normalizing constraint $\hat{\alpha}_{iT}'F'F\hat{\alpha}_{kT} = \delta_{ik}$, where δ_{ik} denotes the Kronecker delta. We get

$$\max_{\alpha} M[\alpha] = \sum_{i=1}^{k} \hat{\mu}_{iT},$$

and the solution in α is

$$\hat{\alpha} = \begin{bmatrix} \hat{\alpha}'_{1T} \\ \vdots \\ \hat{\alpha}'_{kT} \end{bmatrix}.$$

The value of the test statistic follows:

$$\xi_T^k(\alpha) = \hat{b}'\hat{W}^{-1}\hat{b} - \sum_{i=1}^{k} \hat{\mu}_{iT} = \sum_{i=k+1}^{K} \hat{\mu}_{iT}. \tag{8.45}$$

Property 8.46. *The test statistic ξ_T^k and the estimated efficient factor portfolios corresponding to $\hat{\alpha}'_T$ are obtained by a canonical analysis of the matrix $\hat{B}'\hat{\Omega}^{-1}\hat{B}F'F$.*

The statistic may also be computed by using another canonical analysis (see exercise 8.6), since the matrix $\hat{B}'\hat{\Omega}^{-1}\hat{B}F'F$ has the same eigenvalues as the matrix:

$$R^2(F, Y)[Id - R^2(F, Y)]^{-1}, \tag{8.47}$$

with $R^2(F, Y) = (F'F)^{-1}F'Y(Y'Y)^{-1}Y'F$.

Corollary 8.48. *The test statistic ξ_T^k equals*

$$\xi_T^k = T \sum_{i=k+1}^{K} \frac{\hat{\lambda}_{iT}}{1 - \hat{\lambda}_{iT}},$$

where $\hat{\lambda}_{1T} \geq \ldots \geq \hat{\lambda}_{nT}$ are the eigenvalues of the matrix $R^2(F, Y)$ given in (8.47).

This rank test allows for the determination of the efficient factors, since the computation of the statistic requires the estimation of α. If these factors are exogenous, we may deduce the corresponding endogenous factors. From section 8.1, they can be estimated by

$$\hat{A} = \hat{\Omega}^{-1}\hat{B}_0(\hat{B}_0'\hat{\Omega}^{-1}\hat{B}_0)^{-1},$$

where $\hat{B}_0$ is the constrained estimator of B (see subsection 8.1.2).

8.4 Conditional and Historical Performance Measures

8.4.1 The Dynamics of a Model with Endogenous Factors

We now focus on the dynamics of a model with endogenous factors, especially as far as the performance measures are concerned. We consider the nesting model introduced to test for ex-ante efficiency with $X_t = 1$,

$$Y_t = d + BA'Y_t + u_t,$$

with the usual assumptions about the error terms. Changing the basic assets if necessary, we may always assume that $A = [Id_k, 0]$. Introducing the subvectors corresponding to the K first and the $n - K$ latter assets, this system of equations, whose K first equations are redundant (since they are equivalent to $Y_{1t} = Y_{1t}$), may be rewritten

$$Y_{2t} = d_2 + B_{21} Y_{1t} + u_{2t}, \tag{8.49}$$

where the error term u_{2t} has a time independent conditional variance Ω_{22}. Let us study the dynamic resulting from the first two conditional moments. We have

$$m_t = \left[\begin{array}{c} m_{1t} \\ d_2 + B_{21} m_{1t} \end{array} \right], \quad \Sigma_t = \left[\begin{array}{cc} \Sigma_{11t} & \Sigma_{11t} B'_{12} \\ B_{21} \Sigma_{11t} & B_{21} \Sigma_{11t} B'_{21} + \Omega_{22} \end{array} \right].$$

The Sharpe performance of the set of basic assets is (see exercise 8.4)

$$\begin{aligned}
S_t &= m'_t \Sigma_t^{-1} m_t \\
&= [m'_{1t}, d'_2 + m'_{1t} B'_{21}] \left[\begin{array}{cc} \Sigma_{11t}^{-1} + B'_{21} \Omega_{22}^{-1} B_{21} & -B'_{21} \Omega_{22}^{-1} \\ -\Omega_{22}^{-1} B_{21} & \Omega_{22}^{-1} \end{array} \right] \left[\begin{array}{c} m_{1t} \\ d_2 + B_{21} m_{1t} \end{array} \right] \\
&= m'_{1t} \Sigma_{11t}^{-1} m_{1t} + d'_2 \Omega_{22}^{-1} d_2 \\
&= S_{1t} + d'_2 \Omega_{22}^{-1} d_2,
\end{aligned}$$

where S_{1t} is the performance of the set of the K factors portfolios.

Property 8.50. *The factor model (8.49) is such that the performances of the set of assets and the set of factors portfolios depend on time with a time independent difference.*

Similar computations may be performed in an unconditional way. Let us denote

$$m = Em_t, \text{ the marginal mean,}$$
$$\Sigma = E\Sigma_t + Vm_t, \text{ the marginal variance.}$$

We get

$$m = \left[\begin{array}{c} m_1 \\ d_2 + B_{21} m_1 \end{array} \right], \quad \Sigma = \left[\begin{array}{cc} \Sigma_{11} & \Sigma_{11} B'_{12} \\ B_{21} \Sigma_{11} & B_{21} \Sigma_{11} B'_{21} + \Omega_{22} \end{array} \right],$$

and the historical performances satisfy

$$S = S_1 + d'_2 \Omega_{22}^{-1} d_2 = m'_1 \Sigma_{11}^{-1} m_1 + d'_2 \Omega_{22}^{-1} d_2.$$

Property 8.51. *In the nesting model (8.49), the difference between the historical performances equals the difference between the conditional performances.*

8.4.2   Tests for Ex-Ante Efficiency and Performances

To test for the efficiency of the set of the K first assets against the maintained hypothesis (8.49) is equivalent to testing whether d_2 equals zero. The preceding discussion shows that the efficiency hypothesis may be expressed in terms of either conditional or historical performances:

$$H_0 = \{S_t = S_{1t}, \ \forall t\} = \{S = S_1\}.$$

Therefore, the test procedure may likely be expressed from estimated performances. The following result shows that the estimated historical performances appear.

Property 8.52. *The Wald statistic to test for the ex-ante efficiency hypothesis against the maintained hypothesis (8.49) is*

$$\xi_T^d = T \frac{\hat{S} - \hat{S}_1}{1 + \hat{S}_1},$$

where $\hat{S}$ and $\hat{S}_1$ are the estimated historical performances.

Proof. It is sufficient to consider the Wald statistic, whose expression is provided in section 8.3.1 for the model (8.49):

$$\xi_T^d = \sum_i \sum_j \hat{\omega}^{ij} Y_{i2}'(Id - Q_1)e[e'(Id - Q_1)e]^{-1}e'(Id - Q_1)Y_{j2},$$

where ω_{ij} is the (i, j)-th element of the matrix $\hat{\Omega}_{22}^{-1}$, Y_{i2} is the vector of net gains of the i-th asset of the second group, e is the vector of ones and Q_1 is the projector on the net gain vectors of the factor assets. A straightforward computation yields

$$e'(Id - Q_1)e$$
$$= e'[Id - Y_1(Y_1'Y_1)^{-1}Y_1']e$$
$$= T[1 - \hat{m}_1'[\hat{\Sigma}_{11} + \hat{m}_1'\hat{m}_1]^{-1}\hat{m}_1],$$

where $\hat{m}_1$ and $\hat{\Sigma}_{11}$ denote the empirical mean and variances of the net gains of the factor assets. By applying exercise 8.5, we get

$$e'(Id - Q_1)e$$
$$= T\left[1 - \hat{m}_1'\left[\hat{\Sigma}_{11}^{-1} - \frac{1}{1 + \hat{S}_1}\hat{\Sigma}_{11}^{-1}\hat{m}_1'\hat{m}_1\hat{\Sigma}_{11}^{-1}\right]\hat{m}_1\right]$$
$$= T\left(1 - \hat{S}_1 + \frac{\hat{S}_1^2}{1 + \hat{S}_1}\right) = \frac{T}{1 + \hat{S}_1}.$$

We also have

$$Y_{i2}'(Id - Q_1)e$$
$$= T[\hat{m}_{i2}' - \left(\hat{\Sigma}_{i21} + \hat{m}_{i2}\hat{m}_1'\right)^{-1}\left(\hat{\Sigma}_{11} + \hat{m}_1\hat{m}_1'\right)^{-1}\hat{m}_1],$$

where $\hat{\Sigma}_{i21}$ is the row of $\hat{\Sigma}_{21}$ associated with asset i. This formula is simplified into

$$Y_{i2}'(Id - Q_1)e = \frac{T}{1 + \hat{S}_1}\left(\hat{m}_{i2} - \hat{\Sigma}_{i21}^{-1}\hat{\Sigma}_{11}^{-1}\hat{m}_1\right).$$

Taking into account the equality

$$\hat{\Omega}_{22} = \hat{\Sigma}_{22} - \hat{\Sigma}_{21}\hat{\Sigma}_{11}^{-1}\hat{\Sigma}_{12},$$

we deduce that

$$\xi_T^d = \frac{T}{1 + \hat{S}_1}\left(\hat{m}_2 - \hat{\Sigma}_{21}\hat{\Sigma}_{11}^{-1}\hat{m}_1\right)'\left(\hat{\Sigma}_{22} - \hat{\Sigma}_{21}\hat{\Sigma}_{11}^{-1}\hat{\Sigma}_{12}\right)^{-1}\left(\hat{m}_2 - \hat{\Sigma}_{21}\hat{\Sigma}_{11}^{-1}\hat{m}_1\right)$$

$$= T\frac{\hat{S} - \hat{S}_1}{1 + \hat{S}_1}, \text{ according to the formula (7.32).} \qquad \text{Q.E.D.}$$

8.5   Exercises

Exercise 8.1. The linear regression of Y_t on F_t given the past is supposed to be given. Find the explicit form of the linear regression of Y_t on F_t, $A'Y_t$ given the past, where A is a given matrix.

Exercise 8.2. Study how the conditional moments are modified by time aggregation of flows or levels. Two cases have to be distinguished depending upon whether or not the aggregation procedure is also applied to the available information.

Exercise 8.3. Let us assume the conditions of property 8.16.

a) Show that $C'm_t = 0$ and $C'(\Sigma_t - \Omega)C = 0$, with $\Sigma_t - \Omega \gg 0$.

b) Deduce that $m_t \in [RgC]^{\perp}$ and $Ker(\Sigma_t - \Omega) \supset RgC$.

c) Verify that if $\tilde{B}_1, \ldots, \tilde{B}_K$ denotes a basis of $(RgC)^{\perp}$, we have

$$m_t = \sum_{k=1}^{K}\mu_{kt}\tilde{B}_k, \quad (\Sigma_t - \Omega) = \sum_{k=1}^{K}\sum_{l=1}^{K}\lambda_{lkt}\tilde{B}_k\tilde{B}_l'.$$

Exercise 8.4. Σ_t and Ω are two invertible symmetric matrices with dimension (p, p) and (n, n), respectively, and B is an (n, p) matrix; show that

$$\begin{bmatrix} \Sigma & \Sigma B' \\ B\Sigma & B\Sigma B' + \Omega \end{bmatrix}^{-1} = \begin{bmatrix} \Sigma^{-1} + B'\Omega^{-1}B & -B'\Omega^{-1} \\ -\Omega^{-1}B & \Omega^{-1} \end{bmatrix}.$$

Exercise 8.5. Prove the equality $(\Sigma + mm')^{-1} = \Sigma^{-1} - \frac{1}{1+S}\Sigma^{-1}mm'\Sigma^{-1}$, with $S = m'\Sigma^{-1}m$.

Exercise 8.6. (Gouriéroux et al. 1991): The notations of subsection 8.3.2 are used.

i) Find the extended expression of $\hat{B}\hat{\Omega}^{-1}\hat{B}F'F$, and compare it to the one of $R^2(F, Y)$.

ii) Let us introduce the matrix

$$R^2(F, Y) = (YY')^{-1}Y'F(F'F)^{-1}F'Y.$$

Verify that $R^2(F, Y)$ and $R^2(Y, F)$ have the same eigenvalues. Conclude that the rank test could have been performed using the regression of the factors F on the gains of the basic assets. Explain this result.

iii) Verify that the matrix $R^2(F, Y)$ has a basis of eigenvectors $\tilde{\alpha}_{iT}, i = 1, \ldots, K$ that may be normalized by $\tilde{\alpha}_{iT} F' F \tilde{\alpha}_{jT} = \delta_{ij}$.

iv) How can you interpret the eigenvectors of $R^2(F, Y)$?

Exercise 8.7. Let us assume that the initial factors F of a factor model are economic variables with nonfinancial interpretations. Explain how the recursive form (8.9) separates in the dynamics the specific financial part from the influence of the "real sphere" on the "financial sphere".

Exercise 8.8.

i) Explain why the Wald statistic

$$\xi_T^d = T \sum_{i=1}^{n} \frac{\hat{\eta}_{iT}}{1 - \hat{\eta}_{iT}},$$

given in (8.36), could be replaced by

$$\xi_T = T \sum_{i=1}^{n} \hat{\eta}_{iT}$$

or by $\xi_T^* = -T \sum_{i=1}^{n} \log(1 - \hat{\eta}_{iT})$.

ii) Determine the likelihood ratio statistic for the hypothesis $\{D = 0\}$ under the normality assumption for the errors. Verify that it is equal to ξ_T^*.

iii) Determine the score statistic to test $\{D = 0\}$ under the normality assumption of the errors. Verify that it is equal to ξ_T.

iv) Which is the smallest (resp. the largest) of these two statistics?

9
Equilibrium Models

9.1 Capital Asset Pricing Model

9.1.1 Description of the Model

The Capital Asset Pricing Model (CAPM) is obtained by adding to the optimal behavior of the asset demanders an equilibrium condition on supply and demand. This model was derived independently by Sharpe (1964), Lintner (1965) and Mossin (1966). Let us consider the case of a financial market where $n + 1$ assets may be traded, the first one corresponding to the risk-free asset. If m individuals may intervene as demanders in this market, have the same information set and behave optimally with respect to a mean variance plan with risk-aversion coefficient $a_i, i = 1, \ldots, m$, the aggregate demand for risky assets is (see section 7.3.3):

$$\alpha_t^d = \sum_{i=1}^{m} \frac{1}{a_i} (\mathrm{diag}(p_t))^{-1} \Sigma_t^{-1} (m_t - R_{0t} e)$$

$$= \frac{1}{A} (\mathrm{diag}(p_t))^{-1} \Sigma_t^{-1} (m_t - R_{0t} e),$$

where A is the risk-aversion coefficient of the set of demanders.

In addition, let us denote by α_t^s the supply (volume) of assets. This supply may depend on the price evolution, but this dependence will not be used for the moment.

At market equilibrium, the available quantity of assets α_{Mt} will simultaneously equal supply and demand:

$$\alpha_{Mt} = \alpha_t^s = \alpha_t^d = \frac{1}{A} (\mathrm{diag}(p_t))^{-1} \Sigma_t^{-1} (m_t - R_{0t} e). \tag{9.1}$$

The average returns are functions of the available quantities, prices and volatilities:

$$m_t - R_{0t}e = A\Sigma_t \, \text{diag}(p_t)\alpha_{Mt}. \tag{9.2}$$

This relation is the basis of the CAPM. It may also be written in terms of unitary gains:

$$(\text{diag } p_t)(m_t - R_{0t}e) = A(\text{diag } p_t)\Sigma_t(\text{diag } p_t)\alpha_{Mt},$$
$$E_t(\gamma_{t+1}) - (\text{diag } p_t)R_{0t} = AV_t(\gamma_{t+1})\alpha_{Mt}.$$

9.1.2   Market Portfolio

The set of available quantities of the risky assets may be interpreted as a portfolio, called a **market portfolio**. The return of the market portfolio between t and $t + 1$ compared with that of the risk-free asset is

$$R_{M,t+1} - R_{0,t} = R_{t+1}[\alpha_{Mt}] - R_{0t}$$
$$= \frac{\alpha'_{Mt} \, \text{diag}(p_t)(R_{t+1} - R_{0t}e)}{\alpha'_{Mt} \, p_t}$$
$$= \frac{(m_t - R_{0t})'\Sigma_t^{-1}(R_{t+1} - R_{0t}e)}{e'\Sigma_t^{-1}(m_t - R_{0t}e)}.$$

One then obtains the following property.

Property 9.3.   i) *The average returns of the basic assets and market portfolio conditional on date t are*

$$\begin{cases} m_{1t} = E_t(R_{t+1} - R_{0t}e) = m_t - R_{0t}e, \\ m_{2t} = E_t(R_{M,t+1} - R_{0t}e) = \dfrac{(m_t - R_{0t})'\Sigma_t^{-1}(m_t - R_{0t}e)}{e'\Sigma_t^{-1}(m_t - R_{0t}e)}. \end{cases}$$

ii) The conditional volatilities and covolatilities are

$$\begin{cases} \Sigma_{11t} = V_t(R_{t+1} - R_{0t}e) = \Sigma_t, \\ \Sigma_{12t} = \text{Cov}_t(R_{t+1} - R_{0t}e, R_{M,t+1} - R_{0t}) = \dfrac{m_t - R_{0t}e}{e'\Sigma_t^{-1}(m_t - R_{0t}e)}, \\ \Sigma_{22t} = V_t(R_{M,t+1} - R_{0t}) = \dfrac{(m_t - R_{0t}e)'\Sigma_t^{-1}(m_t - R_{0t}e)}{[e'\Sigma_t^{-1}(m_t - R_{0t}e)]^2}. \end{cases}$$

Thus, in the CAPM, the first and second order moments of the net return of the market portfolio can be deduced only from the knowledge of the moments of the basic asset's returns. The market portfolio allocation α_{Mt} is known at date t so that the covariance matrix of $(R'_{t+1} - R_{0t}e', R_{M,t+1} - R_{0t})'$ is not invertible.

Corollary 9.4. *Under the CAPM, the matrix*

$$\begin{bmatrix} \Sigma_{11t} & \Sigma_{12t} \\ \Sigma_{21t} & \Sigma_{22t} \end{bmatrix}$$

is singular.

Another constraint between the moments is given as follows.

Corollary 9.5. *Under the CAPM,*

$$m_{1t} - \Sigma_{12t}(\Sigma_{22t})^{-1}m_{2t} = 0.$$

This condition suggests a simple interpretation in terms of regression. Indeed, let us consider the theoretical linear regression of the basic asset returns on the market portfolio return performed at date t. We may write

$$R_{t+1} - R_{0t}e = \beta_{0t} + \beta_t(R_{M,t+1} - R_{0t}) + u_{t+1}, \tag{9.6}$$

where the residual u_{t+1} has a zero conditional mean $E_t u_{t+1} = 0$ and is not correlated with the market portfolio return:

$$\text{Cov}_t(u_{t+1}, R_{M,t+1} - R_{0t}) = 0.$$

The regression coefficients are given by

$$\beta_t = \Sigma_{12t}(\Sigma_{22t})^{-1},$$
$$\beta_{0t} = m_{1t} - \Sigma_{12t}(\Sigma_{22t})^{-1}m_{2t}.$$

The coefficients β_t are the betas of the basic assets on the market portfolio. The condition of corollary 9.5 is then written in the following form.

Corollary 9.7. *Under the CAPM, the constant terms in the linear regressions of $R_{t+1} - R_{0t}e$ on $R_{M,t+1} - R_{0t}$ (given the past) are zero or, equivalently, the average net returns of the basic assets are proportional to the betas, the proportionality coefficient being the net return of the market portfolio.*

It is usual to plot this linear dependence between expected returns and betas. It results in a straight line whose intercept at the origin is the return of the risk-free asset R_{0t}, and the slope is the expected net return of the market portfolio:

$$E_t R_{j\,t+1} - R_{0t} = \beta_{jt}(E_t R_{M,t+1} - R_{0t}).$$

This straight line is called the (Sharpe–Lintner) **security market line**.

9.1.3 The CAPM as a Factor Model

The relation that links the basic asset returns to the market portfolio return has an equivalent expression in terms of unit gains:

$$\gamma_{t+1} - \gamma_{0t} = \tilde{\beta}_t(\gamma_{M,t+1} - \gamma_{0t}) + \tilde{u}_{t+1},$$

with $\gamma_{0t} = (\text{diag } p_t)R_{0t}e$, $\gamma_{M,t+1} = (\alpha'_{Mt} p_t)R_{M,t+1}$.

$\tilde{\beta}_t$ is the regression coefficient of $\gamma_{t+1} - \gamma_{0t}$ on $(\gamma_{M,t+1} - \gamma_{0t})$ computed conditional to the information available at date t. If the conditional variability of these gains has a structure such that $\tilde{\beta}_t$ and $V_t \tilde{u}_{t+1}$ are time independent, the equation

$$\gamma_{t+1} - \gamma_{0t} = \tilde{\beta}(\gamma_{M\,t+1} - \gamma_{0t}) + \tilde{u}_{t+1}$$

is a factor representation (see chapter 8) including only one factor identifiable as the market portfolio. It is an endogenous factor in the restricted sense of chapter 8 if the composition of the market portfolio α_{Mt} is time independent. This condition is approximately satisfied in practice, where the asset supply varies much less than the prices.

9.1.4 Spectral Decomposition of the Moments

Let us consider the particular case where the instantaneous variability is decomposed on an orthonormal basis of time independent eigenvectors. We may write

$$\Sigma_t = \sum_{j=1}^{n} \lambda_{jt} a_j a'_j,$$

$$m_t - R_{0t} e = \sum_{j=1}^{n} \mu_{jt} a_j.$$

The eigenvectors a_j may be used as basic portfolios. These portfolios have returns equal to

$$\tilde{R}_{j\,t+1} = \frac{a'_j R_{t+1}}{a'_j e}$$

and correspond to weights $\alpha_{jit} = a_{ji}/p_{it}$ $i = 1, \ldots, n$, for the different assets (see section 7.1). These weights are time dependent by means of the prices. The quantities of withheld assets in these basic portfolios vary, but the values of the assets remain constant.

The return of the market portfolio is

$$R_{M,t+1} - R_{0t} = \frac{\sum_j (\mu_{jt}/\lambda_{jt}) a'_j (R_{t+1} - R_{0t} e)}{\sum_j e' a_j (\mu_{jt}/\lambda_{jt})},$$

$$R_{M,t+1} - R_{0t} = \frac{\sum_j (\mu_{jt}/\lambda_{jt}) e' a_j (\tilde{R}_{j\,t+1} - R_{0t})}{\sum_j (\mu_{jt}/\lambda_{jt}) e' a_j},$$

$$R_{M,t+1} = \frac{\left(\sum_j (\mu_{jt}/\lambda_{jt}) e' a_j \tilde{R}_{j\,t+1} \right)}{\left(\sum_j (\mu_{jt}/\lambda_{jt}) e' a_j \right)}. \tag{9.8}$$

The market portfolio net return is a weighted average of the net returns of the portfolios associated with the vectors a_j, $j = 1, \ldots, n$. The correlation between the returns $R_{M,t+1}$ and $\tilde{R}_{j,t+1}$ equals

$$\frac{\mu_{jt}}{\lambda_{jt}^{1/2}} \left(\sum_j \frac{\mu_{jt}^2}{\lambda_{jt}} \right)^{1/2}$$

and is proportional to the Sharpe performance measure of the portfolio a_j, which equals $\frac{\mu_{jt}}{\lambda_{jt}^{1/2}}$. Thus, the market portfolio appears as the most correlated with the best performing portfolios.

Note 9.9. Equation (9.8) is a regression equation of the return $R_{M,t+1}$ on the return $\tilde{R}_{j,t+1}$. Indeed,

$$R_{M,t+1} = cte + \frac{\mu_{jt}}{\lambda_{jt}} e' a_j \tilde{R}_{j t+1} \left(\sum_j \frac{\mu_{jt}}{\lambda_{jt}} e' a_j \right)^{-1} + v_{jt},$$

where the error v_{jt} is uncorrelated with $\tilde{R}_{j\,t+1}$. Do not confuse this regression with the one (9.6) introduced to define the coefficients β_{jt}, the latter one being carried out in the other direction (see exercise 9.1).

9.1.5 Time Dependent Risk Aversion

A natural extension of the mean variance model leads to time dependent risk aversions (see chapter 7). In such a case, the equilibrium equation (9.2) is modified and becomes

$$m_t - R_{0t} e = A_t \Sigma_t \, \text{diag}(p_t) \alpha_{M\,t}, \tag{9.10}$$

where A_t is a function of the past.

This modification has no influence on the link between the returns because the risk-aversion coefficient is eliminated in the computation of the market portfolio return. The constraints in line with the CAPM such as (9.4), (9.5), and (9.7) remain unmodified.

9.2 Test of the CAPM

The theory of optimal behavior of investors and the equilibrium condition imply several constraints between the returns and the quantities, or between the asset returns and the market portfolio return. From the point of view of financial theory, it is important to test some of these constraints. The test procedure obviously depends on the models retained and the available data.

9.2.1   Some Difficulties

i) The CAPM Hypothesis

Chapter 7 and section 9.1 clearly show that the CAPM is based on some strong assumptions:

(*) The investors behave in an optimal way and act according to a mean variance criterion, which implies that they value the risk only by means of the two first moments.

(**) They build their portfolios using n basic assets. Thus, if these n assets are stocks, it is implicitly assumed that they do not consider the possible substitution between this category of assets and, for instance, bonds, currencies or antiques, etc.

(***) These securities are supposed to be tradable in a perfectly competitive market. From a practical point of view, it restricts the type of assets: there exist assets for which no organized market exists, some others for which the market institutionally exists but where the daily trading is weak (in that case, only one demander can make the price vary quickly), etc.

As an example, the table below lists quantities traded for several securities on the Montreal and New York stock exchanges for March 1, 1990.

Stock Exchange	Security	Volume
Montreal	Banque royale	109 770
	BP Can	101 200
	Bow val	109 800
	Mac Lean	479 350
	Wajax. A	100
	Lfrg.Can P	100
	Algo	19
New York	American Express	1 988 300
	General Motors	1 367 800
	Dupont	1 212 000
	AT & T	1 590 200
	Boeing	1 072 000
	BrMYSq	1 089 000
	IBM	1 440 300
	Armc	500
	Bunk	500
	Chemed	100

Naturally, there is a large disparity between the traded volumes of these securities, some of them being frequently and largely bought and sold (**liquid** securities) and others having a very restricted market. It points out that the CAPM can be studied only for particular sets of assets that are both liquid and tradeable on a structured market.

ii) Descriptive and Structural Models

The CAPM can be tested only as a submodel of a larger model, and it is natural to search for this nesting model in the class of the ARCH models. We are nevertheless facing the difficulty of establishing links between a structural formulation, on which the CAPM is based, and a descriptive specification, i.e., the ARCH model.

For instance, let us examine the fundamental equation of the CAPM

$$m_t - R_{0t}e = A \Sigma_t \, \mathrm{diag}(p_t) \, \alpha_{Mt}. \tag{9.2}$$

The ARCH model is essentially defined by selecting a specification of the conditional means and variances as functions of the current or past prices (and eventually of the volumes traded). Under the constraint (9.2), the function of the prices $\frac{1}{A_t}(\mathrm{diag}(p_t)^{-1} \Sigma_t^{-1}(m_t - R_{0t}e)$ should vary just like the observed quantities. This deterministic relation is never satisfied by the data.

Two pragmatic modifications may be proposed, and both consist of testing for an approximated CAPM.

The first one is the usual approach followed in equilibrium models. It implicitly supposes that the quantities α_{Mt} are observed and consists in introducing an error term in the demand equation. This can reflect omitted variables, measurement errors, false evaluation of the available information, nonrational expectations, etc.

Equation (9.2) is then replaced by

$$m_t - R_{0t}e = A \Sigma_t \, \mathrm{diag}(p_t)\alpha_{Mt} + v_{t+1}, \tag{9.11}$$

where (v_{t+1}) is an error process independent of the process of expected error on the returns. The model (9.11) is then nested into a larger specification such as

$$R_{t+1} - R_{0t}e = A \Sigma_t \, \mathrm{diag}(p_t)\alpha_{Mt} + BR_t + \ldots + v_{t+1} + \varepsilon_{t+1},$$

where ε_{t+1} is the forecast error and Σ_t is a function of returns, past volatilities and covolatilities. This specification includes additional explanatory variables like R_t, a variable whose impact should be zero ($B = 0$) if the CAPM were satisfied. This specification looks like an ARCH-M model but is more general since it includes influences of the available quantities.

b) The second solution assumes that the quantities α_{Mt} are not observed and introduces assumptions on their evolution. One often assumes that these quantities are less variable than the prices and may be considered constant across time periods smaller than two or three years. In that case, the null hypothesis is

$$\tilde{H}_0 = \{\exists A, \alpha_M: m_t - R_{0t}e = A\Sigma_t \, \mathrm{diag}(p_t)\alpha_M, \, \forall t\}. \tag{9.12}$$

In terms of unitary gains, the hypothesis becomes

$$\tilde{H}_0 = \{\exists A, \alpha_M: E_t \, \gamma_{t+1} - \gamma_0 = AV_t \, (\gamma_{t+1})\alpha_M, \, \forall t\}.$$

This hypothesis is easy to nest in ARCH models. The tests for the hypothesis $\tilde{H}_0$ will demand a preliminary estimation of the vector α_M and, whether the hypothesis

$\tilde{H}_0$ is accepted or not, it is interesting to study the gap between this estimation and the quantities $\alpha_{M\,t}$ (when the latter ones are available) to locate the periods where the hypothesis is the more (respectively, the less) satisfied. This kind of approach is followed in Engle et al. (1989) or Gouriéroux and Monfort (1990).

iii) The Available Data

The data generally concern asset prices (opening and closing prices, maximal and minimal prices during the day, etc.) and sometimes also volumes traded, interventions (stop of the quotes, central bank interventions in currency markets) and news. However, the CAPM leads us to introduce two kinds of variables, i.e., the quantities supplied and the market portfolio return.

a) **The quantities supplied**

According to the theory, we have to introduce the quantities of assets supplied. For the stocks, this refers to existing quantities of each security and not to traded ones (because the trading that an individual has with himself must be included). For other assets such as, say, corn, this quantity is more difficult to define; indeed, a part of the supply is for consumption, an aspect that does not appear in our model, but it is also an example in which the supply may quickly adjust to prices by means of substitution between corn as a consumption good and corn as an investment good, so that the supply is perhaps more endogenous than assumed in the model.

b) **The market portfolio**

The selection of a market portfolio is also rather tricky, since there exists no market as introduced by economic theory. In practice, one often chooses a portfolio used to construct a market index as a "market portfolio". For the Paris stock exchange, the CAC 40 index may be a proxy for a portfolio built on the 40 support assets with weights equaling the quantities withheld. (The CAC 40 weights do not exactly correspond to these quantities.) The choice of such an index automatically selects the n liquid assets to be considered.

The previous list of these difficulties shows that only modified or partial versions of the CAPM may be tested for and that these versions will likely be rejected. However, we do not have to believe that CAPM theory is useless. For instance, this theory does provide the notion of betas, i.e., the idea of focusing on the link between the asset returns and the market portfolio return. These betas are of important practical interest in comparing asset returns whatever the conclusion of the test for CAPM. For instance, an increasing (not necessarily linear) relation will often be observed between betas and expected returns.

In a similar way, the CAPM theory allows one to point out the interest of the factor notion and has been the basis of APT (see chapter 8). It is also the CAPM theory that leads to the modification of the initial ARCH specification by introducing the impact of lagged quantities or volatility in the explanation of the expected return (ARCH-M models).

iv) The Stationarity Hypothesis

Finally, the basic ARCH models (except those including exogenous effects or unit roots) satisfy weak stationarity properties. One must check whether these properties are approximatively satisfied in practice. Let us suppose weakly stationary returns; the empirical mean $\frac{1}{T} \sum_{t=1}^{T} R_t$ should be close to the common theoretical mean $E R_t$ for large T and independent of the subperiod on which the computation is performed. For instance, Luedecke (1984) has computed the average returns of 392 assets over the periods 1971–1974 and 1975–1978 using daily data. On average, the yearly gains are about -5% for the first subperiod (a loss) and of about 30% for the second. This important difference shows that the stationarity hypothesis will not always be satisfied, and the estimated models will often include unit roots. These nonstationarity features depend on the subperiods considered and especially on their length. Also, recall that the CAPM theory may also be expressed in terms of unit gains and that it would then be necessary to consider the stationarity of the gains.

9.2.2   Testing Procedures in a Static Framework

The easiest way to test for constraints between expected returns and volatilities such as those of the CAPM consists in approximating these quantities by their historical counterpart and investigating whether this counterpart approximately verifies the constraints. In such an approach, the successive returns are considered as independent variables with identical distribution. We have insisted before on the lack of realism of such an assumption. But this simple case provides an easy presentation of the estimation and test methods and allows us to understand the major part of the literature (see the references). We present the test procedures in the following when the returns are i.i.d. A similar approach could be developed if the sequence of unit gains (and not the one of returns) satisfies this assumption.

i) The Basic Condition

Let us consider equation (9.2) in which the conditional moments m_t and Σ_t are time independent, as are the risk-free rate and the available quantities. The constraint becomes

$$\exists A, \alpha : m - R_0 e = A \Sigma (\text{diag } p_t) \alpha.$$

This condition may be satisfied only if the prices are time independent. If, for example, the return of the asset j is constant,

$$R_j = \frac{p_{j,t+1} - p_{j,t}}{p_{j,t}},$$

the constraint can never be satisfied. If the asset prices were constant, we would have

$$\exists A, \alpha : m - R_0 e = A \Sigma (\text{diag } p) \alpha.$$

This system of n equations with $n+1$ unknowns implies no actual constraint. Thus, the hypothesis always appears wrong in the first case and valid in the second.

ii) The Volatility and Covolatility of Basic Assets and of the Market Portfolio

Let us first consider condition (9.4) referring to the variance–covariance matrix of the returns of the basic assets and of the market portfolio. In the i.i.d. case, the condition becomes $\Sigma = \begin{bmatrix} \Sigma_{11} & \Sigma_{12} \\ \Sigma_{21} & \Sigma_{22} \end{bmatrix}$ singular or, equivalently (since Σ_{11} is regular under the absence of arbitrage opportunities),

$$\exists a, b_1, \ldots, b_n : R_{mt} = a + \sum_{j=1}^{n} b_j R_{jt}, \forall t.$$

This is a test for a deterministic relation between the returns. In practice, the return of the market portfolio is computed by

$$R_{mt} = \frac{\sum_{j=1}^{n} c_j p_{jt} R_{jt}}{\sum_{j=1}^{n} c_j p_{jt}},$$

which implies

$$a = 0, \quad b = \frac{c_j p_{jt}}{\sum_{j=1}^{n} c_j p_{jt}}.$$

Once more, the hypothesis is either always rejected (if p_{jt} depends on time) or always satisfied (if the prices are constant over time). It is the same difficulty as with relation (9.2).

iii) Regression Based Test

It remains to study the constraint (9.5) between expected returns and volatilities written in the i.i.d. case. This condition may be written from the regressions

$$R_{t+1} - R_{0t} e = \beta_0 + \beta_1 (R_{M\,t+1} - R_{0t}) + u_{t+1}, \tag{9.13}$$

with $E(u_{t+1}/\underline{R}_t, R_{M,t+1}) = 0$.

It is a system of seemingly unrelated regressions (SURE) with time independent coefficients β_{0j}, $j = 1, \ldots, n$, β_j, $j = 1, \ldots, n$, because of the i.i.d. assumption. The condition (9.5) gives

$$H_0 = \{\beta_0 = 0\} \Leftrightarrow H_0 = \{\beta_{0j} = 0, j = 1, \ldots, n\}. \tag{9.14}$$

Therefore, we test whether the market portfolio return is a factor that summarizes the dynamics of the asset returns. This problem has been solved in chapter 8.

The test for the null hypothesis H_0 may be carried out in the usual way. Since we have a SURE with the same explanatory variables 1 and $R_{M,t+1} - R_{0t}$, the unknown parameters β_{0j}, β_j, $j = 1, \ldots, n$, may be estimated equation by equation by ordinary least squares (equivalent to generalized least squares). The estimators are

$$\begin{cases} \hat{\beta}_j = \dfrac{\text{Cov}_{emp}(R_{j,t+1} - R_{0t}, R_{M,t+1} - R_{0t})}{V_{emp}(R_{M,t+1} - R_{0t})}, \\ \hat{\beta}_{0j} = \bar{R}_{j,t+1} - \bar{R}_{0t} - \hat{\beta}_j(\bar{R}_{M,t+1} - \bar{R}_{0t}), \end{cases}$$

where Cov_{emp}, V_{emp}, $\bar{R}$ denote the empirical covariances, variances and means, respectively. These estimators are consistent and asymptotically normal:

$$\begin{bmatrix} \hat{\beta}_0 \\ \hat{\beta} \end{bmatrix} \approx N\left[\begin{pmatrix} \beta_0 \\ \beta \end{pmatrix}, \Omega \right]. \tag{9.15}$$

The matrix Ω may be estimated easily by standard formulas for SURE. If $\hat{\Omega}$ denotes this estimated matrix, the test statistic is

$$\xi = \hat{\beta}_0' \hat{\Omega}_{00}^{-1} \hat{\beta}_0, \tag{9.16}$$

where $\hat{\Omega}_{00}$ denotes the upper left block of $\hat{\Omega}$: $\hat{\Omega}_{00} = V_{as}(\hat{\beta}_0)$.

The test procedure consists in

$$\begin{cases} \text{accepting the null hypothesis if } \xi < \chi^2_{95\%}(n), \\ \text{rejecting it otherwise,} \end{cases}$$

where $\chi^2_{95\%}(n)$ denotes the 95% quantile of a chi-square distribution with n degrees of freedom.

This procedure is global, and we may extend it to distinguish the different assets. A feasible procedure consists in testing for a subhypothesis:

$$H_{0,B} = \{\beta_{0j} = 0, \, j \in B\},$$

where B is a subset of $[1, \ldots, n]$.

iv) Security Market Line Based Tests

There exist empirical procedures based on the security market line. Indeed, we may compute the average returns of the assets $\hat{R}_{j,t+1}$ and the estimated $\hat{\beta}_j$. These values may then be plotted with average returns on the y axis and estimated betas on the x axis. A line can be drawn that summarizes the cloud obtained. Under the null hypothesis, this line should pass through the intercept $(0, \bar{R}_{0t})$ and have slope $\bar{R}_{M,t+1} - \bar{R}_{0t}$.

The null hypothesis may be rejected in several cases, particularly in the cases illustrated in figures 9.1, 9.2 and 9.3.

(*) The estimated straight line goes through $(0, \bar{R}_{0t})$ and has the slope $\bar{R}_{M,t+1} - \bar{R}_{0t}$, but some points of the cloud are far from the line. The residual corresponding to (at least) an asset j_0 is large, and the relation is not satisfied for this asset.

(**) The estimated straight line does approximate the cloud, has approximate slope $\bar{R}_{M,t+1} - \bar{R}_{0t}$, but does not pass through $(0, \bar{R}_{0t})$. This kind of configuration may be compatible with the CAPM but reveals a wrong definition of the risk-free asset. Thus, instead of taking the return of a risk-free asset, which in practice may be traded in another market, one could have taken the

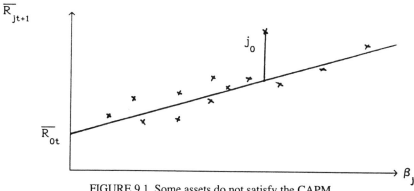

FIGURE 9.1. Some assets do not satisfy the CAPM.

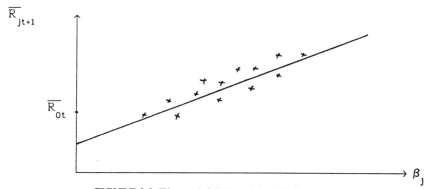

FIGURE 9.2. Wrong definition of the risk-free asset.

return of the least risky portfolio constituted within the n basic assets, with allocation:

$$\alpha_t^{**} = (\text{diag } p_t)^{-1} \frac{\Sigma_t^{-1} e}{e' \Sigma_t e}. \qquad \text{(see section 7.2.1).}$$

(***) The estimated line fits the cloud well and passes through $(0, \bar{R}_{0t})$, but its slope significantly differs from $\bar{R}_{M,t+1} - \bar{R}_{0t}$. Before rejecting the hypothesis deduced from the C.A.P.M., it must be checked whether the portfolio selected as a market portfolio is a good proxy of the underlying market portfolio.

Note 9.17. The sign of the beta is another characteristic of the assets that is often examined. Indeed, under the null hypothesis, we have

$$\beta_j = \frac{E(R_{j,t+1} - R_{0t})}{E(R_{M,t+1} - R_{0t})},$$

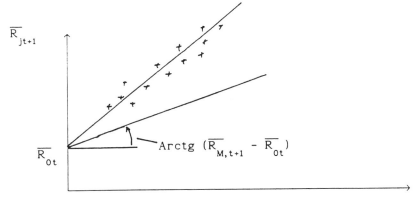

FIGURE 9.3. The effect of the choice of the market portfolio.

and, the risky assets having to pay on average more than the risk-free asset, we expect positive betas. Negative betas may then reveal a misspecification or a non-satisfied CAPM hypothesis.

v) Interpretation of the Regression Based Test

To test for condition (9.14) is to test not for the entire CAPM but simply for a consequence of this theory. It is therefore interesting to examine whether this consequence has its own interpretation. For this purpose, we will establish a link between the factor model and efficiency as presented in chapter 7.

If the condition (9.14) is satisfied, we may write

$$R_{j,t+1} = (1 - \beta_j)R_{0t} + \beta_j R_{M,t+1} + u_{j,t+1},$$

with $E(u_{j,t+1}) = 0$, $\text{Cov}(u_{j,t+1}, R_{M,t+1}) = 0$, $\forall j$.

Let us then consider a portfolio with unitary cost, which is built using the n basic assets and the risk-free asset. Assuming the purchase prices equal 1, the portfolio return is equal to $\sum_{j=1}^{n} a_j R_{j,t+1}$, with $\sum_{j=1}^{n} a_j = 1$. This return is then

$$\sum_{j=1}^{n} a_j R_{j,t+1} = \sum_{j=1}^{n} a_j(1 - \beta_j)R_{0t} + \sum_{j=1}^{n} a_j \beta_j R_{M,t+1} + \sum_{j=1}^{n} a_j u_{j,t+1}.$$

We deduce the two first order moments

$$E\left(\sum_{j=1}^{n} a_j R_{j,t+1}\right) = E\left(\sum_{j=1}^{n} a_j(1 - \beta_j)R_{0t} + \sum_{j=1}^{n} a_j \beta_j R_{M,t+1}\right),$$

$$V\left(\sum_{j=1}^{n} a_j R_{j,t+1}\right) = V\left(\sum_{j=1}^{n} a_j(1 - \beta_j)R_{0t} + \sum_{j=1}^{n} a_j \beta_j R_{M,t+1}\right)$$
$$+ V\left(\sum_{j=1}^{n} a_j u_{j,t+1}\right)$$

$$\geq V\left(\sum_{j=1}^{n} a_j(1 - \beta_j)R_{0t} + \sum_{j=1}^{n} a_j\beta_j R_{M,t+1}\right).$$

Thus, if the hypothesis is satisfied, one may, using only the risk-free asset and the market portfolio, constitute a portfolio having the same cost and return and a lower risk than the initial portfolio. This portfolio with the composition $\sum_{j=1}^{n} a_j(1 - \beta_j)$, $\sum_{j=1}^{n} a_j\beta_j$ in the risk-free asset and the market portfolio is preferable to the initial portfolio. If the asset associated with the market portfolio physically exists and is tradeable, one may then forget the n basic assets (see section 7.5). This interpretation is essentially carried out in terms of portfolio efficiency and does not require the underlying equilibrium idea of the CAPM. Therefore, regression based tests are sometimes called **tests for market portfolio efficiency**. In fact, they concern efficiency tests of the proxy portfolio retained in order to approximate the market portfolio.

vi) Nonstationary Frameworks

The efficiency test based on the statistic (9.16) remains valid under weaker assumptions than i.i.d. returns. In particular, it is valid in some nonstationary cases, for instance, when the market return is nonstationary, but the links between the market return and the returns of the other assets remain stationary.

Furthermore, the procedure could be extended to cases where the betas depend on time. Thus, we could consider the regression model

$$R_{j,t+1} - R_{0t} = a_j + (b_j + c_t)(R_{M,t+1} - R_{0t}) + u_{j,t},$$

with $\sum_{t=1}^{T} c_t = 0$, so as to introduce a time effect c_t common to the betas of the different assets. However, the estimation of such models requires a rather important number of assets.

9.2.3   Test for Efficiency of the Market Portfolio in a Dynamic Framework with Constant Betas

Let us consider a case where the returns of the basic assets and of the market portfolio satisfy a heteroscedastic dynamic model:

$$\begin{cases} R_{t+1} - R_{0t}e = BZ_t + u_{1,t+1}, \\ R_{M,t+1} - R_{0t} = b'Z_t + u_{2,t+1}, \end{cases} \tag{9.18}$$

where Z_t denotes a set of observable variable functions of the past, and B and b are matrices of parameters with adequate dimensions. The errors $u_{1,t+1}$ and $u_{2,t+1}$ are orthogonal to the past, conditionaly zero mean, with conditional variance:

$$V_t\begin{pmatrix} u_{1,t+1} \\ u_{2,t+1} \end{pmatrix} \equiv \begin{bmatrix} \Sigma_{11t}(\theta) & \Sigma_{12t}(\theta) \\ \Sigma_{21t}(\theta) & \Sigma_{22t}(\theta) \end{bmatrix}.$$

Moreover, the betas of the basic assets on the market portfolio are time independent:

$$\Sigma_{12t}(\theta)\Sigma_{22t}(\theta)^{-1} = \beta(\theta). \tag{9.19}$$

The model (9.18) may then be written under a recursive form:

$$\begin{cases} R_{t+1} - R_{0t}e = [B - \beta(\theta)b']Z_t + \beta(\theta)(R_{M,t+1} - R_{0t}) + v_{t+1} \\ R_{M,t+1} - R_{0t} = b'Z_t + u_{2,t+1}, \end{cases} \tag{9.20}$$

where the error term $v_{t+1} = u_{1,t+1} - \beta(\theta)u_{2,t+1}$ is orthogonal to $R_{M,t+1} - R_{0t}$.
    We have indeed

$$\mathrm{Cov}_t(R_{M,t+1}, v_{t+1}) = \mathrm{Cov}_t(u_{2,t+1}, u_{1,t+1} - \beta(\theta)u_{2,t+1}) = \Sigma_{21t} - \beta(\theta)\Sigma_{22t} = 0,$$

according to (9.19). The first subsystem of (9.20) therefore provides the regression of $R_{t+1} - R_{0t}e$ on Z_t and $R_{M,t+1} - R_{0t}$.
    Let us then examine the efficiency constraint deduced from the CAPM:

$$m_{1t} - \Sigma_{12t}(\Sigma_{22t})^{-1}m_{2t} = 0, \ \forall t,$$
$$\Leftrightarrow \quad BZ_t - \beta(\theta)b'Z_t = 0, \quad \forall t,$$
$$\Leftrightarrow \quad\quad\quad B - \beta(\theta)b' = 0.$$

Property 9.21. *The efficiency condition is satisfied if and only if the coefficients of Z_t in the theoretical regression of $R_{t+1} - R_{0t}e$ on Z_t and $R_{M,t+1} - R_{0t}$ are zero.*

This condition means that the best forecast of the returns R_{t+1} given the past Z_t and the market return $R_{M,t+1}$ coincide with the best forecast based on the return $R_{M,t+1}$ only. Thus, the condition is realized if the return $R_{M,t+1}$ is a sufficient summary of the past. The whole dynamics of the returns R_{t+1} is included in $R_{M,t+1}$, and the model is a one factor model (see chapter 8) with a simple interpretation.
    As in the i.i.d. case, the test may be performed directly using the SURE:

$$R_{t+1} - R_{0t}e = CZ_t + \beta(R_{M,t+1} - R_{0t}) + v_{t+1}. \tag{9.22}$$

The test for the null hypothesis $\{C = 0\}$ must be performed taking into account the correlations between the several components of the error v_{t+1} and the heteroscedasticity because

$$V_t(v_{t+1}) = \Sigma_{11t} - \Sigma_{12t}(\Sigma_{22t})^{-1}\Sigma_{21t}$$
$$= \Sigma_{11t} - \beta\Sigma_{21t}$$

generally depends on time.

9.2.4   Tests in the General Case

i) Market Portfolio Efficiency Test

When the betas are time dependent, there exists no regression method similar to the one presented in the previous section. We then have to start from the most general formulation,

$$\left\{ \begin{array}{l} R_{t+1} - R_{0t}e = m_{1t}(\theta) + u_{1,t+1}, \\ R_{M,t+1} - R_{0t} = m_{2t}(\theta) + u_{2,t+1} \end{array} \right. , \qquad (9.23)$$

with

$$V_t \left(\begin{array}{c} u_{1,t+1} \\ u_{2,t+1} \end{array} \right) \equiv \left[\begin{array}{cc} \Sigma_{11t}(\theta) & \Sigma_{12t}(\theta) \\ \Sigma_{21t}(\theta) & \Sigma_{22t}(\theta) \end{array} \right].$$

For each date, we may consider the parameter function

$$g_t(\theta) = m_{1t}(\theta) - \Sigma'_{12t}(\Sigma_{22t}(\theta))^{-1} m_{2t}(\theta),$$

in which the past variables are considered fixed and equal to their observed values.

This function may be estimated by $g_t(\hat{\theta}_T)$, where $\hat{\theta}_T$ is an estimator based on the complete model (9.23). If this estimator is consistent, asymptotically normal with variance–covariance matrix $\Omega(\theta)$:

$$\sqrt{T}(\hat{\theta}_T - \theta) \approx N[0, \Omega(\theta)],$$

we get asymptotically by the δ method

$$\sqrt{T}[g_t(\hat{\theta}_T) - g_t(\theta)] \approx N\left[0, \frac{\partial g_t(\theta)}{\partial \theta'} \Omega(\theta) \frac{\partial g_t'(\theta)}{\partial \theta} \right],$$

and

$$T[g_t(\hat{\theta}_T) - g_t(\theta)]' \left[\frac{\partial g_t(\hat{\theta}_T)}{\partial \theta'} \Omega(\hat{\theta}_T) \frac{\partial g_t'(\hat{\theta}_T)}{\partial \theta} \right]^{-1} [g_t(\hat{\theta}_T) - g_t(\theta)]$$

follows a chi-square distribution with n degrees of freedom. Under the null hypothesis $H_{0t} = \{g_t(\theta) = 0\}$, we have with probability 95%

$$\xi_t = T g_t(\hat{\theta}_T)' \left[\frac{\partial g_t(\hat{\theta}_T)}{\partial \theta'} \Omega(\hat{\theta}_T) \frac{\partial g_t'(\hat{\theta}_T)}{\partial \theta} \right]^{-1} g_t(\hat{\theta}_T) < \chi^2_{95\%}(n),$$

where $\chi^2_{95\%}(n)$ denotes the 95% quantile of the χ^2 distribution.

In a more descriptive way, we could also examine the efficiency hypothesis date by date, reporting in a diagram ξ_t as a function of time as in figure 9.4. The dates where the efficiency hypothesis is not rejected are the ones for which $\xi_t < \chi^2_{95\%}$.

Such an approach allows for a partition of the set of the dates into efficiency and nonefficiency subperiods.

Note 9.24. The tests are carried out separately date by date without readjusting the errors of the type I. More global tests of the hypothesis $H_0 = \{g_t(\theta) = 0, t = 1, \ldots, T\}$ could also be introduced, but they are simple only in the particular cases where the set of constraints $g_t(\theta) = 0, t = 1, \ldots, T$ is equivalent to a finite number of constraints on θ, independent of T. Such a simplification, for instance, existed in the model described in section 9.2.3.

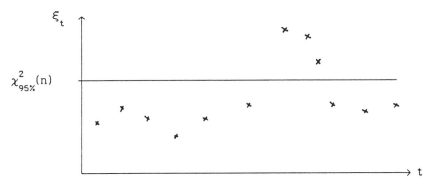

FIGURE 9.4. Rolling analysis of the efficiency hypothesis.

ii) Test for the Basic CAPM Relation

Let us assume that the available quantities α_{Mt} are observable. The basic equation

$$m_t - R_{0t}e = A\,\Sigma_t\,(\mathrm{diag}(p_t))\alpha_{Mt} \tag{9.2}$$

may be analyzed from the framework of descriptive ARCH models. Thus, we could write

$$R_{t+1} - R_{0t}e = CZ_t + A\Sigma_t(\mathrm{diag}(p_t))\alpha_{Mt} + v_{t+1}, \tag{9.25}$$

with $E_t v_{t+1} = 0$, $V_t v_{t+1} = \Sigma_t(\theta)$, and test the null hypothesis

$$H_0 = \{C = 0\}$$

by the likelihood ratio test, for instance. It is thus sufficient to introduce the quantities $(\mathrm{diag}\, p_t)\alpha_{Mt}$ in the expression of the variances to obtain an ARCH model that includes the CAPM.

9.3 Examples of Structural Models

A dynamic structural model compatible with the CAPM can only be built by specifying simultaneously the demand and supply for assets. Such models are generally more complex than the descriptive models considered previously because they must take into account the behavior of different agents intervening on the market.

9.3.1 A Model with Speculative Bubbles

i) The Model

Such a model has been studied in Broze et al. (1985). We consider a commodity such as coffee, which can either be consumed or bought for speculative purposes.

If the speculators build their portfolios in an optimal mean variance way using this commodity and the risk-free asset, the demanded quantity at date t is

$$X_t = \frac{E(p_{t+1}/I_t) - R_0 p_t}{AV(p_{t+1}/I_t)},$$

where p_t is the price of the good, R_0 is the return of the risk-free asset and A is the risk-aversion coefficient.

Market supply is constituted from

- the stock of the speculators δX_{t-1}, where δ measures the depreciation rate, $1 > \delta > 0$;

- the excess of supply over domestic demand, which is written as an increasing linear function of the price $\alpha p_t + u_t$, where α is a positive coefficient and u_t a summary of the exogenous variables.

The total available quantity is

$$\alpha_{Mt} = \delta X_{t-1} + \alpha p_t + u_t$$
$$= \delta \frac{E(p_t/I_{t-1}) - R_0 p_{t-1}}{AV(p_t/I_{t-1})} + \alpha p_t + u_t.$$

Even if the quantities α_{Mt} are not observable, the equilibrium condition allows us to derive the price dynamics. The equation satisfied by the price is

$$\frac{E(p_{t+1}/I_t) - R_0 p_t}{AV(p_{t+1}/I_t)} = \delta \frac{E(p_t/I_{t-1}) - R_0 p_{t-1}}{AV(p_t/I_{t-1})} + \alpha p_t + u_t, \quad \forall t. \qquad (9.26)$$

This is an implicit equation in the price, which also appears in the information I_t available at date t. The equation admits a large number of solutions for the price dynamic.

Property 9.27. *Let (ε_t) be a martingale difference sequence $E(\varepsilon_t/I_t) = 0$. Then, a price process (p_t) solution of*

$$\frac{p_{t+1} - \varepsilon_{t+1} - R_0 p_t}{AE(\varepsilon_{t+1}^2/I_t)} = \delta \frac{p_t - \varepsilon_t - R_0 p_{t-1}}{AE(\varepsilon_t^2/I_{t-1})} + \alpha p_t + u_t, \quad \forall t,$$

is also the solution of equation (9.26).

Proof. Let us take the expectation of both sides of equation (9.27) given the information I_t:

$$\frac{E(p_{t+1}/I_t) - R_0 p_t}{AE(\varepsilon_{t+1}^2/I_t)} = \delta \frac{E(p_t/I_{t-1}) - R_0 p_{t-1}}{AE(\varepsilon_t^2/I_{t-1})} + \alpha p_t + u_t, \quad \forall t.$$

By subtracting from the initial equation, we get that $\varepsilon_{t+1} = p_{t+1} - E(p_{t+1}/I_t)$, and ε_t is necessarily the forecast error of the price. Finally, by substituting the process ε_{t+1} by its expression $p_{t+1} - E(p_{t+1}/I_t)$ in (9.27), we find equation (9.26). Q.E.D.

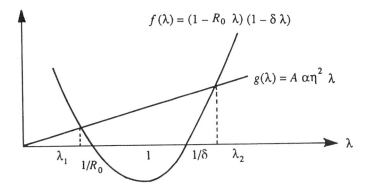

$$f(\lambda) = (1 - R_0 \lambda)(1 - \delta \lambda)$$

$$g(\lambda) = A \alpha \eta^2 \lambda$$

FIGURE 9.5. Location of the roots.

ii) Some Particular Models

To any martingale difference sequence model for (ε_t) there corresponds a price model that is compatible with the equilibrium condition.

a) Homoscedastic models

Let us first impose conditional homoscedasticity: $V(p_{t+1}/I_t) = E(\varepsilon_{t+1}^2/I_t) = \eta^2$, time independent. Then, we get

$$p_{t+1} = (R_0 + \delta + A\alpha\eta^2)p_t - \delta R_0 p_{t-1} + \varepsilon_{t+1} - \delta\varepsilon_t + A\eta^2 u_t. \qquad (9.28)$$

This is an ARMAX (2,1) model with exogenous variables u_t. If these exogenous variables are stationary, the price evolution is itself stationary when the roots of the autoregressive polynomial

$$1 - (R_0 + \delta A\alpha\eta^2)\lambda + \delta R_0 \lambda^2 = 0$$

lie outside the unit circle. The characteristic equation may be rewritten as

$$(1 - R_0\lambda)(1 - \delta\lambda) = A\alpha\eta^2\lambda.$$

Because $0 < \frac{1}{R_0} < 1 < \frac{1}{\delta}$, one of the two roots is smaller than 1 and one is greater than 1 (see figure 9.5).

Therefore, the price process is nonstationary with some explosion. It is a consequence of the speculative aspect which leads to an increase of the commodity price much quicker than that of the risk-free asset ($\lambda_2 > \frac{1}{R_0}$) in order to compensate both the risk and the depreciation of the stock.

b) Heteroscedastic models

Let us now consider a price model with ARCH error. We introduce a martingale difference sequence such that $E(\varepsilon_t/I_{t-1}) = 0$, $E(\varepsilon_t^2/I_{t-1}) = a + b\varepsilon_{t-1}^2 = h_{t-1}$. The price model becomes

$$p_{t+1} = R_0 p_t + \delta A p_t h_t + \alpha A p_t h_t h_{t-1} - \delta R_0 h_t p_{t-1}$$
$$+ A u_t h_t h_{t-1} + \varepsilon_{t+1} - A\delta\varepsilon_t h_t,$$

with $E(\varepsilon_t^2/I_{t-1}) = h_t$. It is an ARCH-M model with much more complicated volatility effects than those introduced in the descriptive ad hoc ARCH-M models, like cross effects $p_t h_t$ (already met in the CAPM), cross effects $h_t h_{t-1}$, and so on.

iii) Asymmetric Information

The model may be easily extended to the case of asymmetric information. Let us consider two groups of speculators with risk aversions A_1 and A_2 and information sets I_{1t} and I_{2t}, respectively. It is assumed that $p_t \in I_{1t} \subset I_{2t} \subset I_{1t+1}$. Consequently, the second group is always more informed than the first group, and each group disposes of the minimal information contained in the sequence of past prices. The equilibrium model becomes

$$\frac{1}{A_1} \frac{E(p_{t+1}/I_{1t}) - R_0 p_t}{AV(p_{t+1}/I_{1t})} + \frac{1}{A_2} \frac{E(p_{t+1}/I_{2t}) - R_0 p_t}{AV(p_{t+1}/I_{2t})}$$
$$= \delta \left(\frac{1}{A_1} \frac{E(p_t/I_{1t-1}) - R_0 p_{t-1}}{AV(p_t/I_{1t-1})} + \frac{1}{A_2} \frac{E(p_t/I_{2t-1}) - R_0 p_{t-1}}{AV(p_t/I_{2t-1})} \right)$$
$$+ \alpha p_t + u_t.$$

Let us consider the homoscedastic case

$$V(p_t/I_{1t-1}) \text{ and } V(p_t/I_{2t-1}) \text{ are time independent.} \tag{9.29}$$

Taking the expectation conditional to the information I_{1t} of both sides of the equilibrium equation and subtracting from the initial equation, we see that

$$E(p_{t+1}/I_{2t}) = E(p_{t+1}/I_{1t}). \tag{9.30}$$

Thus, although the two groups possess different information sets, *they make the same forecast in equilibrium*. This may be explained by the fact that the useful information of the more informed agents is transmitted to the less informed ones through the prices p_t, whose observation is common to the two groups. Thus, *in equilibrium and under some conditions, it is not necessary to take into account the asymmetry of information*.

Nevertheless, this result is not valid if the price is not common knowledge and, above all, *if there is conditional heteroscedasticity*.

9.3.2   The Consumption Based CAPM

i) Intertemporal Optimization Behavior

In the previous section, we discussed the evolution of the equilibrium prices when several categories of agents intervene, among whom some have pure speculative behavior. Other equilibrium models may be designed in which some agents perform substitutions between their investments in several financial assets and, for instance, their consumption. The consumption based CAPM (CCAPM) is one of the first models of this type that has been described (Rubinstein 1976; Lucas 1978; Breeden

1979). It is based on the description of the optimal behavior of a consumer who intertemporally maximizes his or her expected utility.

More precisely, the assumptions are the following. We consider an economy with one consumption good and one consumer. The consumer consumes the quantity C_t at date t. It is supposed that the good cannot be stocked and consequently cannot be used for interperiodic transfer. Its price is conventionally fixed to 1 at all dates. This good can be produced by n distinct production units indexed by $i, i = 0, \ldots, n$. The production at date t of the unit i is Y_{it}.

In the following, the framework of an exchange economy is considered. The consumer income essentially comes from the shares of firms that he or she owns. We denote by $\alpha_{1t}, \ldots, \alpha_{nt}$ the shares held at date t. These shares may be traded on the financial market at a unit price $p_t = (p_{1t}, \ldots, p_{nt})'$ and ensure the owner the possession of the corresponding proportion of the output.

We assume that the consumer has time separable preferences represented by a utility function U at each date. We introduce a subjective discount rate β. The optimization program of the consumer is

$$\left\{ \begin{array}{l} \text{Max } E\left[\sum_{t=0}^{\infty} \beta^t U(C_t) \right] \\ \text{subject to } C_t + p_t' \alpha_{t+1} \leq \alpha_t' Y_t + \alpha_t' p_t, \forall t. \end{array} \right. \tag{9.31}$$

The maximization is performed on the consumption patterns c_t and asset allocations (α_t), which have to be determined with respect to the available information: α_t and C_t must be functions of the current and past values of Y and p only. The inequality constraint in (9.31) is nothing more than the budget constraint at date t.

ii) Solution of the Optimization Problem

This optimization problem is easy to solve using dynamic programming when the predetermined variables satisfy a Markov property of order one. More precisely, we suppose that the current value of the production Y_t summarizes all of the information useful to forecast Y_{t+1} and that the price p_t is also a function of this quantity: $p_t = p(Y_t)$. In order to solve the problem, we introduce the **value function**, which gives the value of the objective function of the problem (9.31) as a function of the initial conditions α_0 and Y_0. This function v is such that

$$v(\alpha, y) = \max_{C,x} \left\{ U(C) + \beta \int v(x, y') \, dF(y', y) \right\}, \tag{9.32}$$

where the maximization is with respect to the quantities C, x constrained by

$$C + \alpha p(y).x \leq \alpha' y + \alpha' p(y), \tag{9.33}$$

and where $dF(y', y)$ denotes the conditional probability density function of Y_{t+1} given $Y_t = y$. The standard conditions of increasing and concave utility functions ensure that the constraint (9.33) is binding at the optimum and that the solutions can be determined from the first order conditions. We have

$$v(\alpha, y) = \max_x \left\{ U(\alpha'y + \alpha'p(y) - x'p(y)) + \beta \int v(x, y')\, dF(y', y) \right\}.$$

Deriving the function between brackets with respect to x, we have at the optimum

$$U'(C)p(y) = \beta \int \frac{\partial v}{\partial x}(x, y')\, dF(y', y),$$

where U' denotes the derivative of U. Deriving with respect to α, we have at the optimal x

$$\frac{\partial v(\alpha, y)}{\partial \alpha} = [y + p(y)]U'(C).$$

By reintroducing the time subscripts, we find the so-called **Euler equations:**

$$U'(C_t)p(Y_t) = \beta E[U'(C_{t+1})(Y_{t+1} + p(Y_{t+1}))/Y_t]. \tag{9.34}$$

These equations may be written in terms of returns. The return of the asset i is

$$R_{i,t+1} = \frac{Y_{i,t+1} + p_i(Y_{t+1})}{p_i(Y_t)}.$$

We have

$$E\left[\frac{U'(C_{t+1})}{U'(C_t)} R_{i,t+1}/Y_t \right] = \frac{1}{\beta}, \forall i.$$

This relation is especially valid taking for $i = 0$ the risk-free asset if it exists. It implies

$$E\left[\frac{U'(C_{t+1})}{U'(C_t)}(R_{i,t+1} - R_{0,t+1})/Y_t \right] = 0. \tag{9.35}$$

Therefore, the modification of the marginal utility must be orthogonal to the net return.

iii) The Equilibrium Condition

The model may then be closed by adding the equilibrium conditions both on the good market $C_t = \sum_{i=0}^{n} Y_{it}$ and on the financial asset markets: $\alpha_{it} = 1, i = 0, \ldots, n$.
    These conditions, introduced in the Euler equation (9.34), give

$$U'\left[\sum_{i=0}^{n} Y_{it} \right]p(Y_t) = \beta E\left\{ U'\left[\sum_{i=0}^{n} Y_{it+1} \right](Y_{t+1} + p(Y_{t+1}))/Y_t \right\}. \tag{9.36}$$

If the utility function and the evolution of the production are given, the system (9.36) is a rational expectation model which theoretically allows us to deduce the paths of the equilibrium prices.

iv) Approximation of the Euler Conditions and Constant Relative Risk Aversion

If the modification of the consumption between two successive dates is small, we may write

$$\frac{U'(C_{t+1})}{U'(C_t)} \approx 1 - \left[-C_t \frac{U''(C_t)}{U'(C_t)} \right] \frac{C_{t+1} - C_t}{C_t}$$

$$\approx 1 - \left[-C_t \frac{U''(C_t)}{U'(C_t)} \right] \Delta \log C_{t+1}.$$

The function $-C_t \frac{U''(C_{t+1})}{U'(C_t)}$ is nothing more than the Arrow–Pratt relative risk aversion.

In order to continue the computation, it is interesting to consider utility functions with constant risk aversion, i.e., power functions:

$$U(C) = \frac{B}{B-1} C^{1-1/B}, \quad B > 0.$$

Then, we have $-C \frac{U''(C_t)}{U'(C_t)} = \frac{1}{B}$, and the Euler condition is approximatively

$$E\left([1 - \frac{1}{B} \Delta \log C_{t+1}](R_{i,t+1} - R_{0,t+1}) \right)/I_t = 0,$$

$$E\left(R_{i,t+1} - R_{0,t+1})/I_t \right) = \frac{1}{B} E\left[\Delta \log C_{t+1}(R_{i,t+1} - R_{0,t+1})/I_t \right]. \tag{9.37}$$

The expected net return is a function of the links between the net returns and the growth rate of aggregated consumption. This property will naturally incite us to introduce this latter variable $\Delta \log C_{t+1}$ in the models describing the evolution of the returns or, in the framework of factor models, to search for it as a potential factor.

v) Testable Constraints induced by the CCAPM

As with the CCAPM model studied in sections 9.1 and 9.2, the constraints (9.37) or some of their consequences can be tested. For this purpose, we have to introduce a modelling for the joint evolution of the net returns and the growth rates of the consumption and then deduce the constraints on the parameters induced by (9.37). For instance, we may consider a static case and introduce the regression of $R_{i,t+1} - R_{0,t+1}$ on $\Delta \log C_{t+1}$:

$$R_{i,t+1} - R_{0,t+1} = a_i + b_i \Delta \log C_{t+1} + u_{i,t}.$$

The coefficients a_i and b_i are such that

$$a_i = E(R_{i,t+1} - R_{0,t+1}) - b_i E(\Delta \log C_{t+1}),$$

$$b_i = \frac{\text{Cov}(\Delta \log C_{t+1}, R_{i,t+1} - R_{0,t+1})}{V(\Delta \log C_{t+1})}.$$

Equation (9.37) then implies

$$E(R_{i,t+1} - R_{0,t+1}) = \frac{1}{B}\{\text{Cov}(\Delta \log C_{t+1}, R_{i,t+1} - R_{0,t+1})$$
$$+ E(\Delta \log C_{t+1})E(R_{i,t+1} - R_{0,t+1})\}$$

$$E(R_{i,t+1} - R_{0,t+1}) = \frac{1}{B + E(\Delta \log C_{t+1})} \text{Cov}(\Delta \log C_{t+1}, R_{i,t+1} - R_{0,t+1}),$$

$$a_i = b_i \left[E(\Delta \log C_{t+1}) + \frac{V(\Delta \log C_{t+1})}{B - E(\Delta \log C_{t+1})} \right].$$

Therefore, a consequence of the CCAPM is that the two vector coefficients (a_i) and (b_i) should be proportional.

References

Chapter 2: LINEAR AND NONLINEAR PROCESSES

Ashley, R. and D. Patterson (1986) "A Nonparametric Distribution Free Test for Serial Dependence in Stock Returns", *Journal of Financial and Quantitative Analysis*, 21, 221–227.

Ashley, R. and D. Patterson (1987) *Linear Versus Nonlinear Macroeconomics: A Statistical Test*, Discussion Paper. Blacksburg: Blacksburg University.

Ashley, R., Patterson, D. and M. Hinich (1986) "A Diagnostic Test for Nonlinearity Serial Dependence in Time Series Fitting Errors", *Journal of Time Series Analysis*, 7.

Box, G. and G. Jenkins (1970) *Time Series Analysis, Forecasting and Control*, San Francisco: Holden–Day.

Box, G. and D. Pierce (1970) "Distribution of Residual Autocorrelation in Autoregressive Integrated Moving Average Time Series Models", *Journal of the American Statistical Association*, 70, 70–79.

Clark, P. (1973) "A Subordinated Stochastic Process Model with Finite Variance for Speculative Prices", *Econometrica*, 41, 135–155.

Corrado, C. and J. Schatzberg (1990) "A Nonparametric Distribution Free Test for Serial Independence in Stock Returns: a Correction", *Journal of Financial and Quantitative Analysis*, 25, 411–416.

Dacarogna, M., Gauvreau, N., Muller, U., Olsen, R. and O. Piclet (1994) "Changing Time Scale for Short Term Forecasting in Financial Market", Discussion Paper. Zurich: Olsen and Associates.

Davies, N. and J. Petrucelli (1986) "Detecting Nonlinearity in Time Series", *The Statistician*, 35, 271–280.

Engle, R. (1995) *ARCH Selected Readings*, Oxford: Oxford University Press.

Garbade, K. (1977) "Two Methods for Examining the Stability of Regression Coefficients", *Journal of the American Statistical Association*, 72, 54–63.

Ghysels, E., Gouriéroux, C. and J. Jasiak (1995) "Trading Patterns, Time Deformation and Stochastic Volatility in Foreign Exchange Markets", Discussion Paper 9542. Montréal: Centre interuniversitaire de recherche en analyse des organisations.

Godfrey, L. (1978) "Testing Against General Autoregressive and Moving Average Error Models when the Regressors Include Lagged Dependent Variables", *Econometrica*, 46, 1293–1302.

Granger, C. and A. Andersen (1978) *An Introduction to Bilinear Time Series Models*, Göttingen: Vandenhoeck et Ruprecht.

Granger, G.W.J. and P. Newbold (1976) "Forecasting Transformed Series", *Journal of the Royal Statistical Society B*, 38, 189–203.

Hasselman, K., Munk, W. and G. McDonald (1963) *Bispectrum of Ocean Waves, Time Series Analysis* (M. Rosenblatt, Ed.), New York: Wiley. pp. 125–139.

Hinich, M.J. (1982) "Testing for Gaussianity and Linearity of a Stationary Time Series", *Journal of Time Series Analysis*, 3, 169–176.

Hinich, M. and D. Patterson (1985) "Evidence of Nonlinearity in Daily Stock Returns", *Journal of Business and Economic Statistics*, 3, 69–77.

Keenan, D.M. (1985) "A Tukey Nonadditivity-Type Test for Time Series Non Linearity", *Biometrika*, 72, 39–44.

Lawrance, A.J. and P.A. Lewis (1985) "Modelling and Residual Analysis of Nonlinear Autoregressive Time Series in Exponential Variables", *Journal of the Royal Statistical Society B*, 47, 165–202.

Ljung, G.M. and G.E. Box (1978) "On a Measure of Lack of Fit in Time Series Models", *Biometrika* 65, 297–303.

Mc Leod, A.I. and W.K. Li (1983) "Diagnostic Checking ARMA Time Series Models Using Squared Residual Autocorrelations", *Journal of Time Series Analysis*, 4, 269–273.

Maravall, A. (1983) "An Application of Nonlinear Time Series Forecasting", *Journal of Business and Economic Statistics*, 1, 66–74.

Nisio, M. (1960) "On Polynomial Approximation for Strictly Stationary Processes", *Journal of the Mathematical Society of Japan*, 12, 207–226.

Nisio, M. (1961) "Remarks on the Canonical Representation of Strictly Stationary Time Series", *American Statistician*, 37, 323–324.

Patterson, D. (1983) "BISPEC, A Program to Estimate the Bispectrum of a Stationary Time Series", *American Statistician*, 37, 323–324.

Priestley, M. (1978) "Nonlinear Models in Time Series Analysis", *The Statistician*, 27, 159–176.

Raftery, A.E. (1980) "Estimation efficace pour un processus autorégressif exponentiel à densité discontinue," *Publication de l'Institute Statistique de l'Université de Paris*, 25, 64–91.

Raftery, A.E. (1981) "Un processus autorégressif ... loi marginale exponentielle: propriétés asymptotiques et estimation du maximum de vraisemblance", *Annales Scientifiques de l'Université Clermont*, 69, 149–160.

Rosenblatt, M. and J.W. Van Ness (1964) *Estimates of the Bispectrum of Stationary Random Processes*, Discussion Paper. Providence, RI: Brown University.

Stock, J. (1988) "Estimating Continuous Time Processes Subject to Time Deformation", *Journal of the American Statistical Association*, 83, 877–884.

Subba Rao, T. (1981) "On the Theory of Bilinear Models", *Journal of the Royal Statistical Society B*, 43.

Subba Rao, T. and M. Gabr (1980) *An Introduction to Bispectral Analysis and Bilinear Time Series Models*, New York: Springer-Verlag.

Tong, M. and K. Lin (1980) "Threshold Autoregressions, Limit Cycles and Cyclical Data", *Journal of the Royal Statistical Society B*, 42, 245–292.

Whittle, P. (1963) *Prediction and Regulation*, The English University Press.

Chapter 3: UNIVARIATE ARCH MODELS

Bera, A. and M. Higgins (1993) "A Survey of ARCH Model Properties, Estimation and Testing", *Journal of Economic Surveys*, 7, 305–366.

Bera, A. and S. Lee (1988) *Interaction Between Autocorrelation and Conditional Heteroskedasticity: A Random Coefficient Approach*, Urbana: University of Illinois.

Bollerslev, T. (1986) "Generalized Autoregressive Conditional Heteroscedasticity", *Journal of Econometrics* 31, 307–327.

Bollerslev, T. (1987) "A Conditional Heteroscedastic Time Series Model for Speculative Prices and Rates of Return", *Review of Economics and Statistics*, 69, 542–547.

Bollerslev, T. (1988) "On the Correlation Structure for the Generalized Autoregressive Conditional Heteroskedastic Process", *Journal of Time Series Analysis*, 9, 121–131.

Bollerslev, T., Chou, R. and K. Kroner (1992) "ARCH Modelling in Finance: A Review of Theory and Empirical Evidence", *Journal of Econometrics*, 52, 5–60.

Bollerslev, T., Engle, R. and D. Nelson (1993) "ARCH Models", in *Handbook of Econometrics, Volume IV*, Amsterdam: North-Holland.

Chou, R.Y. (1988) "Volatility Persistence and Stock Valuations: Some Empirical Evidence Using GARCH", *Journal of Applied Econometrics*, 3, 279–294.

Diebold, F.X. (1986) "Modelling the Persistence of Conditional Variance: A Comment", *Econometric Reviews*, 5, 51–56.

Diebold, F.X. (1986) *Temporal Aggregation for ARCH Processes and the Distribution of Asset Returns*, Discussion Paper. Philadelphia: University of Pennsylvania.

Diebold, F.X. (1988) *The Time Series Structure of Exchange Rate Fluctuations*, Ph.D. thesis. Philadelphia: University of Pennsylvania.

Diebold, F.X., Im, J. and C.J. Lee (1989) "Conditional Heteroskedasticity in the Market Model", *Journal of Accounting, Auditing and Finance*.

Diebold, F.X. and M. Nerlove (1988) "The Dynamics of Exchange Rate Volatility: A Multivariate Latent Factor ARCH Model", *Journal of Applied Econometrics* 4, 1–22.

Diebold, F.X. (1988) *Empirical Modelling of Exchange Rate Dynamics,* New York: Springer-Verlag.

Domowitz, I. and C.S. Hakkio (1985) "Conditional Variance and the Risk Premium in the Foreign Exchange Market", *Journal of International Economics*, 19, 47–65.

Duan, J. and M. Hung (1991) "Modelling the GARCH Process with Maturity Effect", Discussion Paper. Montréal: McGill University.

Engle, R.F. (1982) "Autoregressive Conditional Heteroscedasticity with Estimates of the Variance of U.K. Inflation", *Econometrica*, 50, 987–1008.

Engle, R.F. (1983) "Estimates of Variance of U.S. Inflation Based Upon the ARCH Model", *Journal of Money, Credit and Banking*, 15, 286–301.

Engle, R. (1995) *ARCH, Selected Readings*, Oxford: Oxford University Press.

Engle, R.F. and T.P. Bollerslev (1986) "Modelling the Persistence of Conditional Variances", *Econometric Review*, 5, 1–50.

Engle, R.F. and D.F. Kraft (1983) "Multiperiod Forecast Error Variances of Inflation Estimated from ARCH Model", in *Applied Time Series Analysis of Economic Data*, (A. Zellner, Ed.) Washington, DC: U.S. Bureau of the Census. pp. 293–302.

Engle, R.F., Lilien, D. and R. Robbins (1987) "Estimating Time Varying Risk Premia in the Term Structure: the ARCH-M Model", *Econometrica*, 55, 391–407.

Engle, R.F. and W.L. Lin (1988) "Meteor Showers on Heat Waves Heteroskedastic Intra-Daily Volatility in the Foreign Exchange Market", Publ. 2609. Washington, DC: National Bureau of Economic Research.

French, K.R., Schwert, G.N. and R.F. Stambaugh (1987) "Expected Stock Returns and Volatility", *Journal of Financial Economics*, 19, 3–29.

Harvey, A., Ruiz, E. and N. Shepard (1991a) "Modelling Volatility: Some Alternatives to ARCH", Discussion Paper. Athens: Athens University.

McCulloch, J.M. (1983b) "Interest-Risk Sensitive Deposit Insurance Premia Adaptive Conditional Heteroskedastic Estimates", Discussion Paper. Columbus: Ohio State University.

Milhoj, A. (1985) "The Moment Structure of ARCH Processes", *Scandinavian Journal of Statistics*, 12, 281–292.

Milhoj, A. (1987) "A Conditional Variance Model for Daily Deviations of an Exchange Rate", *Journal of Business and Economic Statistics*, 5, 99–103.

Nemec, A.F. (1984) "Conditionally Heteroscedastic Autoregression", Tech. Rep. 43. Seattle: University of Washington, Dept. of Statistics.

Nelson, D.B. (1987) *Conditional Heteroskedasticity in Asset Returns: A New Approach*, Discussion Paper. Chicago: University of Chicago.

Nicholls, D.F. and A.R. Pagan (1983) "Heteroscedasticity in Models with Lagged Dependent Variables", *Econometrica*, 51, 1233–1242.

Pantula, S. (1984) *Autoregressive Conditionally Heteroscedastic Models*, Discussion Paper. Raleigh: North Carolina State University.

Sampson, M. (1988) "A Stationarity Condition for the GARCH (1,1) Process", Discussion Paper. Montréal: Concordia University.

Tsay, R.S. (1987) *Order Selection and Leptokurtosis in ARCH Models of Exchange Rates*, Discussion Paper. Philadelphia: University of Pennsylvania.

Weiss, A.A. (1983) *Time Series Models with Varying Coefficients and Variances*, Ph.D. thesis. Sydney: Sydney University.

Weiss, A.A. (1984) "ARMA Models with ARCH Errors", *Journal of Time Series Analysis*, 5, 129–143.

Weiss, A.A. (1985) "On the Stability of a Heteroskedastic Process", *Journal of Time Series Analysis*, 7, 303–310.

Weiss, A.A. (1986) "ARCH and Bilinear Time Series Models: Comparison and Combination", *Journal of Business and Economic Statistics,* 4, 59–70.

Chapter 4: ESTIMATION AND TEST

Pseudo maximum likelihood method

Amemiya, T. (1985) *Advanced Econometrics*, Oxford: Blackwell.

Gallant, R.A. (1987) *Non Linear Statistical Models,* New York: Wiley.

Gouriéroux, C. and A. Monfort (1995) *Statistics and Econometric Models*, 2 volumes, Cambridge: Cambridge University Press.

Gouriéroux, C., Monfort, A. and A. Trognon (1984) "Pseudo Maximum Likelihood Methods: Theory", *Econometrica*, 52, 681–700.

White, H. (1981) "Maximum Likelihood Estimation of Misspecified Models", *Econometrica*, 50, 1–25.

Heteroscedasticity Tests

Breusch, T.S. and A.R. Pagan (1979) "A Simple Test for Heteroskedasticity and Random Coefficient Variation", *Econometrica*, 47, 1287–1294.

Breusch, T.S. and A.R. Pagan (1981) "The Lagrange Multiplier Test and its Applications to Model Specification in Econometrics", *Review of Economic Studies*, 47, 239–254.

Chesher, A. (1984) "Testing for Neglected Heterogeneity", *Econometrica*, 52, 865–872.

Cragg, J.C. (1982) "Estimation and Testing in Time Series Regression Models with Heteroscedastic Disturbances", *Journal of Econometrics*, 20, 135–157.

Glejser, H. (1969) "A New Test for Heteroskedasticity", *Journal of the American Statistical Association*, 64, 316–323.

Godfrey, L.G. (1978) "Testing for Multiplicative Heteroskedasticity", *Journal of Econometrics*, 8, 227–231.

Silvey, S.D. (1970) *Statistical Inference*, Harmondsworth: Penguin Books.

Srzoeter, J. (1978) "A Class of Parametric Tests for Heteroskedasticity in Linear Econometrics Models", *Econometrica*, 46, 1311–1328.

White, H. (1980) "A Heteroscedasticity Consistent Covariance Matrix Estimation and a Direct Test for Heteroscedasticity", *Econometrica*, 48, 817–838.

Statistical Inference for ARCH Models

Bera, A. and S. Lee (1988), *Information Matrix Test, Parameter Heterogeneity and ARCH*, Urbana: University of Illinois.

Bera, A.K. and M.L. Higgins (1989) "A Joint Test for ARCH and Bilinearity in the Regression Model", *Econometric Reviews*, 8.

Bollerslev, T. (1986) "Generalized Autoregressive Conditional Heteroskedasticity", *Journal of Econometrics*, 31, 307–327.

Bollerslev, T. and J.M. Wooldridge (1992) "Quasi-Maximum Likelihood Estimation Dynamic Models with Time Varying Covariances", *Econometric Reviews*, 11, 143–172.

Engle, R.F. (1982) "Autoregressive Conditional Heteroscedasticity with Estimates of the Variance of U.K. Inflation", *Econometrica*, 50, 987–1008.

Engle, R.F., Hendry, D.F. and D. Trumble (1985) "Small Sample Properties of ARCH Estimators and Tests", *Canadian Journal of Economics*, 18, 66–93.

Geweke, J. (1989) "Exact Predictive Densities for Linear Models with ARCH Disturbances", *Journal of Econometrics*, 40, 63–86.

Granger, C.W.J., White, H. and M. Kamstra (1989) "Interval Forecasting: An Analysis Based Upon ARCH-Quantile Estimators", *Journal of Econometrics*, 40, 87–96.

Gregory, A.W. (1989) "A Nonparametric Test for Autoregressive Conditional Heteroscedasticity: A Markov Chain Approach", *Journal of Business and Economic Statistics*, 7, 107–115.

Harvey, A. and N. Shepard (1993a) "The Econometrics of Stochastic Volatility", Discussion Paper. London: London Stock Exchange, Financial Market Groups.

Harvey, A. and N. Shepard (1993b) "Estimation and Testing of Stochastic Variance Models", London: London Stock Exchange.

Lee, J. and M. King (1993) "A Locally Most Mean Powerful Based Score Test for ARCH and GARCH Regression Disturbances", *Journal of Business and Economic Statistics*, 11, 17–28.

Lin, S. and B. Brorsen (1995) "Maximum Likelihood Estimation of a GARCH-Stable Model", *Journal of Applied Econometrics*, 10, 273–286.

Ruiz, E. (1992) "Heteroscedasticity in Financial Time Series", Ph. D. thesis, London: London School of Economics.

Ruiz, E. (1994) "Quasi-Maximum Likelihood Estimation of Stochastic Volatility Models", *Journal of Econometrics*, 63, 289–306.

Weiss, A.A. (1986) "Asymptotic Theory for ARCH Models: Estimation and Testing", *Econometric Theory*, 2, 107–113.

Whistler, D. (1988) *Semi-parametric ARCH Estimates of Intra Daily Exchange Rate Volatility*, Discussion Paper R 17. London: London School of Economics.

Chapter 5: SOME APPLICATIONS OF UNIVARIATE ARCH MODELS

Leptokurtic Aspects of Financial Series and Time Aggregation

Drost, F. and T. Nijman (1993) "Temporal Aggregation of GARCH Processes", *Econometrica*, 61, 909–927.

Taylor, S. (1985) *Modelling Financial Time Series,* Amsterdam: North-Holland.

Thomas, A. (1989) *Modèles à variance conditionnelle et applications aux modèles d'évaluation financière*, Ph.D. thesis. Toulouse: Toulouse University.

ARCH Processes as Approximations of Continuous Time Processes

Duffie, D. and K. Singleton (1993) "Simulated Moments Estimation of Markov Models of Asset Prices", *Econometrica*, 61, 929–952.

Gouriéroux, C. and A. Monfort (1996) *Simulated Estimation Methods*, Oxford: Oxford University Press.

Nelson, D. (1990) "ARCH Models as Diffusion Approximations", *Journal of Econometrics*, 45, 7–38.

Nelson, D. (1992) "Filtering and Forecasting with Misspecified ARCH Models: Getting the Right Variance with the Wrong Model", *Journal of Econometrics*, 25, 61–90.

Nelson, D. (1996) "Asymptotically Optimal Smoothing with ARCH Models", *Econometrica*, 64, 531–573.

Nelson, D. and D. Foster (1994) "Asymptotic Filtering Theory for Univariate ARCH Models", *Econometrica*, 62, 1–41.

Stroock, D. and S. Varadhan (1979) "Multidimensional Diffusion Processes", Berlin: Springer-Verlag.

The Random Walk Hypothesis

Bachelier, L. (1900) "Theory of Speculation", *The Random Character of Stock Market Prices* (P. Cootner, Ed.), Cambridge: MIT Press. pp. 17–78.

Diebold, F. (1986) "Testing for Serial Correlation in the Presence of ARCH", Proceedings of the American Statistical Association, Business and Economic Statistic Section, 323–328.

Fama, E.F. (1965) "The Behaviour of Stock Market Prices", *Journal of Business*, 38, 34–105.

Fama, E.F. (1976) *Foundations of Finance*, Basil Blackwell: Oxford.

Kim, K. and P. Schmidt (1989) "Unit Root Tests with Conditional Heteroskedasticity", Discussion Paper. East Lansing: Michigan State University.

Milhoj, A. (1985) "The Moment Structure of ARCH Processes", *Scandinavian Journal of Statistics*, 12, 281–292.

Samuelson, P. (1973) "Proof that Properly Discounted Present Values of Assets Vibrate Randomly", *Bell Journal*, 4.

Solnik, B. (1973) "Note on the Validity of the Random Walk for European Stock Prices", *Journal of Finance*, 28, 1151–1160.

Wooldridge, J. (1991) "On the Application of Robust, Regression Based Diagnostics to Models of Conditional Means and Conditional Variances", *Journal of Econometrics,* 47, 5–46.

Threshold ARCH Models and Nonparametric Approaches

Black, F. (1976) "Studies in Stock Price Volatility Changes", Proceedings of the 1976 Business Meeting, American Statistical Association, pp. 177–181.

Cai, J. (1994) "A Markov Model of Switching Regime ARCH", *Journal of Business and Econometric Statistics*, 12, 309–316.

Engle, R. and G. Gonzales Rivera (1991) "Semi-Parametric ARCH Models", *Journal of Business and Econometric Statistics*, 9, 345–359.

Gallant, R. (1981) "On the Bias in Flexible Functional Forms and an Essentially Unbiased Form: The Fourier Flexible Form", *Journal of Econometrics*, 15, 211–244.

Gallant, R., Hansen, L.P. and G. Tauchen (1990) "Using Conditional Moments of Assets Payoffs to Infer the Volatility of Intertemporal Marginal Rates of Substitution", *Journal of Econometrics*, 45, 141–180.

Gallant, R. and G. Tauchen (1989) "Semi-nonparametric Estimation of Conditionally Constrained Heterogeneous Processes: Asset Pricing Applications", *Econometrica*, 57, 1091–1120.

Gouriéroux, C. and A. Monfort (1992) "Qualitative Threshold ARCH Models", *Journal of Econometrics*, 52, 159–200.

Hafner, C. (1996) "Estimating High Frequency Foreign Exchange Rate Volatility with Nonparametric ARCH Models", Discussion Paper. Berlin: Humboldt University.

Hentschel, L. (1994) "Alternative Models of Asymmetric Volatility in Stock Returns", Ph.D. dissertation, Princeton, NJ: Princeton University.

Higgins, H.L. and A.K. Bera (1988) "Non Linear ARCH Models Properties, Testing and Applications", Australian Meeting of the Econometric Society.

Higgins, M. and A. Bera (1992) "A Class of Nonlinear ARCH Models", *International Economic Review*, 33, 137–158.

Pagan, A. and W. Schwert (1990) "Alternative Models for Conditional Stock Volatility", *Journal of Econometrics*, 45, 267–290.

Rabemananjara, R. and J.M. Zakoïan (1993) "Threshold ARCH Models and Asymmetries in Volatility", *Journal of Applied Econometrics*, 47, 67.

Watt, W. and P. Yadav (1993) "An Empirical Analysis of Alternative Parametric ARCH Models", Discussion Paper. Glasgow: University of Glasgow.

Zakoïan, J.M. (1994) "Threshold Heteroskedastic Models", *Journal of Economics Dynamics and Control*, 18, 931–956.

Integrated ARCH Models

Bollerslev, T. (1988) "Integrated ARCH and Cointegration in Variance", Evanston, IL: Northwestern University.

Bollerslev, T. and Engle, R. (1989) "Common Persistence in Conditional Variances", Discussion Paper. La Jolla: University of California—San Diego.

Chou, R.Y. (1987) "Persistent Volatility and Stock Returns", Discussion Paper. La Jolla: University of California—San Diego.

Engle, R.F. and R. Bollerslev (1986) "Modelling the Persistence of Conditional Variances", *Econometric Reviews*, 5, 1–50.

French, K., Schwert, G.W. and R. Stambaugh (1987) "Expected Stock Returns and Volatility", *Journal of Financial Economics*, 19, 3–29.

Geweke, J. (1986) "Comment on Modeling the Persistence of Conditional Variances", *Econometric Reviews*, 5, 57–62.

Hansen, B. (1990) "Regression Theory when Variances are Non Stationary", Discussion Paper. Rochester, NY: University of Rochester.

Hansen, B. (1990) *Regression Theory When Variances are Non Stationary*, Discussion Paper. Rochester: University of Rochester.

Hendry, D.F. (1986) "Comment on Modeling the Persistence of Conditional Variances", *Econometric Reviews*, 5, 63–70.

Hong, C.H. (1987) "The IGARCH-Model: the Process Estimation and Some Monte Carlo Experiments", Report 87–32. La Jolla: University of California—San Diego.

Lumsdaine, R. (1995) "Finite Sample Properties of the Maximum Likelihood Estimator in GARCH(1,1) and IGARCH(1,1) Models: A Monte Carlo Investigation", *Journal of Business and Economic Statistics*, 13, 1–10.

Lumsdaine, R. (1996) "Consistency and Asymptotic Normality of the Quasi-Maximum Likelihood Estimator in IGARCH(1,1) and Covariance Stationary GARCH(1,1) Models", *Econometrica*, 64, 575–596.

Lamoureux, C. and W. Lastrapes (1990) "Persistence in Variance Structure Change and the GARCH Model", *Journal of Business and Economic Statistics*, 8, 225.

Melvin, M. and B. Peiers (1996) "Volatility Persistence in High Frequency Data: Evidence from the Mark and the Yen", Discussion Paper. Tempe: Arizona State University.

Nelson, D. (1990) "Stationarity and Persistence in the GARCH (1,1) Models", *Econometric Theory*, 6, 318–334.

Pantula, S. (1986) "Modelling the Persistence of Conditional Variances: a Comment", *Econometric Reviews*, 5, 71–73.

Poterba, J. and L. Summers (1986) "The Persistence of Volatility and Stock Market Fluctuation", *American Economic Review*, 76, 1142–1151.

Chapter 6: MULTIVARIATE ARCH MODELS

Statistical Inference

Attanasio, O. (1988) "A Note on Estimation and Hypothesis Testing in Multivariate ARCH Models", Discussion Paper.

Basawa, I., Feigin, P. and C. Heyde (1976) "Asymptotic Properties of Maximum Likelihood Estimators for Stochastic Processes", *Sankya, Serie A*, 38, 259–270.

Crowder, M. (1976) "Maximum Likelihood Estimation with Dependent Observations", *Journal of the Royal Statistical Society B*, 38, 45–53.

Gouriéroux, C. and A. Monfort (1990) "Séries Temporelles et Modéles Dynamiques," *Economica*, 750.

Gouriéroux, C., Monfort, A. and A. Trognon (1984) "Pseudo Maximum Likelihood Theory", *Econometrica*, 52, 681–700.

Kroner, K.F. (1987) "Estimating and Testing for Factor ARCH", Mimeograph. La Jolla: University of California—San Diego.

White, H. (1982) "Maximum Likelihood Estimation of Misspecified Models", *Econometrica*, 50, 126.

Models and Applications

Baba, Y., Engle, R., Kraft, D. and K. Kroner (1987) "Multivariate Simultaneous Generalized ARCH", Discussion Paper. La Jolla: University of California—San Diego.

Baillie, R. and T. Bollerslev (1987) "Multivariate GARCH Processes and Models of Time Varying Risk Premia in Foreign Exchange Markets", Mimeograph.

Bera, A., Bubuys, E. and H. Park (1988) "Conditional Heteroskedasticity in the Market Model and Efficient Estimates of Betas", *The Financial Review*, 23, 201–204.

Bera, A. and S. Lee (1989) "On the Formulation of a General Structure for Conditional Heteroskedasticity", Discussion Paper. Urbana: University of Illinois.

Bollerslev, T. (1987a) *A Multivariate GARCH Model with Constant Conditional Correlations for a Set of Exchange Rates*, Discussion Paper. Evanston, IL: Northwestern University.

Bollerslev, T. (1987b) "A Conditionally Heteroskedastic Time Series Models for Security Prices and Rates of Return Data", *Review of Economics and Statistics*, 69, 542–547.

Bollerslev, T. (1990) "Modelling the Coherence in Short Run Nominal Exchange Rates: A Multivariate Generalized ARCH Models", *Review of Economics and Statistics*, 72, 498–505.

Bollerslev, T., Engle, R. and J. Wooldridge (1988) "A Capital Asset Pricing Model with Time Varying Covariance", *Journal of Political Economy*, 96, 116–131.

Diebold, F. and M. Nerlove (1986) "Factor Structure in a Multivariate GARCH Model of Exchange Rate Fluctuations", Discussion Paper. Philadelphia: University of Pennsylvania.

Diebold, F. and M. Nerlove (1989) "The Dynamic of Exchange Rate Volatility: A Multivariate Latent Factor ARCH Model", *Journal of Applied Econometrics*, 4, 1–22.

Diebold, F. and P. Pauly (1988) "Endogenous Risk in a Portfolio Balance Rational Expectation Model of the Deutschmark-Dollar Rate", *European Economic Review*, 32, 27–53.

Engle, R. (1987) "Multivariate ARCH with Factor Structure. Cointegration in Variance", Discussion Paper. La Jolla: University of California—San Diego.

Engle, R., Granger, C.W. and D. Kraft (1984) "Combining Competing Forecasts of Inflation Using a Bivariate ARCH Model", *Journal of Economic Dynamics and Control*, 6, 151–165.

Engle, R., Ito, T. and W. Lin (1990) "Meteor Showers on Heat Waves Heteroskedastic Intra-Daily Volatility in the Foreign Exchange Market", *Econometrica*, 58, 525–542.

Engle, R. and D. Kraft (1982) "Autoregressive Conditional Heteroskedasticity in Multiple Time Series Models", Discussion Paper 82–2. La Jolla: University of California—San Diego.

Engle, R. and A. Rodrigues (1987) "Tests of International CAPM with Time Varying Covariances", Discussion Paper 2054. Washington, DC: National Bureau of Economic Research.

Engle, R., Ng, V. and M. Rothschild (1990) "Asset Pricing with a Factor ARCH Covariance Structure: Empirical Estimates for Treasury Bills", *Journal of Econometrics*, 45, 213–237.

Granger, C., Robins, R. and R. Engle (1984) "Wholesale and Retail Prices: Bivariate Time Series Modelling with Forecastable Error Variance", in *Model Reliability*, (D.A. Belsley and E. Kuh, Eds.) Cambridge: MIT Press.

Harmon, R. (1988) *The Simultaneous Equations Model with Generalized Autoregressive Conditional Heteroskedasticity: the S.E.M. GARCH Model*, Discussion Paper. Washington, DC: Georgetown University.

Harvey, A., Ruiz, E. and N. Shepard (1994) "Multivariate Stochastic Variance Models", *Review of Economic Studies*, 61, 247–264.

Karolyi, A. (1995) "A Multivariate GARCH Model of International Transmission of Stock Returns and Volatility: The Case of United States and Canada", *Journal of Business and Economic Statistics*, 13, 11–25.

King, M., Sentana, E. and S. Wadhwani (1994) "Volatility and Links Between National Stock Markets", *Econometrica*, 62, 901–934.

Kroner, K.F. (1988) *Finding the Optimal Currency Composition of External Debt Using Multivariate ARCH*, Discussion Paper. Geneva: World Bank.

Lin, W. (1992) "Alternative Estimators for Factor GARCH Models. A Monte Carlo Comparison", *Journal of Applied Econometrics*, 7, 259–279.

Nelson, D. (1991) "Conditional Heteroskedasticity in Asset Return: A New Approach", *Econometrica*, 59, 347–370.

Nerlove, M., Diebold, F., Van Beeck, H. and Y. Cheung (1988) *A Multivariate ARCH Model of Foreign Exchange Rate Determination*, Discussion Paper. Philadelphia: University of Pennsylvania.

Chapter 7: EFFICIENT PORTFOLIOS AND HEDGING PORTFOLIOS

Mean Variance Efficiency

Arrow, K.J. (1953) *Le rôle des valeurs boursières pour la répartition la meilleure des risques*, Paris: CNRS Econométrie.

Arrow, K.J. (1963) "The Role of Securities in the Optimal Allocation of Risk-Bearing", *Review of Economic Studies*, 31, 91–96.

Chamberlain, G. (1983) "A Characterization of the Distribution that Imply Mean-Variance Utility Functions", *Journal of Econometric Theory*, 29, 185–201.

Copeland, T. and F. Weston (1984) *Financial Theory and Corporate Policy*, Reading, MA: Addison–Wesley.

Hanoch, G. and H. Levy (1969) "The Efficiency of Choice Involving Risk", *Review of Economic Studies*, 36, 335–346.

Huang, C.F. and R. Litzenberger (1988) *Foundations for Financial Economics*, Amsterdam: North-Holland.

Kroll, Y., Levy, H. and H. Markowitz (1984) "Mean-Variance Versus Direct Utility Maximization", *Journal of Finance*, 39, 47–62.

Lee, S. and A. Lerro (1973) "Optimizing the Portfolio Selection for Mutual Funds", *Journal of Finance*, 28, 1087–1102.

Levy, H. and H. Markowitz (1979) "Approximating Expected Utility by a Function of Mean and Variance", *American Economic Review*, 69.

Lintner, J. (1965) "Valuation of Risk Asset and the Selection of Risky Investments in Stock Portfolios and Capital Budgets", *Review of Economics and Statistics*, 47, 13–37.

Malinvaud, E. (1969) "First Order Certainty Equivalence", *Econometrica*, 37, 706–718.

Markowitz, H. (1952) "Portfolio Selection", *Journal of Finance*, 7, 77–91.

Markowitz, H. (1976) *Portfolio Selection*, New Haven, CT: Yale University Press.

Markowitz, H. (1992) *Mean-Variance Analysis in Portfolio Choice and Capital Markets*, Oxford: Blackwell.

Merton, R. (1972) "An Analytical Derivation of the Efficient Portfolio Frontier", *Journal of Financial and Quantative Analysis*, 7, 1851–1872.

Pulley, L. (1981) "A General Mean-Variance Approximation to Expected Utility for Short Holding Periods", *Journal of Financial and Quantitative Analysis*, 16, 361–373.

Rothschild, M. (1986) "Asset Pricing Theories", in *Essays in Honor of Arrow*, (Heller et al., Eds.) Cambridge: Cambridge University Press.

Ross, S. (1978) "Mutual Fund Separation in Financial Theory. The Separating Distribution", *Journal of Economic Theory*, 17, 254–286.

Roy, A. (1952) "Safety First and the Holding of Assets", *Econometrica*, 20, 431–449.

Samuelson, P. (1970) "The Fundamental Approximation Theorem of Portfolio Analysis in Terms of Means, Variances, and Higher Moments", *The Review of Economic Studies*, 37, 537–542.

Sharpe, W.F. (1963) "A Simplified Model for Portfolio Analysis", *Management Science*, 9, 277–293.

Sharpe, W.F. (1964) "Capital Asset Prices: A Theory of Market Equilibrium under Conditions of Risk", *The Journal of Finance*, 19, 425–442.

Sharpe, W.F. (1970) *Portfolio Theory and Capital Markets*, New York: McGraw-Hill.

Sharpe, W.F. (1984) "Factor Models, CAPM's and the A.P.T.", *Journal of Portfolio Management*, 11, 21–25.

Treynor, J.L. (1961) "Towards a Theory of Market Values of Risky Assets", Mimeograph.

Performance Measures and Tests for Efficient Portfolios

Carlson, R. (1967) "Aggregate Performance of Mutual Funds", *Journal of Financial and Quantitative Analysis*, 5, 1–51.

Gendron, M. (1988) "Mesures de performance et économie de l'information. Une synthése de la littérature théorique", in *Incertain et Information*, (G. Dionne, Ed.) Economica.

Gouriéroux, C. and F. Jouneau (1995) "Fitted Efficient Portfolios", Discussion Paper. Paris: Centre de Recherche en Economie et Statistique.

Jensen, M. (1968) "The Performance of Mutual Funds in the Period, 1945–1964", *Journal of Finance*, 23, 389–416.

Jobson, J. and R. Korkie (1980) "Estimation for Markowitz Efficient Portfolios", *Journal of the American Statistical Association*, 75, 544–554.

Jobson, J. and R. Korkie (1981) "Performance Hypothesis Testing with the Sharpe and Treynor Measures", *Journal of Finance*, 36, 889–908.

Jobson, J. and R. Korkie (1982) "Potential Performance and Tests of Portfolio Efficiency", *Journal of Financial Economics*, 10, 433–466.

Jobson, J. and R. Korkie (1989) "A Performance Interpretation of Multivariate Tests of Assets Set Intersection, Spanning and Mean-Variance Efficiency", *Journal of Financial and Quantitative Analysis*, 24, 183–204.

Roll, R. (1977) "A Critique of the Asset Pricing Theory's Test", *Journal of Financial Economics*, 4, 129–176.

Roll, R. (1980) "Performance Evaluation and Benchmark Errors", *Journal of Portfolio Management*, 5–11.

Ross, S. (1980) "A Test of the Efficiency of a Given Portfolio", presented at ESEM, Aix en Provence.

Hedging

Black, F. and M. Scholes (1973) "The Pricing of Options and Corporate Liabilities", *Journal of Political Economy*, 81, 637–654.

Gouriéroux, C. and J.P. Laurent (1995) "Estimation of a Dynamic Hedge", Discussion Paper 95. Paris: Centre de Recherche on Economie et Statistique.

Koopmans, T. (1951) *Analysis of Production as an Efficient Combination of Activities*, New Haven, CT: Yale University Press.

Treynor, J. (1965) "How to Rate Management Funds", *Harvard Business Review*, 43, 36–75.

Chapter 8: FACTOR MODELS, DIVERSIFICATION AND EFFICIENCY

Arbitrage Pricing Theory

Chamberlain, G. and M. Rothschild (1983) "Arbitrage, Factor Structure and Mean Variance Analysis on Large Asset Markets", *Econometrica*, 51, 1281–1301.

Chamberlain, G. (1983) "Funds, Factors and Diversification in Arbitrage Pricing Models", *Econometrica*, 51, 1305–1323.

Chen, N. and J. Ingersoll (1983) "Exact Pricing in Linear Factor Models with Infinitely Many Assets: A Note", *Journal of Finance*, 38, 985–988.

Dybvig, P. (1983) "An Explicit Bound on Deviations from A.P.T. Pricing in a Finite Economy", *Journal of Financial Economics*, 12, 483–496.

Ehrardt, M. (1987) "A Mean-Variance Derivation of a Multi-factor Equilibrium Model", *Journal of Financial and Quantitative Analysis*, 22, 227–236.

Huberman, G. (1952) "A Simple Approach to Arbitrage Pricing Theory", *Journal of Economic Theory*, 28, 183–191.

Ingersoll, J. (1984) "Some Results in the Theory of Arbitrage Pricing", *Journal of Finance*, 39, 1021–1039.

Milne, F. (1988) "Arbitrage and Diversification in a General Equilibrium Asset Economy", *Econometrica*, 56, 815–840.

Ross, S.A. (1976) "The Arbitrage Theory of Capital Asset Pricing", *Journal of Economic Theory*, 17, 254–286.

Trzcinka, C. (1986) "On the Number of Factors in the Arbitrage Pricing Model", *The Journal of Finance*, 2, 347–368.

Dynamic Factor Models

Connor, G. (1984) "A Unified Beta Pricing Theory", *Journal of Economic Theory*, 34, 13–31.

Connor, G. and R. Korajczyk (1988) "Risk and Return in an Equilibrium A.P.T.", *Journal of Financial Economics*, 21, 255–289.

Gouriéroux, C., Monfort, A. and E. Renault (1991a) "Modèles Dynamiques á Facteurs", Discussion Paper. Paris: Centre pour la Recherche en Economie Mathematique Appliquée à la Planification.

Gouriéroux, C. Monfort, A. and E. Renault (1991b) "A General Framework for Factor Models", Discussion Paper. Paris: Institute Nationale de la Statistique et des Etudes Economiques.

Grinblatt, M. and S. Titman (1983) "Factor Pricing in a Finite Economy", *Journal of Financial Economics*, 12, 497–508.

Grinblatt, M. and S. Titman (1984) "The Relationship Between Mean Variance Efficiency and Arbitrage Pricing", Discussion Paper 4-83. Los Angeles: University of California—Los Angeles.

Huberman, G., Kandel, S. and R. Stambaugh (1987) "Mimicking Portfolios and Exact Arbitrage Pricing", *Journal of Finance*, 42, 1–9.

Tests

Affleck-Graves, J. and B. McDonalds (1990) "Multivariate Tests of Asset Pricing: The Comparative Power of Alternative Statistics", *Journal of Financial and Quantitative Analysis*, 25, 163–185.

Black, F., Jensen, M. and M. Scholes (1972) "The Capital Asset Pricing Model: Some Empirical Tests", in *Studies in the Theory of Capital Markets*, (M. Jensen, Eds.) New York: Praeger. pp. 79–121.

Brown, S. (1989) "The Number of Factors in Security Returns", *The Journal of Finance*, 44, 1247–1262.

Burmeister, E. and M. McElroy (1991) "The Residual Market Factor, the APT and Mean Variance Efficiency", *Review of Quantitative Finance and Accounting*, 1, 27–50.

Cheng, P. and R. Grauer (1980) "An Alternative Test of the Capital Asset Pricing Model", *American Economic Review*, 70, 660–671.

Fama, E. and J. MacBeth (1973) "Risk, Return and Equilibrium: Empirical Tests", *Journal of Political Economy*, 81, 607–636.

Ferson, W. (1983) "Expected Real Interest Rates and Consumption in Efficient Financial Markets: Empirical Tests", *Journal of Financial and Quantitative Analysis*, 18, 477–498.

Ferson, W., Kandel, S. and R. Stambaugh (1987) "Tests of Asset Pricing with Time Varying Expected Risk Premiums and Market Betas", *Journal of Finance*, 42, 201–220.

Gibbons, M. (1982) "Multivariate Tests of Financial Models: A New Approach", *Journal of Financial Economics*, 10, 3–27.

Gibbons, M., Ross, S. and J. Shanken (1989) "A Test of the Efficiency of a Given Portfolio", *Econometrica*, 57, 1121–1152.

Jobson, J. and R. Korkie (1980) "Estimation of Markowitz Efficient Portfolio", *Journal of the American Statistical Association*, 75, 544–554.

Jobson, J. and R. Korkie (1982) "Potential Performance and Tests of Portfolio Efficiency", *Journal of Financial Economics*, 10, 433–466.

Jobson, J. and R. Korkie (1989) "A Performance Interpretation of Multivariate Tests of Asset Set Intersection, Spanning and Mean Variance Efficiency", *Journal of Financial and Quantitative Analysis*, 24, 183–204.

Kandel, S. (1986) "The Geometry of the Maximum Likelihood Estimator of the Zero-Beta Return", *The Journal of Finance*, 2, 339–346.

Lehmann, B. and D. Modest (1985) "Mutual Fund Performance Evaluation: A Comparison of Benchmarks and Benchmarks Comparisons", *Journal of Finance*, 42, 233–266.

Shanken, J. (1982) "The Arbitrage Pricing Theory: Is it Testable?", *Journal of Finance*, 37, 1112–1140.

Stambaugh, R. (1982) "On the Exclusion of Assets from Tests of the Two Parameters Model: A Sensitivity Analysis", *Journal of Financial Economics*, 10, 237–268.

Stambaugh, R. (1983) "Arbitrage Pricing with Information", *Journal of Financial Economics*, 12, 357–370.

Performance Measures

Carlson, R. (1970) "Aggregate Performance of Mutual Funds", *Journal of Financial and Quantitative Analysis*, 5, 1–31.

Cranshaw, T. (1977) "The Evaluation of Investment Performance", *Journal of Business*, 50, 468–485.

McDonald, J. (1973) "French Mutual Fund Performance: Evaluation of Internationally Diversified Portfolios", *The Journal of Finance*, 28, 1161–1180.

Dybvig, P. and S. Ross (1985) "Differential Information and Performance Measurement Using a Security Market Line", *The Journal of Finance*, 40, 383–399.

Fama, E. (1972) "Components of Investment Security Performance", *Journal of Finance*, 27, 63–72.

Gendron, M. (1988) "Mesures de performance et économie de l'information, une synthèse de la littérature théorique", in *Incertain et Information*, (G. Dionne, Ed.) Paris: Economica.

Good, W. (1983) "Measuring Performance", *Financial Analysis Journal*, 39, 19–23.

Jensen, M. (1968) "The Performance of Mutual Funds in the Period 1945–1964", *Journal of Finance*, 23, 389–416.

Jensen, M. (1972) "Optimal Utilization of Market Forecasts and the Evaluation of Investment Performance", in *Mathematical Models in Investment and Finance*, (G. Szego and K. Shell, Eds.) Amsterdam: North-Holland.

Mayers, D. and E. Rice (1979) "Measuring Portfolio Performance and the Empirical Content of Asset Pricing Models", *Journal of Financial Economics*, 7, 3–28.

Moses, E., Cheyney, J. and T. Veit (1987) "A New and More Complete Performance Measure", *Journal of Portfolio Management*, 4, 24–33.

Roll, R. (1978) "Ambiguity when Performance is Measured by the Securities Market Line", *The Journal of Finance*, 33, 1031–1069.

Roll, R. (1980) "Performance Evaluation and Benchmarks Errors", *Journal of Portfolio Management*, 5–11.

Sharpe, W. (1966) "Mutual Fund Performance", *Journal of Business*, 39, 119–138.

Additional References on Statistical Methods

Asymptotic Least Squares

Gouriéroux, C. and A. Monfort (1995) *Statistics and Econometric Models*, Cambridge: Cambridge University Press.

Canonical Analysis

Anderson, T.W. (1958) *An Introduction to Multivariate Analysis*, New York: Wiley.

Muirhead, R. (1982) *Aspects of Multivariate Statistical Theory*, New York: Wiley.

Bootstrap

Bickel, J. and D. Freedman (1981) "Some Asymptotic Theory for the Bootstrap" *Annals of Statistics*, 9, 1196–1217.

Efron, B. (1982), *The Jacknife, the Bootstrap and Other Resampling Plans*, Philadelphia: Society for Industrial and Applied Mathematics.

Chapter 9: EQUILIBRIUM MODEL

Historical Papers on CAPM

Admati, A.R. (1985) "A Noisy Rational Expectation Equilibrium for Multi Assets Securities Markets", *Econometrica*, 53, 629–648.

Lintner, J. (1965) "The Valuation of Risk Assets and the Selection of Risky Investments in Stock Porfolios and Capital Budgets", *Review of Economics and Statistics*, 41, 13–37.

Merton, R. (1973) "An Intertemporal Capital Asset Pricing Model", *Econometrica*, 41, 867–886.

Mossin, J. (1966) "Equilibrium in Capital Asset Market", *Econometrica*, 35, 768–783.

Sharpe, W. (1964) "Capital Asset Prices: A Theory of Market Equilibrium Under Conditions of Risk", *The Journal of Finance*, 19, 425–442.

Sharpe, W. (1966) "Mutual Fund Performance", *Journal of Business*, Suppl. 1, part 2, 119–138.

Testing for CAPM in a Static Framework

Black, F., Jensen, M. and M. Scholes (1972) "The Capital Asset Pricing Model: Some Empirical Tests", in *Studies in the Theory of Capital Markets*, (M. Jensen, Ed.) New York: Praeger.

Blume, M. and I. Friend (1973) "A New Look at the Capital Asset Pricing Model", *Journal of Finance*, 28, 19–33.

Fama, E. and J. McBeth (1973) "Risk, Return and Equilibrium: Empirical Tests", *Journal of Political Economy*, 81, 607–636.

Gibbons, M. (1982) "Multivariate Tests of Financial Models: A New Approach", *Journal of Financial Economics*, 10, 3–27.

Krauss, A. and R. Litzenberger (1976) "Skewness Preference and the Valuation of Risk Assets", *Journal of Finance*, 31, 1085–1100.

MacKinlay, A. (1987) "On Multivariate Test of the CAPM", *Journal of Financial Economics*, 18, 341–371.

Shanken, J. (1985) "Multivariate Tests of the Zero-beta CAPM", *Journal of Financial Economics*, 14, 326–348.

Testing for CAPM in a Dynamic Framework

Bollerslev, R., Engle, R. and J. Wooldridge (1988) "A Capital Asset Pricing Model with Time Varying Covariance", *Journal of Political Economy*, 96, 116–131.

Engle, R., Ng, V. and M. Rothschild (1990) "Asset Pricing with a Factor ARCH Covariance Structure: Empirical Estimates for Treasury Bills", *Journal of Econometrics*, 45, 213–237.

Engle, C. and A. Rodrigues (1987) "Tests of International C.A.P.M. with Time Varying Covariances", Report No. 2303. Washington, DC: National Bureau of Economic Research.

Gibbons, M. and W. Ferson (1985) "Testing Asset Pricing Models with Changing Expectations and an Unobservable Market Portfolio", *Journal of Financial Economics*, 14, 217–236.

Gouriéroux, C. and A. Monfort (1992) "Qualitative Threshold ARCH Models", *Journal of Econometrics*, 52, 159–199.

Structural Models

Broze, L., Gouriéroux, C. and A. Szafarz (1986) "Bulles spéculatives et transmission d'information sur le marché d'un bien stockable", *Actualité Economique*, 62, 166–184.

Grossman, S.J. (1976) "On the Efficiency of Competitive Stock Markets where Traders Have Diverse Information", *Journal of Finance*, 31, 573–585.

Grossman, S.J. and J.E. Stiglitz (1980) "On the Impossibility of Informationally Efficient Markets", *American Economic Review*, 70, 393–408.

Hellwig, M.F. (1982) "Rational Expectations Equilibrium with Conditioning on Past Prices: A Mean-Variance Example", *Journal of Economic Theory*, 26, 279–312.

Consumption Based CAPM

Breeden, D. (1979) "An Intertemporal Asset Pricing Model with Stochastic Consumption and Investment Opportunities", *Journal of Financial Economics*, 7, 265–296.

Brenden, D., Gibbons, M. and R. Litzenberger (1989) "Empirical Tests of the Consumption Oriented CAPM", *The Journal of Finance*, 2, 231–262.

Cox, J., Ingersoll, J. and S. Ross (1985) "An Intertemporal General Equilibrium Model of Asset Prices", *Econometrica*, 53, 363–384.

Duffie, D. and W. Zame (1988) "The Consumption Based Capital Asset Pricing Model", Discussion Paper No. 922. Stanford, CA: Stanford University.

Grossman, S. and G. Laroque (1987) "Asset Pricing and Optimal Portfolio Choice in the Presence of Illiquid Durable Consumption Goods", Discussion Paper. Paris: Institut Nationale de la Statistique et des Etudes Economiques.

Lucas, R. (1978) "Asset Prices in Exchange Economy", *Econometrica*, 46, 1429–1445.

Rubinstein, M. (1976) "The Valuation of Uncertain Income Streams and the Pricing of Option", *Bell Journal of Economics*, 7, 407–425.

Index

Springer Series in Statistics

(continued from p. ii)